D/2021/45/582 – ISBN 978 94 014 7210 4 – NUR 801

Cover and interior design: Peer De Maeyer
Cover illustration: Axelle Vanquaillie
Back cover portrait: An Clapdorp
Ecosystem Canvas visuals (p. 226 / fragments
on p. 246-249, p. 263, p. 283, p. 329 /
p. 318 / p. 330 / p. 332 / back cover):
Tim Tondeleir | Big Boom

LannooCampus Publishers is a subsidiary
of Lannoo Publishers, the book and multimedia division
of Lannoo Publishers nv.

LannooCampus Publishers
Vaartkom 41 box 01.02   P.O. Box 23202
3000 Leuven   1100 DS Amsterdam
Belgium   Netherlands
www.lannoocampus.com

RIK VERA

The Guide to the Ecosystem Economy

Sketchbook for Your Organisation's Future

Lannoo
Campus

*"Start as a brush
and become the canvas."*

Dendermonde, 18th June 2021
(I almost wrote the year 2 AC, C designating Corona)

Intro

Damned hard work

The most difficult part of writing a book is (surprise) actually writing the book; the second most difficult part is finishing it.

In my younger days, I enjoyed painting. I remember that every time I painted, there came a moment when I could say: this is it. One more stroke of the brush would ruin the whole thing. It is what it is; let us call this a finished painting. I had absolutely no problem with stepping back, leaving the painting on its own, out there in the open, naked and vulnerable, to be seen, perceived and judged by others.

Writing a book seems to be more difficult. If I had to guess why, I would say that it has something to do with the overview. One can take a step back and look at a painting. Squinted eyes, a frown on your face, head tilted a little to the left, leaning backwards, your right hand under your chin and a brush held in your left. In that moment, you can almost trade places with the person who will see the painting – you are no longer the painter. But you can't do that with a book. I can't in any case. I don't see the whole book. I see fragments, bits and pieces, extracts and ideas. (If you asked me where I refer to antifragility, my best estimate would be that it is somewhere in Chapter 5.) I can't step into the shoes of the reader. Whenever I try to see it through a reader's eyes, I am inclined to write some extra lines here and there. It seems like a book is never ready to be perceived and judged by the wild wide world out there.
But you can't keep on writing. About a week ago, I called *The Guide to the Ecosystem Economy* a book. I said it was done. I had it printed in the format of a book, smiled, relaxed and promised myself that this was it. I would not touch it any more.

The only thing I still needed to do was write a foreword. You know, the "thank people introduction" to the book where you have to credit everybody who contributed to the book and try not to forget anyone.

In other words: that minefield of human interaction. The book itself was finished, I pressed "send" and the manuscript was in the book publisher's inbox. That was it. A heavy weight fell off my shoulders. I had not slept much in those last few weeks. A few days after saying "here you go" to the book, my body told me that it had been a hell of a journey and stole my most important instrument for a couple of days: my voice. For a while, I was the voiceless keynote speaker. Nature always wins.

Hurricane

Today, on 18th June 2021, I had a conversation about ecosystems with Nina at nexxworks, Jeroen and Esther at Bol.com (a company I refer to in this book) and Matthew Brennan, a renowned speaker and writer focusing on Chinese mobile technology and innovation. His book, *Attention Factory* (the story of TikTok & China's ByteDance), is a must-read. You can try to draw links between my view on ecosystems and that "attention factory". It is an overwhelming illustration of the building blocks and dynamics I describe.

It was the type of conversation one could have recorded to be viewed by the whole world, because it grew organically into a deep and profound session on all things related to big data, AI, algorithms, the potential creepiness of being too close to customers (who want to be treated like an individual), double flywheels, partnerships, engaged customers, user-generated content, the building blocks of an ecosystem and of course how to build one. We were five like-minded souls with the same drive and passion, inspiring one another.

For the duration of that conversation, I knew I had to hold my horses. I told myself: "Rik, your book is finished. You are not going to touch it any more. Don't even think about it. No. No. No." It was a perfect storm inside my head, but in some way I could find the very eye, the place full of calm. I was pretty proud of myself. I would not have to run to the publisher and shout out loud: "Stop the printing process, I have some new stuff that needs to be in the book no matter what."

But just when I thought I had survived this hurricane of thoughts, ideas and insights, Matthew said one thing, one little thing, that was enough to push me out of the eye of the storm and into internal mayhem. I was dragged into the danger zone, my head spinning, my feet unable to stay on the ground, my body being lifted into the air to be thrown down to earth, bruised and battered.

What he said felt like the very summary of my book. It was the key to my struggle in chapter 9. I admit that I had originally envisioned chapter 9 as a manual, a recipe, a step-by-step guide on how to build an ecosystem. But building an ecosystem is not about following a recipe. Matthew was talking about TikTok and said: "They started like the brush, and evolved into the canvas."

The summary

And I just knew: that is the summary. That is what my book is all about: why and how to evolve from being a simple brush into a canvas on which anything can happen.

As you might have guessed, seeing as you are reading this in my book, I shouted: "Dear publisher, stop for a moment! There is something that needs to make the book no matter what."

I told Matthew Brennan that, by providing me with this metaphor, I had to thank him for ruining and making my day at the same time. "Can I quote you on this?" I asked. "I will refer to you and your book," I said. (I almost said please, a word I hardly ever use.) He agreed. In my head I was dancing.

Straight after this energising conversation, I grabbed my computer and started doing what I had sworn I wouldn't do: I wrote a few hundred extra words for the book that was supposed to be finished. While I was writing I received an email from Matthew.

Before I turn to the quote itself, I have to share something else that struck me in his email: "It's in Chapter 5 somewhere."

This quote by Alex Zhu, the former CEO of TikTok, is exactly what the over 250 pages of my book are all about: *"When you want to grow early on, you want to be a brush, meaning you have to be very specific; you have to solve a specific need very well… Later you want to be a canvas; you want all kinds of things to happen on this blank canvas."*

Preface

I bring good news for companies big and small. If, after reading the first chapters, you want to become an ecosystem, a canvas on which all types of stuff can happen (business models that bring money), or you want to become some of that stuff that happens on the canvas, the simple message is this: yes, you can. Is there a better way to open this book than by saying that you can do it?

Because right now, you are a brush.

Read the book, get to know and understand the building blocks and the dynamics of an ecosystem and then... just start building it. Like a surfer riding one of those gigantic waves in Nazaré, there is no stopping halfway.

This is a preface, so I need to start to thank people.

As I said in the preface of my first book, I am a dreamer. Writing *The Guide to the Ecosystem Economy*, I have not only been writing about crazy surfer dudes, I have been one myself.

Managers The Day After Tomorrow was a calm sea when I compare it to the content and dynamics of this book. I have had the guts (and the complete and utterly stupid craziness) to surf this gigantic wave of platforms, ecosystems, canvasses, big data, AI, customer-centricity, engaged and empowered people and their impact on people, business and society and I have to admit that there have been many moments when I thought "What the heck was I thinking?", but I knew I had to surf that whole wave. There was no giving up.

I am a dreamer. When dreamers want to realise their crazy dreams, they need warmth, love and support. Many people have been patient enough to live with the many mood swings of a writer, which are worse than four seasons in one day (or they have just ignored them), and have not stopped pampering me with warmth and love: my wife Christel (who is also kind of acting as the CFO of my business) and my children Lisse and Lore. Without Stephanie, who is running my company as if it were her own, I would have been drowning in all the practicalities that are part of being a keynote speaker, off- and online; and without Alanah (only she knows how important she has been in the writing process), this book would have been finished in 2035 (that is: never).

If I had never met Peter and Steven sometime in 2015, my business life might have taken a completely different direction, I guess. They were, and still are, my heroes and role models. Thanks buddies, and thanks to the whole nexxworks crew and community. Speaking of communities: in January 2021 I wrote a white paper called *2020. The year of inspiration*, which you can still download from my website www.rikvera.com. That led to a tsunami of online events, webinars, jam sessions or whatever we called those digital meetings. I have to thank all those who participated and shared ideas, challenges, questions and remarks, as all of them contributed to my writing process.

Finally, I want to repeat the words I used in the preface of *Managers The Day After Tomorrow*, which is a long version of the preface of this new book.

"We have a crushing responsibility. We need to shape the world for the sake of our children and grandchildren. All of us. Including the managers of today and tomorrow. I hope they will do so with The Day After Tomorrow in mind. I hope that they can help their companies adapt to the new world in which my grandchildren will grow up."

With this in mind, I dedicate this book to Sam, Line and Nout, my grandchildren.

Contents

11. Exemplify

11.5. Work

? There is a lot i didn't know
i didn't know

He is silent for a minute, sipping his drink ?? some before
he continues:

"How many ??? I. I have put round ??? There is
quite a lot I didn't know I didn't know. At all.

There is a whole new world happening here;
it has been happening for years and I had no clue.
What I have learned is ~~that automotive~~ about automotive to be about automotive
is it is not even about automotive mobility, it is about
smart cities and another society in which all industries
will melt down into ... some ??? that we have never seen
before. And it is not going to happen. It is happening. Right here. Right now.

We are going in the most direction. What we
we don't have a clue. And if we do, it
is how we innovate, within our business model
on our industry, we have to invent a whole
??????? and a new industry, we
??????? to do that it is what we don't
will not be able to do that it is ??? we don't
embrace the technology that we have discovered.
oh. oh. Oh
complete
shit?

AUTOMOTIVE → A MOBILITY B → SMART CITIES → NEW SOCIETY

1

Reality

"Either you deal with what is the reality,
or you can be sure that the reality
is going to deal with you."
ALEX HALEY

---

featuring:
a black swan
the end of horse(-)power
a broken system
the gift of time
a metal burden
the chicken or the egg
a dead-end train

San Francisco, March 2020

It's the first week of March 2020. I'm on a ferry in San Francisco Bay. As the day draws to a close, the air is calm with hardly any wind. The water in the bay is as dark and flat as a black mirror. It's getting cold out on the upper deck where we are drinking that Mexican beer, the one with the same name as the virus that has just escalated to a pandemic. We are laughing and having fun. In that moment, we don't realise how serious this big virus with a little name is nor how devastating it will be for people, society and business. How could we know that this thing would change our world and have such an overwhelming impact?

The sky is blue and as the sun sets over the Golden Gate Bridge to our left, we take pictures with our smartphones. No social distancing yet. No masks. Just a bunch of people having fun, enjoying the moment and the stunning view. The boat leaves a V-shaped wake behind it, stark white in the dark blue ice-cold water. In the distance, San Francisco bathes in the waning orange glow of the sun. As we celebrate this powerful moment, a whale's tail fin breaks the surface of the water. We have another beer and realise that this may be our last trip for a long time. Since 2015, I have travelled to this vibrant city a few times a year. It's like my second home. I am in love with the spirit of the Valley

and the no-nonsense attitude of the people who live here – how conquering the world and beating old and sleepy companies and business
models is just what they do. It hurts to know I will not be back before
summer. Little did I know at the time that it would end up being much
longer than that.

Dendermonde, December 2020

I am rewriting this first chapter for the seventeenth time just before
2020 turns into 2021. Since March, I have barely left the house, making
only one trip to Vienna. Yesterday we started the first round of vacci-
nations in Belgium. I built a studio at home so that I could continue
giving my keynotes. My words and ideas are travelling the planet, but
my body is locked inside this small bubble. Sometimes I feel as restless
as a lion in a zoo. I have nothing to worry about, but I miss the thrill of
survival.

San Francisco, March 2020

Two days ago, I celebrated my 57th birthday in San Francisco. This
evening, however, we are having dinner at a small harbour on the other
side of the Bay. We enjoy our aperitifs on the restaurant's terrace over-
looking the harbour and San Francisco in the far distance. This evening,

a girl in our group is celebrating her birthday. She is half my age. She is part of the lucky generation that is going to design a new society with the leftover mess my generation has created. It's a fun evening. We laugh, drink, share stories, crack jokes, momentarily forgetting about the dark shadow of the virus and the mind-blowing ideas we have been bombarded with on our visits to various tech companies during the week – so much information that we have yet to digest.

Before we take an Uber back to the hotel, the CEO of the company I am guiding that week takes me by the shoulder, leads me to a table in the corner of the bar downstairs, orders two glasses of excellent Californian wine and starts to talk about the lessons he has learnt. He is one of the most vibrant CEOs I have ever met, full of pure energy, drive and passion, but that night, in a bar on the other side of San Francisco Bay, he is quiet and philosophical.

"Tomorrow, I will have to announce a travel ban," he says in a low voice. "This thing is way more serious than we could have imagined. We are going to fly back to Europe at the end of this week and then... I just don't know... All I know is that I don't know what I don't know yet. We will have to prepare the company for the worst. This is the famous Black Swan. We thought that it was a concept. It has become our reality. We are no longer going to talk about how we can make our company more agile; it is going to be a matter of survival now."

"But what is even more devastating is this: in your book *Managers The Day After Tomorrow* you use the automotive industry and Mary Barra as an example of how disruptive technology can be to an industry. I met Mary once and she is a truly inspirational woman. I asked you to guide this group here in San Francisco because I hoped it would wake my team up, give us a sense of urgency to speed up our innovation. But boy..."

He is silent for a minute, sipping his dark red wine before he continues:

"How wrong was I. I have just realised that there is quite a lot that I didn't know I didn't know. At all. There is a whole new world happening

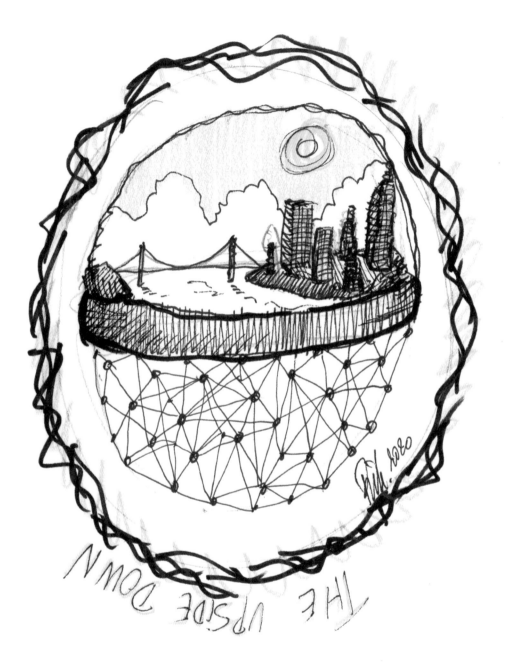

THE UPSIDE DOWN

here; it has been happening for years, and I had no clue. What I have learnt is that automotive is no longer about automotive, it is not even about mobility, it is about smart cities and another society in which all industries will melt down into... something that we have never seen before. And it is not going to happen. It is happening right here, right now.

"We were going in the wrong direction. What we were doing was a dead-end street. We don't have to innovate within our business model or our industry; we have to invent a new business model and a new industry. We will not be able to do that if we don't embrace the technology that we have discovered over the last couple of days. Digitisation. Big data. Artificial intelligence. Robotisation. Internet of Things. We have no clue about this parallel universe, but it is the new universe. We need to realise that trying to offer new services for new customers is of no use any more. We need to dive deep into changed and changing customer behaviour, new customer needs and dreams, and how we can find better answers to questions we have never asked before. We need to involve the customer and make them part of our mission. We don't need to offer them cars or mobility; we need to facilitate how they want to travel from A to B. And finally, Rik, we need to stop being a link in a dying chain. We need to become an ecosystem."

I listen and realise that he has just referred to my TREE principle* of exponential growth without realising, but I don't mention it.

Before I can open my mouth, the CEO continues with his stream of thought:

"This is... huge. We can no longer follow the rules of an industry. We can't even try to be creative with those rules. We need to write completely new ones and we don't even know how to do that. We have never been trained to do that. Where do we start?"

I inhale deeply and try to come up with an answer, but he doesn't wait for my reply.

---

* I didn't elaborate much on this formula in my first book *Managers The Day After Tomorrow.* It was one of those bursts of inspiration that came quite late. In the end, it only just made it into the book but wasn't given the time nor attention it deserved. That is something I will rectify in this book.

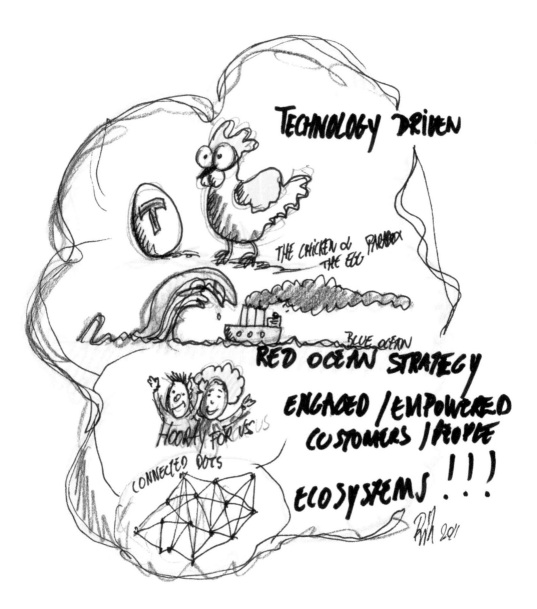

"We need to better understand society and customers and our future role, function and functionality; we need to not only understand technology, we need to become a technology-first company, a company that breathes technology. That means that we need to build a completely new ecosystem. It's a harsh conclusion, but a pretty easy decision to make. The big question is: what is an ecosystem and how do we build it? What building blocks can we reuse? How do we involve others in the ecosystem? What do we bring to the table? What do they need to bring to that table and how do we trade these assets, services or information? And by the way, how long before the Uber arrives?"

Finally able to get a word in, I say: "I still have to order one; maybe we'd better pay the bill. Shall I?"

The Uber arrives five minutes later.

It is late and already morning in Europe. We both call home from our Uber while crossing the Golden Gate. The news from Europe is terrifying. In our countries there are rumours about a lockdown like the one in Wuhan where it all started. We spend the rest of our journey in deep thought and exchange not a single word. Sometimes words are not needed.

San Francisco, March 2020

The next morning, after a sleepless night in the Fairmont Hotel, my forehead rests against the cold window of my room with a view. On my far left, the Golden Gate Bridge is just a greyish shadow in the early morning mist. At that very moment, I decide to write a book about ecosystems and how to build them. Little did I know that this was an easy decision to make, but a hard nut to crack. The alarm on my smartwatch starts to beep. Time for breakfast. That afternoon, we will visit the Tesla factory in Fremont to meet with a couple of executives to discuss their future strategy. We're all very excited.

In the morning, however, we are visiting Aurora, a three-year-old start-up. On the bus over there, I give the group a brief introduction to this company they know little to nothing about – a company formed by brilliant people who want to become leaders in the autonomous driving sector.

At our meeting with Aurora's CEO in Mountain View, we "shake hands" by bumping elbows or feet (we jokingly called it the San Francisco way) and use hand sanitiser before being led into a meeting room the size of a bedroom – way too small for 35 people. It felt like trying on the suit I wore at my wedding 35 years ago: hard to breathe and at risk of falling to pieces.

It can be difficult to imagine a revolution coming from such cramped quarters. In their introduction, Aurora presents their claims as something that was expected, the new normal.

It's easy to forget that this company, seemingly made up of a small army of nerdy coders sitting in front of oversized screens filled with numbers and dashboards, hiding in their cocoon of fancy headphones and drinking Coca-Cola alternatives, could turn the world upside down with bleeding edge technology. To me, they seemed like the black swans at work.

After that meeting, while on the bus on the way to the Tesla factory in Fremont, we discuss what we have seen. Was this just an example of the San Francisco way – "fake it until you make it" – or was a company this small capable of disrupting the automotive industry in the near future? The conclusion was simple: this may have been our early warning moment, that wake-up call right before the shark fin of exponential change slaps you right in the face, the early warning as mentioned by Larry Downes and Paul Nunes in *Big Bang Disruption*. We all know that we shouldn't ignore this.

Dendermonde, December 2020

As 2020 comes to a close, I am writing the book I had envisioned in that hotel room back in San Francisco. It has been a difficult ride so far. I had a well-developed writing routine in my non-routine chaotic life. Waiting in airport lounges, sitting on a plane, spending empty hours in hotel lobbies or behind the scenes at an event waiting for my turn in the spotlight, sleepless nights in San Francisco, Shanghai, Singapore or Sao Paolo: that was "the zone" for me. In COVID-19 times, I have to plan writing time, something I have never planned before, and that's not my thing. As I struggle to put pen to paper, or rather finger to keyboard, a message pops up in the WhatsApp group we set up back in March: "Uber sells self-driving car division to Aurora."

That week we spent in San Francisco in March 2020 seems like a century ago.

The message contains a link to an article. Instead of continuing to develop self-driving cars on their own, Uber sold their ATG (Advanced Technologies Group) to Aurora and invested $400 million in the start-up, which was already backed by Amazon.[1] Together they will form a new partnership, with Uber's CEO joining the board at Aurora, led by former Google, Tesla and Uber executives, boasting partners such as Hyundai and Kia. These five companies – Aurora, Amazon, Uber, Kia and Hyundai – are all members of this perfect storm of new technologies and potential business models. The ecosystem economy is happening and moving under our very noses. Fiat Chrysler also had a partnership with Aurora, which they concluded in June 2020 after eighteen months of collaboration.[2] That's how ecosystems function. Partners come and go, but the ecosystem survives. It's happening. Now's the time to really finish the book.

As a new chapter opens, another closes

Noise pollution, air pollution, traffic accidents, cities that become uninhabitable… these modern day problems are not as modern as we may think. They were also a scourge for urban dwellers in the 19th century. Back then, cars weren't the issue. Horses were the main mode of transport for people and goods. Some of us maintain a romantic vision of the simplicity of this time, but it wasn't all rosy. Just look at the facts. Horses excrete, on average, over a litre of urine and between seven and fifteen kilograms of manure every day.[3] This wasn't really a problem at first – the city earned money by selling this manure to farmers – but supply soon outstripped demand with 100,000 horses travelling the streets of cities such as New York and London, transporting people and goods. Even more horses were needed to collect and transport all that manure. In fact, it was kind of exponential.

NEW YORK IN DEEP SH*T

The maths is simple. 100,000 horses x 7-15kg of manure = between 700,000 and 1.5 million kilograms of manure per day left on city streets. In 1894, *The Times of London* supposedly dubbed this the Horse Manure Crisis,* predicting that every street in London would be buried under three metres of manure within 50 years if nothing changed. General panic led to a ten-day horse manure crisis conference being convened, but cancelled after only three days. The problem was easy to identify, but participants found that it was too big and all-encompassing to solve.

Nevertheless, at the time of the conference, the car had already been invented. Gottlieb Daimler installed a combustion engine on a carriage in 1886 and Karl Benz developed the first three-wheel car later the same year.[4] However, these new vehicles remained a luxury reserved only for

HORSE SHIT CRISIS

the privileged, due to their price tag of roughly two years of a worker's salary. The revolution came later, but relatively quickly, in 1908, when Henry Ford introduced the Model T.

---

* There has been some debate as to whether this article ever existed as records of it have not been found.

THE END OF HORSE POWER

The revolution that city residents so badly needed wasn't the invention of the car itself, but rather the invention of mass produced cars.

Ford chose to earn a small profit margin on each car and, by creating an efficient manufacturing system, managed to reduce production time of the Model T from 12.5 hours to 1.5 hours. As a result, he was able to sell at scale and lower the price from $2,500 in 1914 to $260 in 1924.

Technology saved the day.

This is how the automotive industry was born, evolving over the years to become what it is today – on the cusp of something huge.

Has the automotive chapter of history come to a close?

How did this paradigm – the automotive industry as we know it today – become a dead-end street? Whether we want to admit it or not, a transformation is on the horizon. In 2016, Mary Barra, CEO of General Motors, predicted exponential change in a speech at the Consumer Electronics Show in Las Vegas: "I have no doubt that the automotive industry will change more in the next five to ten years than it has in the last 50. The convergence of connectivity, vehicle electrification, and evolving customer needs demands new solutions."[5]

With the benefit of hindsight which is always easier, one can say that on the whole Barra was around 90% correct in her projection. However, the change will be even greater than she predicted or perhaps wanted or dared to envision. The automotive industry isn't going to change; it's going to disappear. It's going to be devastating.

When talking about society's needs and frustrations in an interview with Business Insider,[6] Barra pointed out that people still need to get from point A to point B (=need), but driving can be a pain (=frustration). Take New York as an example: residents are for the most part reluctant to own a car and not just because driving in the city, attempting to navigate your own hunk of metal among many others surrounded by honking horns and angry drivers, is comparable to hell on earth. Extortionate parking rates, heavy congestion and elevated insurance premiums have also contributed to making ride-sharing services a welcome alternative.

As a result, self-driving cars will probably surge in popularity in a big city like New York. Barra said that time would be the main benefit: "Time is almost a currency for many people and so we will be giving back that time." Thanks to reduced congestion and the fact that you are not operating the vehicle yourself, time will be on your side: time in

---

I'd recommend that you go back and read the last few paragraphs again. Take your time to digest what Mary Barra said: "I have no doubt that the automotive industry will change more in the next five to ten years than it has in the last 50. The convergence of connectivity, vehicle electrification, and evolving customer needs demands new solutions."

She spoke those words in 2016, which was five years before the time of writing. Those words weren't uttered by some futurist or thought leader or ambitious and slightly reckless entrepreneur, but by the CEO of an incumbent company. Look at your company, your industry, right now. Do you have the guts to say it out loud? "My industry is going to see more change in the next ten years than it has in the last 50." Once you've come to terms with that, you can do something about it.

---

the vehicle to spend as you please (probably in a highly customisable environment) and more time at your destination (thanks to less traffic) to do what really matters.

COVID-19 didn't break the system; it exposed the broken system

In March 2020, when I was in San Francisco with that group of company executives and workers to explore upcoming innovation in the automotive industry, COVID-19 was a dark cloud hanging over us. It hadn't yet hit Europe or the United States with full force, but we knew it was on the horizon. While we were in San Francisco, the virus sowed chaos: countries implemented travel bans and lockdown became a reality.

Although this wasn't what we had envisioned, COVID-19 was the source of the first lesson we learnt during that trip. The unexpected can happen. Our environment was now out of our control and we had no scripts telling us how to deal with it. Governments and companies reeled from the impact, trying to get their feet back on solid ground. We tend to build our companies based on a rigid structure designed to prevent risks. They are made to be in a constant state of slow transition, moving forward in an environment we can control. This is the problem that COVID-19 exposed: how can our companies cope in an environment that is beyond our control?

The meteorite 65 million years ago didn't kill the dinosaurs; it changed the ecosystem the dinosaurs were a part of. What ultimately led to their demise was their failure to adapt to the new environment around them, the changed ecosystem.

We are limiting our company's potential to adapt by creating a rigid structure, a linear (or circular) chain of links. If one link in the chain breaks, we're in trouble. That one link is vital to the rest of the processes in the company. An ecosystem, however, where every link is connected to every other link, is resilient. It's flexible. It's a series of interconnected dots that gives us a greater chance of rebounding if one link in the system fails.

The automotive industry is a dinosaur

The second lesson we learnt in San Francisco revolved around this interconnectedness, a network of links. Some members of the company I travelled with had already made the trip, but had failed to impress the reality on those who hadn't seen it with their own eyes. Armed with people from across the spectrum of the company, we set out to discover the future of the automotive industry together. Instead we learnt that it was going to disappear. Industry lines are blurring. The future of automotive lies elsewhere.

You can wait, cross your fingers and hope that the meteorite will not hit the planet, or you can search for it in the sky and spot it on time. Some devastating events, like the changes in the automotive industry, are not even a black swan or a meteorite. The destruction of a whole industry and, in its slipstream, the transformation of a whole society is a pretty devastating event, but we can't say that we didn't see it coming. Mary Barra did in 2016; Elon Musk saw it years earlier. But he wasn't the first.

In the 1990s, Toyota's management tasked a team with designing the car of the future – the car of the 21st century.[7] They didn't just have to design a new model; the team also had to approach the job differently. To create something completely new, using technology that didn't yet exist, they couldn't possibly follow standard procedure conducting market research and seeing what competitors were doing. They needed to reinvent the wheel. Senior management put immense pressure on the development team, publicly announcing a release date before they had even created a working prototype.

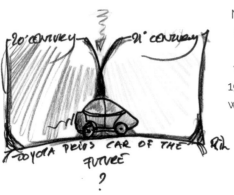

Nevertheless, Toyota succeeded in launching the Prius in time for the Third Conference of the Parties to the United Nations Framework Convention on Climate Change held in December 1997, which led to the Kyoto Protocol.[8] Their idea was to create an energy efficient car to respond to the social challenges of energy and the environment. By setting seemingly impossible targets and establishing checkpoints along the way, the development team managed to create a new type of vehicle - the hybrid car.

The Prius was hailed by many as an innovative revolution, but let's face it, it was still a car with an engine. The only way for it to make a real impact and become a revolution was for it to be widely adopted by society.

Society is the foundation of business

January 2020 brought another grand announcement from Toyota, not at the Motor Show in Brussels but at the Consumer Electronics Show in Las Vegas (just like Mary Barra's in 2016). The fact that it has become normal for news relating to the automotive industry to be revealed at CES rather than at an automotive event is a clear indication that technology-first companies are dominating the sector.

Toyota unveiled their idea to build a real-life experiment – a smart hyper-connected city known as the "woven city" – where smart utilities, smart buildings, smart transport and connected people intertwine. Thanks to underground infrastructure, there would be no more delivery trucks and lorries on the roads. Mobility above ground would be split into three: roads built exclusively for electric vehicles, tree-lined lanes for slower traffic such as bicycles and park-like green pathways for pedestrians. It sounds like an oasis.

The future of the automotive industry is about society, not about cars.

Society is frustrated. The daily commute to work, most of which is spent in traffic jams, is a waste of time and is detrimental to our overall wellbeing. Mary Barra was right. Time is money. Congestion now means that, on average, the speed of a car in city centres is the same as the horses we used over a century ago to get around.[9] There's also the space we have to make for cars; the infrastructure they require – roads, car parks, fuel stations – takes up a lot of valuable space in our city centres while also occupying prime real estate in our homes. Think of how you could use that garage space if you didn't need it for your car.

On top of the time and space problems, cars are a huge expense, not just to buy but to run: fuel, insurance, road tax, maintenance, cleaning... That's not to mention the pressure to buy a new car after just a few years because the mileage is too high or the latest model has new and so-called innovative features. Cars are also dangerous and notoriously bad for the planet, polluting the air and polluting our wellbeing with constant traffic noise. We don't even use them 90% of the time! They just sit there, taking up space and waiting for us to need them again.

If we're honest with ourselves, cars are a hassle. What if all that space could be given back to the public to use in a way that adds value rather than being an eyesore? What if there were less traffic on the road despite the growing population? What if we no longer had to bear the burden of owning a car but shared one instead?

We don't need to ask these what-if questions; this is the future of the automotive industry. Instead of being automotive, it will be about mobility for society. We won't own cars any more, we will call a car to take us home from work. While bringing us home, it may also replace a delivery van by delivering something to our neighbour. Another neighbour may then take the car to travel somewhere else. Maybe someone a little further away needs the car? Well, that's not a problem: you're not the one driving the car, it's driving itself.

In San Francisco, they say that autonomous cars will create an explosion of new innovation and game-changing technologies, due to the fact that garages, freed from having to store those useless, dangerous and expensive things called cars, will instead be filled with young start-ups and entrepreneurs building their businesses in there from scratch, like many did before (think IBM, Amazon, Google, Microsoft, Facebook, YouTube).

The future of mobility is ACES

Cars of the future will be connected, driven by data and, of course, autonomous. They will be ACES: autonomous, connected, electrical and shared.

Autonomous because they will drive themselves. Connected because they will constantly be sending data back to the central computer to improve comfort, safety and connectivity with the cars around them. Electrical because... well it's clear that the oil industry is a dinosaur and clean energy is the future. And finally shared, because why have a personal car if you can share one and forego all the hassle of actually owning one?

Israeli start-up Ree has come up with a completely modular electric car.[10] Rather than having the crucial parts needed to run the car spread throughout a fixed chassis in the shape of a car as we know it now, they have designed a new type of vehicle with small motors in the wheels. Replacing the complex network of up to 30,000 parts in modern cars, people could build their own cars like a computer. Ree's car is essentially a giant skateboard.

Ree's idea is to have different "cabins" that you can lower onto the electric vehicle base as needed. For those who want to use the time to work, there's the office module. For those who want to rest, there's the high-comfort option. Thanks to interchangeable settings, cars are soon going to become much more personalised.

Ree is a new breed. They create a platform that is only of value in an ecosystem, where other parties are using the platform.

The new automotive reality is all about ecosystems.

Rather than designing the next generation car, manufacturers now need to imagine mobility in the 21st century. How will people want to travel? What will be important to them: comfort, speed, safety, ownership, the environment? How can manufacturers adapt to this changing reality?

Responding to what the customer wants

What about us – the potential users of this new mobility? Can we adapt? I often get asked this question, and not just in the case of autonomous vehicles. Is there a use case? In other words: do users really want this technology or would we just be investing in something that nobody needs?

I bet that if you asked 100 people on the street right now if they were willing to be driven around by a car, most of them would say "no" or maybe even "never". There are many reasons why people might respond this way, and while some of them may be rational, most will be emotional.

So if we asked people what they wanted right now, they would probably say no to autonomous electric cars. Some people would take that as proof that it's never going to happen. But the customer doesn't know what they don't know. They have no idea about something they've never experienced until they've experienced it for themselves. It's plain and simple.

Over the last year, during the countless (really, I've lost count) webinars, keynotes and other online sessions I've held, I've had more interaction with participants than was ever possible at an in-person event. And much of that interaction has been resistance. "Yes, but Rik, we are customer-centric." "Yes, but Rik, how do we know that's what the customer wants?" "Yes, but Rik, doesn't this spell the end for us?" This interaction has been wonderful; it has challenged me no end. And that's what I'm here to do with you. So I'm going to warn you. This book will make you question how you've been running your business and thinking of customers and innovation.

Later in this book, when I tell you that you need to drastically overhaul your business model, decomposing it and building a whole new one, you may want to resist. It's highly likely that you'll refer to the customer and say there's no business case for this new model because customers aren't asking for it. Rather than waiting until we get to that point, I'm simply going to address this now.

If you want to be customer-centric, don't ask the customer

Yes really. I know that Steve Jobs once said: "You've got to start with the customer experience and work back toward the technology – not the other way around." But he also said this: "Some people say, 'Give the customers what they want.' But that's not my approach. Our job is to figure out what they're going to want before they do. I think Henry Ford once said, 'If I'd asked customers what they wanted, they would have told me, "A faster horse!"' People don't know what they want until you show it to them. That's why I never rely on market research. Our task is to read things that are not yet on the page."

It's an important paradox that we need to clarify right now. Yes, you need to start with the customer and ask yourself how you can serve them, but that doesn't involve asking the customer what they want. It involves collecting data and insights so that you can find a way to serve the customer and resolve their frustrations. That's what we're going to work on in this book: creating a human-like*, sensitive, open-minded,

---

* We need to compare our organisations to humans, build them so that they resemble that smallest unit within our companies, and without a doubt the most important part – people. By creating organisations that resemble humans, we create something that truly fits with what people want and need. The digital age provides us with the toolkit to do this; not just to digitise our existing business model, but to make something that really works for people.

receptive, interactive, ever-learning business model that can read people's minds and almost predict the future without actually asking customers.

Reimagining mobility through the lens of customer-centricity

Imagine this perhaps familiar scenario. You need to travel from Brussels to Berlin for a conference. At the moment, the simplest option is to take a plane (although this is not actually that simple): it involves getting to the airport (early and probably the day before), spending time being subjected to some quite irritating but useful procedures like check-in and security, waiting to board, boarding like cattle on a wagon, the flight itself, disembarking, picking up your luggage and then travelling to your hotel. We all know that this can't be the best option: of course taking a plane to travel less than 1000km is bad for the planet.

What if there were another option? Night trains are now making a comeback in Europe. They're more environmentally friendly and although it takes longer than flying, this is time that you spend sleeping. Why not use that time to travel?

However, what if there were an even better option? What about a hotel room on wheels? Imagine a vehicle that picks you up from your door, but it's actually a hotel room. You can spend the evening catching up on some work, enjoying a nice meal, watching your favourite streaming service and then getting a good night's sleep in a comfortable bed. The next morning, you wake up, shower, have breakfast and you're in Berlin, bright and ready for your conference. You could have all the benefits of a night in a hotel room to make sure you're well-rested, while travelling to your destination at the same time.

What if there were an even better solution? Just imagine an app on your phone that allows you to make your very own choices: faster or slower; greener or not; more or less luxurious; more or less expensive; more or less entertainment on the journey; sightseeing tour or fastest route… If this is what you're dreaming of, then have hope. This app is being developed. I would be inclined to say that it is being built by a company, but it is not. It is no longer about companies.

In order to successfully make this a reality, companies would need partners – an ecosystem of players. In this case, an airline could partner with a car manufacturer, a hotel, a caterer or renowned chef, a streaming service, a telecommunications company. Or better yet, several of each to create a fluid, hyperconnected ecosystem that is flexible and can adapt to changes in the system, or one player falling away.

Toyota's Prius was not a revolution. The electric car was not a revolution. Even the car itself was not a real revolution. The revolution will be marked by a new type of mobility, one that doesn't simply involve replacing horse power with a combustion engine or a battery or something else, but instead uses the combined power of empowered people and an interconnected world.

Reinvent the business model to stay relevant

The business model needs to change and adapt to a society that is not even there yet. By doing that, it will reshape society.

The automotive industry has been a stalwart pursuer of tradition. Cars are made with parts that are manufactured in different factories, which are then put together and sold in dealerships dotted around the world.

Without these dealerships, it was impossible (or so it seemed) to sell cars. This made it very difficult for new players to break into the market; the infrastructure needed to sell a car was expensive. As a result, the automotive industry has had the same giants for years and years. Some companies fell off the map, but new ones didn't take their place.

However, this status quo ended when Elon Musk reinvented it with Tesla. His revolution was not the Tesla car, but the business model. Tesla is a closed ecosystem. All the car's parts are made by Tesla, from start to finish, including the supercharger itself (electric vehicle charging station). Musk wanted to take his car global, but without the infrastructure and expense of local dealerships and mass communication campaigns. Instead, he decided to use the internet. He broke the rules of the game.

Traditional brands felt safe; they thought that entering the market with both brand-new technology and a whole new business model was impossible. But they were wrong.

Rather than relying on the traditional supply chain, Musk removed that complex factor from the equation. Rather than making sales in showrooms and dealerships, Tesla was the first car to be sold online. Rather than investing in marketing, Musk relied on the fuss he could generate on social media. He knew that both lovers and haters would spread the news, and thus spread the word.

This was a revolution. Selling cars online meant that large, expensive showrooms weren't needed. Using social media meant that Tesla didn't have to invest in expensive, showy advertising campaigns. Elon Musk used the power of community to spread Tesla's message.

Tesla is a software-first, data-driven company. All Tesla cars are connected to the central brain. They gather data as they go and send it back to the central system. Driving a Tesla feels like driving a car 20 years ahead of its time. Even if you turn off the autopilot system, the car still gathers data, it learns from what you do, how you react and compares data across the network. Tesla is not a car manufacturer. It's a data company.

In order to survive and thrive in this new era, the traditional rigid and linear structure of companies has to be transformed into a flexible network of interconnected dots. If you want to start connecting the dots, you need data. In order to collect data, you need new expertise: artificial intelligence, big data, robotisation, the ecosystem economy.

Existing industries will be devastated

Let's go back to the hotel room on wheels. This could be devastating for airlines, hotels and other companies that resist the change and try to maintain the status quo of the traditional business model. It could be life-changing for those who embrace potential. By working with artificial intelligence companies, government and local authorities, utility companies, giants like Apple, Microsoft and IBM, and other partners, you can develop a smart ecosystem that is data-driven and ready to adapt to the future.

Ecosystems will start at a local level with local entities. It would take at least fifteen years to program a car that could drive anywhere in the world. These cars need data, real-time information and experience of human reactions. It takes less time, however, to prepare a car for a determined environment – one city for example. Platforms will be needed so that cities can provide an overview of transport, optimise commute times and manage the remaining power of each vehicle. Charging time

and battery life have been obstacles to the widespread adoption of electric cars since they were invented; having a fleet of cars available solves that problem. By planning the downtime of every vehicle in the fleet, cities can ensure that they have enough cars on the road at any given time.

The face of our cities has changed considerably since the 19th century. Streets are no longer littered with manure, urine and horse carcasses (due to the strain put on working horses, they only lived for around three years).[11] We no longer hear the cacophony of horses whinnying while their shoes clatter on the paved streets or smell the foul stench of excrement. Instead, the streets are littered with parked cars. We hear the constant drone of traffic, punctuated by squealing brakes and beeping horns, as we inhale the potent odour of car fumes. Instead of manure attracting flies and spreading typhoid fever, air pollution infiltrates our respiratory systems and spreads illnesses like asthma.

The next transformation won't be replacing horses with an engine; it will be putting computers on wheels. It will be empowering people to use these autonomous, connected electric vehicles when and how they want. Most people view new breakthroughs with an old lens: people don't need that, don't want that, the old way is better, there's no need to change. When Steve Jobs presented the iPhone in 2007, he said, "iPhone is like having your life in your pocket." Many people shrugged it off as a niche product. Those people have long been proven wrong.

Even I was reluctant to change. I liked my Blackberry and its keyboard; I was a pro at typing on those tiny keys. I was wary of the new-fangled notion of a touchscreen. I remember writing articles, all those years ago, about how using a touchscreen felt like trying to tie my shoelaces with gloves on. Now, however, I couldn't do without it. Now, without a touchscreen I feel like I am missing a limb. Steve Jobs created the easiest interface ever and Apple's reluctance to integrate this feature into their laptops is baffling. I can barely work with my MacBook; not being able to combine a mouse, keyboard and touchscreen makes it so much harder for me to work. Being able to use our fingers to navigate our devices was a game changer.

Will you throw in the towel?

Life as we know it may be coming to an end, but that doesn't spell the end for your business. Some businesses will adapt and thrive while others will crash and burn. It all comes down to mentality, the mindset you adopt to approach business. This is a fast-changing environment. Business models and paradigms are being transformed. You can easily find yourself stuck in quicksand if your mindset no longer keeps up with the transformations in the outside world. That's what the CEO who I was with in San Francisco realised. The change is not coming; it's here. You just need to have the guts to see it. The sooner the better. But whether sooner or later, it will always be painful.

Businesses and society are intertwined. All businesses have an impact on our everyday lives as individuals, while people affect how business is done. Businesses are not independent entities that can stand alone on an island. They are part of an ecosystem, a connected dot in the ocean. It's the riddle of the chicken and the egg. Are businesses responsible for changing consumer habits, or are consumers pushing businesses to cater to their new habits? How can we know what came first? It's all connected.

Data is the new currency. It is infinitely valuable, not as a commodity to sell but as a tool. Information will be essential to help you integrate and drive the new economy. Data is the key to unlocking the future: what's the end game? What do your customers want?

Traditionally, business owners are inadvertently shaped to fit the mould. Existing paradigms and norms that guide how business should be done exert enormous pressure on how you manage your own business. Business books, training courses, publications, KPIs and peer pressure cement these practices. We implement tips and tricks we learn from others without stepping back and evaluating what our business actually needs.

Many people laugh at conspiracy theorists and their unwavering conviction that what we see is a scam. However, sticking to the old-fashioned ways of business is just like believing in conspiracy theories. You are convinced that something is wrong with new businesses, that they are just trying to benefit and that you are the victim. The problem is that old business models are just that. Old. Hanging on to them, believing that so-called innovations are truly innovative, makes you just as susceptible as a conspiracy theorist.

Currently, most of us are on the same train, moving forward at a steady speed. The problem is that everything is changing, everything will be different. Where will your train be able to go? How long will it be able to keep going? In this environment, you can't just hang on and hope for the best. It's time to jump off the train and get on another one. There's just a small hitch. There currently is no other train. You need to build it first. But you can't build a new train while you're still on the old one.

It's time to leave the old business model behind and build a new one. It's time to create the new economy. At this point, you should have plenty of questions. That's good. Curiosity is the key to this new world.

What do we need to know in order to create these new ecosystems? What will this new environment of ecosystems look like? How will the ecosystem economy work? As a company, how do we become a part of the new economy?

COVID-19 has given us an opportunity. It's been a wake-up call, showing us that the old system is no longer workable. It's time to leave the train, jump into the void and ask the hard questions.

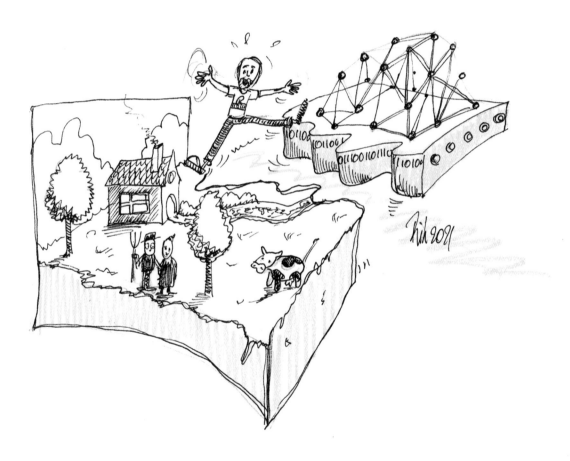

CHAOS — UNWANTED BUT NECESSARY —

Chaos tends to be feared. It is seen as an opposing force to companies' processes and procedures which are specifically designed to minimise the risk of chaos. We implement systems to ensure their operations can continue to run smoothly, even when problems and unforeseen (of foreseen) scenarios arise.

So here is the catch. We need chaos.

I repeat:

WE
NEED
CHAOS.

Yes, you heard it right. Chaos is good.

Chaos is the driver of change. Companies continuously claim to have "innovative" ideas at their fingertips. Every new release has supposedly innovative features: a new camera, better battery life, a slimmer model. Some have even gone so far as to say that innovation has become a commodity. That's not true. The innovation we have seen across the board in recent years can simply be described as incremental improvements, part of a company's plan for steady growth.

2

Undoing

**"Blinding ignorance does mislead us.
O! Wretched mortals, open your eyes!"**
LEONARDO DA VINCI

featuring:
chaos
a frozen dinosaur
the flat earth
the digital twin
stolen internet
an emaciated planet
the end of the world

Chaos – unwanted but necessary

Chaos tends to be feared. It is seen as an opposing force to companies' processes and procedures which are specifically designed to minimise the risk of chaos. We implement systems to ensure that operations can continue to run smoothly, even when problems and unforeseen (or foreseen) scenarios arise.

So here is the catch. We need chaos.

I repeat:

WE

NEED

CHAOS.

Yes, you heard that right. Chaos is good.

Chaos is the driver of change. Companies continuously claim to have "innovative" ideas at their fingertips. Every new release has supposedly innovative features: a new camera, better battery life, a slimmer model. Some have even come so close as to say that innovation has become a commodity. That's not true. The innovation we have seen across the board in recent years can simply be described as incremental improvements, part of a company's plan for steady growth. No, adding a fourth camera to a phone is not innovative. It's just Gilette razors revisited. What's next? Five cameras?

This is where companies have been going wrong. They are headed down the wrong path and they do it knowingly. The problem is that it seems like they can't do anything about it. All they seem to be able to do is keep going on the same misguided path, locked in by rigid processes, strict KPIs and balanced scorecards, also known as risk control. Change has not come, because without chaos there can be no change. If only we could pull chaos out of a hat when we need it. It's a Catch 22: companies know that they need to change but seem to be unable to do anything about it.

Then came 2020 and, with it, COVID-19. The coronavirus created chaos, throughout the world, bringing every country to a standstill. Global trade was disrupted, businesses had to adapt to employees working from home, non-essential shops and restaurants were closed.

We knew that there was a change underway; the age-old way of doing business was obsolete. When COVID-19 shook the world, people said that the tables had turned, that the world couldn't continue as it was. However, we had already reached the tipping point long before the

pandemic even though most of us didn't realise it. The problem is that we were not looking at reality through the right lens. COVID-19 came and changed our prescription, giving us the right glasses to open our eyes and see the true reality. COVID-19 was a wake-up call, but not the critical moment itself.

To rephrase Prince, it's time for businesses to stop partying like it's 1999. The business model that we have maintained for centuries is no longer valid. This was key to my first book, *Managers The Day After Tomorrow*, published in 2018. It took on new relevance in 2020. Even then, I was highlighting the change that was inevitable. Tesla, for example, was already making waves in the automotive industry. Archaic "competitors", however, turned a blind eye, convinced that if they maintained their course, continuing business as usual, Elon Musk's grand ideas would soon peter out.

The problem with this attitude is that the very nature of business has changed. Entrepreneurs can't just put their heads in the sand and wait until the disruption in their industry has blown over. They can't just freeze the dinosaur: put their model on ice and wait until the situation has died down. The dinosaurs were killed by their inability to adapt, not by the meteorite. This could kill you too. Whether you like it or not, consumer habits, expectations and needs are changing. You can freeze your model and wait, but it will no longer be relevant once thawed.

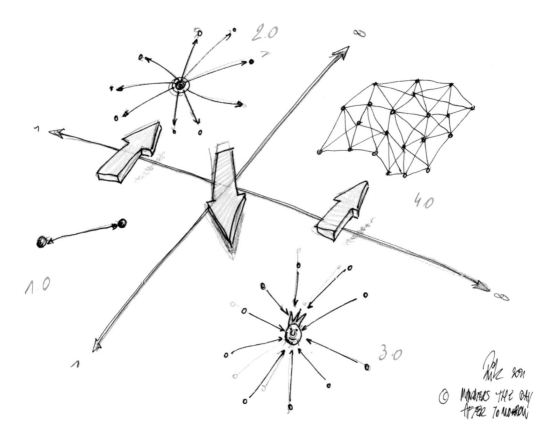

The world has changed drastically. The internet has transformed how we communicate. Our online world has merged with our offline world. And our planet is suffering the consequences of our greed.

1. Communication – from analogue to digital and back (or not?)

This may come as a shock, but I must insist: The world is no longer flat. It's got dimension, or rather several dimensions.

1.0

When you walk into your local restaurant, you take in all of the infrastructure: the tables, kitchen, general aesthetics, entrance, waiters and so on. It feels familiar. It sets the scene. Actually, it is the scene, just like in a play, for what is going to happen that evening. All of these items are part of the context, the backdrop. It is the environment and it has an impact on you.

A good customer experience is one that exceeds expectations. But just like in a play, our restaurant experience doesn't simply depend on the setting or even the food (of course, it helps if the food is better than expected).

You could enjoy a spectacular meal, delectable dishes that delight and surprise your taste buds, but still have a bad experience.

Imagine if you walked into your local restaurant, a place you visit every couple of weeks, and all of a sudden the people there no longer recognised you. Imagine if you were treated like a stranger. That's not what you want; you would feel awful. When you walk into your local restaurant, you expect two-way data transmission – otherwise known as having a two-way conversation with your waiter. You expect personalisation – not a personalised menu, but someone to talk you through it and perhaps offer suggestions. You expect surveillance - you want the waiter to not just keep an eye on the whole room but in particular to see that you need more water before you even realise that you need it. These are all aspects of a good experience; they're not just details, they're make or break. The food may be some of the best you've ever had, but if you have to flag down a waiter because you've run out of water and they ignore you, you'll leave with a bad taste in your mouth nonetheless.

It's not the setting or the food that makes the evening what it is; it is the whole of the happening* that makes the difference.

In the old normal, we just enjoyed being recognised. Facial recognition was normal. When I was a child, my dad would pick us up from school every Friday afternoon and we would go to the bank where the teller knew and recognised my dad. He didn't have to prove his identity in any way. It was easy. They also enjoyed two-way conversation, once upon a time known as small talk. The teller gathered more information about my dad than just his banking details. Did he use that information? Probably. It's likely that he used it to build a better relationship with the customer and perhaps identify that my dad needed some service he didn't know about. But it wasn't just about the return on his time investment. They enjoyed this chit-chat because it was fun and natural. It feels good to have a normal conversation. We all enjoy(ed) this one-to-one communication.

2.0

Nevertheless, companies want to grow. It's a truth we're all familiar with: if you're not moving forward, you're moving backwards; if companies don't grow, they will die. A small restaurant could become a larger one or turn into a chain of restaurants. For companies, the next step is scaling. I remember that we walked into that bank one day and it had literally grown: there were more counters and the teller who served my dad wasn't the same one as before. As a result, my dad had to show his ID. I remember his face like it was yesterday. I can't describe the emotion I witnessed, but I know for sure that it wasn't delight. There was no small talk, just business.

---

* The use of the word happening may seem a bit odd, so allow me to explain. I quite like the Collins Dictionary definition – "an improvised or spontaneous display or performance consisting of bizarre and haphazard events" – but it still doesn't quite encompass what I mean. The word happening goes beyond something that we experience, often passively, to something that we are involved in, something active. It is an unscripted interaction (improvised or spontaneous) between individuals; it is the result of what each participant brings to the table.

It's the same with restaurants. If your local restaurant scales, you can walk into the "same" restaurant in another city but it won't feel the same – it won't feel like home – if no one recognises you. It was always the same mechanism when companies scaled: they took the happening and turned it into a formula.

All of this – scaling, turning happenings into processes – took place on the old flat earth. We had no other option, which is why we opted for a blue ocean strategy: do the same for more customers or, to rephrase it, find new customers for what you do. Either you stayed small or you moved into mass production. But in doing so, you lost touch with your customers. Companies created advertising campaigns aimed at a wide audience, putting the company at the centre of its universe. In this one-to-many communication model, there was no two-way dialogue; the relationship between the company and the customer was completely disconnected. Most companies still live in this optic, surviving on the flat earth, detached from the end user. By scaling their business, they fell into the trap of one-directional communication: they hardly ever listen, there's no more interaction and there's no real communication (one-way communication is not communication).

In B2B2C, the situation is even worse. Companies have made the mistake of confusing their distribution channel with their customers. (However, it must be pointed out that this wasn't really a mistake on the flat earth because there was no other option to be had.) The distribution channel buys the company's goods to sell to end users, so companies called the distribution channel their customer because they were the ones buying their goods. The distribution channel is not your customer. The end user is your customer. On the flat earth, in the analogue physical world, you needed the distribution channel to sell your goods to the end user. It was a linear model where every person, from the initial product designer to the end user, was a link in the chain. However, with this model, your understanding of the chain as a whole is limited, if not non-existent. Many companies made the mistake of using the distribution channel (their next link) as a means to establish communications with the end user (a link further down the chain). However, if you want to communicate, and I mean really communicate, you cannot do it through the distribution channel.

In the 2000s, I managed a company that produced carpet tiles for hotels, offices and airports. When I joined the company in 2003, they were acting like the internet didn't exist. Rather than use the new tools, they continued to do business with the outside world as they had done for the last 15 years. The result was easy to predict: their market share was marginal and their profitability was in the red. Manager after manager tried to improve results, to turn a profit, but their efforts were in vain. It's not hard to discover why. They didn't change the paradigm, the algorithm, the business model. They just tried to exert better control over the input into the model. We all know the drill: more salespeople, better salespeople, more distribution channels, more products, cheaper, more expensive, new channels, enhanced quality, lower quality, more production, less production. These changes often seemed to work for a while, but they weren't sustainable and when the parameters shifted again, the business model stayed stuck. That model was identical throughout the industry, where market shares had remained stable for years. No surprise there.

When I was brought on as manager, they asked me to make the business profitable. I was stuck in a vicious circle: we could only become profitable if we sold more, and we could only sell more if we could produce more to sell at a lower price until our market share was large enough for us to raise prices and make real profits. I would never have been able to get out of that Catch-22 if I didn't develop another business model, and in particular another type of interaction with the people who were the end users of my product. Managers throughout the industry were stuck in the 2.0 world: their communication followed the flow of goods, it was one-directional and sales-oriented. It was all about mass communication and using salespeople to sell and I would always be outnumbered. I didn't have the marketing budget nor the salespeople and I didn't have the money to pay for more.

At the same time, the internet was growing quickly and new business models that used it were conquering the world. The World Wide Web gave me a present: access to information or, in other words, inspiration free of charge.

I won't go into unnecessary details, but in 2004 we launched an ambitious programme called "3 in 3". We wanted to become the third biggest player in the market within three years, rising from our then position of number 17. We knew that that meant tripling our volume in a market that had not been shaken up in 15 years. To do this, we needed a few key ingredients that everyone in the company needed to abide by:

1. Know our customers better than we know ourselves.
2. Customers decide which channels are best.
3. Embrace new technologies.
4. Be the industry's pirates, the new kids in town, the rebels.
5. Have the guts to go against the tide.
6. See no competition, only customers.
7. Foresee that it will be a bumpy and winding road. We know our target, but not exactly how we'll get there.
8. Customers will guide us, but may speak in riddles.
9. Love to experiment.
10. Celebrate every little win until we win big.

We had to start somewhere, so I shared two sources of inspiration with my management team which we translated into a model designed for our industry and market position.

The first source of inspiration was Dell. In 2004, Dell was the rising star; their business model was completely new to us and many other companies. The second source of inspiration was the tobacco industry. They were forced to change their interaction with the end user because one-to-many mass communication was made illegal. They had to be extremely creative and so did we. For us, it wasn't illegal but we didn't have the budget for mass communications. I found some interesting examples on the internet and we used all that information to our benefit.

Without knowing it, we actually built a business model that could now be described as the early days, or a rather primitive version, of 3.0 and 4.0 customer interaction, leading to some of the first signs of 5.0. We designed a model that started with the customer, which we called "reverse outside-in thinking". We started to build a network using the emerging technology toolkit (phones, computers etc.), the growing impact of the internet and Dell's e-commerce model.

Two years later, we achieved that third position. Or at least we think so. In any case, we reached the volume we wanted to reach and one year later we further doubled that volume. If you want to be able to grow in a red ocean – a crowded market where competition is fierce and dominant positions are taken – apply technology. Know your customers better than you know yourself, engage them and build a community. In other words, build a platform and become an ecosystem.

3.0

In 2021 I say that the world isn't flat any more, because it's no longer just about the physical world – there is also the digital world. There is what we see, in the upper world, and there is what is connected, in the under world. Most companies still try to do business on the flat earth, but others like Amazon and Netflix have left the flat earth behind and developed their business in the new dimension just like Dell did in 2004 and Tesla has been doing for the past few years. They are outrunning traditional companies thanks to information and data flows. The internet has enabled us to create a digital twin of the earth.

What Netflix and Amazon have done is collect data about us through our devices and how we use them, sending that data to a central brain which can identify trends and improve suggestions. Thanks to their devices, customers are empowered. They're constantly using their devices and thus leaving traces all the time. Companies flock to the consumer, trying to be bigger and better than the competition. It's a many-to-one world, in which companies target the individual consumer. It's the opposite of using mass media to emit a mass message; the customer has put themselves at the centre.

We have become sensitive nodes.

4.0

The digital world has also made us hyperconnected, where the nodes are creating connections. If that sounds like how we grow a brain to you, then that's about right. Humanity is growing a gigantic "brain" with a few billion connected and sensitive nodes, which has never happened before. The end of *The Hitchhiker's Guide to the Galaxy* (incidentally a source of inspiration for the name of this book) was right: we have become a supercomputer.

The internet has developed an interconnected network. Everybody is connected to everybody. Everyone can share their experiences, their thoughts on companies and their products with everyone else. We live in a world where it is no longer about one company communicating with the masses, but about the masses communicating with the masses. Rather than listening to the messages conveyed by the company's marketing department, customers are sharing the brand's message. The middleman has been removed from play.

5.0

At the bank, I never saw my dad ask for the right to be forgotten. That would have been foolish. My dad knew that he could meet that guy outside the bank – the same person who knew details about his family and financial situation – but he trusted him not to share that information. He didn't have proof, but he trusted him. Before the internet, we didn't mind other people knowing about us, our likes and dislikes, our family… what if the digital space could treat our data in the same way? Perhaps then, we could progress to a new yet nostalgic one-to-one communications model – a world of mass personalisation.

Let's go back to our local restaurant. Imagine if your waiter were a robot, connected to all the other robots throughout the chain of restaurants. In the beginning, they would probably be clumsy. But if they were programmed to make their customers smile and do whatever it takes to make the customer smile, they would do that. If all the robots throughout the chain were connected, they'd learn much faster. Instead of serving a handful of customers every evening, they would be serving thousands and learning from thousands. This kind of optimisation is impossible on the flat earth, but the internet has given us the tools to do it. Thanks to digitisation, everything can become a sensor. Everything that can be measured can or will be measured. In the past, traces would only be left with an immediate observer (if you have a conversation in a restaurant, the only trace lies with the other person). Now, however, everything is captured and collected (like my heartrate and temperature via my wearable watch). In coming years, we'll probably measure much more. If it's measured, it leaves traces, thus leaving room to learn.

Companies like Netflix and Amazon are doing this: multiple sensors, fast two-way communication, a central brain that collects all the data, learns from it and then improves customer interaction. Those robot waiters are the sensors, collecting information from their customers, which the central brain uses to learn what customers want and what certain types of customer want. This information is then not limited to one robot, one sensor, but shared with every sensor.

Now what if those sensors were people? What if people could benefit from all the information collected by other sensors and processed in the central brain? By putting together the best of human intelligence and artificial intelligence, we would have augmented intelligence. If we fed people with all of this knowledge, they would be able to react faster than a robot or computer. People are good at improvising and learn faster.

I don't have to ask you to know that you, like myself, miss the flat earth world of one-to-one personal communication. I remember visiting my local record shop once a month, with the pocket money I had saved, to buy a new record. After a couple of visits, the shop assistant came to learn my tastes and started offering me personalised suggestions that I could listen to before buying. But then the local record shop became a chain. I was given a customer number and a loyalty card, but I lost the personalised advice. Now, Spotify has filled that gap. It knows our tastes and offers suggestions. Sometimes they hit the mark, sometimes they don't.

2. The internet was stolen

Are we really this gigantic brain of connected dots? It certainly seems so. However, the condition for this to be so is that all the connections between dots are pure and organic. If something or someone were to control these connections (how and who we connect with), it could be extremely dangerous. As people, we are simply the dots; we can't control the connection.

The internet, as we know it, is disappearing. The first pioneers of the internet had a rather idealistic view of how the internet could transform the world, how it could be used as a tool to connect people and build a better world. They imagined the internet as a means to enable conversation and thus to liberate the world from a singular authority.

Creating knowledge together

The creator of Wikis, Ward Cunningham, imagined a primarily collaborative tool.[12] Before the internet, Cunningham created a HyperCard system with screens that connected to other screens, so that people within a company could search for ideas. He also wanted to make it boundless. If you wanted to know more about a certain concept, but that concept didn't yet exist, he programmed the system to automatically make a new information sheet about that concept. In this way, people could keep pushing the boundaries and creating new cards with new information. It was such a fascinating idea that Cunningham often found people gathered around his desk, wanting to see how it worked and learn more. Until the internet came along.

The internet allowed Cunningham to take this HyperCard system and transform it into the WikiWikiWeb, commonly known as Wikis. He wanted everyone to be able to add their own insight to build a knowledge base that is founded not on a single perspective, but on a multitude. It is a system where everyone can add and edit content, but is encouraged not to sign their work. Cunningham believed that it should be like a gift of knowledge. People from around the world were able to infuse their own perspective, providing a global overview of the topic by not basing it solely on one person's background. This was Cunningham's vision for the internet: a place of distributed authority, transparent and unfiltered, a place that is much closer to reality.

This ideology was victim to three severe mistakes; the creators of the internet underestimated human nature, the commercial potential of the internet and the sheer number of people who would write content on it. Participation couldn't be expressed in terms of thousands or millions, but rather in billions.

Mirroring the real world

Mark Zuckerberg, the founder of Facebook, was quick to identify the potential of the internet. He originally created "The Facebook" as an online directory of students at Harvard. Using this directory, you could find out information about other students at the college. Zuckerberg started small, first expanding "The Facebook" to Yale, Stanford and Columbia before widening the scope to other colleges as well. In his first interview with CNBC,[13] Zuckerberg described "The Facebook" as an online directory where you could "find interesting information about people". He stated that the most important aspect of the directory was being able to see who people's friends were, although it also gathered other personal details such as your interests, favourite books and college major.

In another early interview, Mark Zuckerberg said that his aim for this directory of students was not to create an online community but rather a mirror of real-life community. His idea was that people would use Facebook to see who knew who and thus use this information as an icebreaker to initiate conversations in real life. Facebook wasn't about connecting people, it was about gleaning information about people. The key to making this work was to make the site interesting enough so that people would want to use it and eventually become addicted.

Mark Zuckerberg saw the potential of using the community aspect to make people addicted to Facebook, gather their data and sell it for a return. Other companies, such as Google and Amazon, also saw this potential and started to use the internet as a tool to make money. The internet was originally designed as a communications tool, but it became a tool for commerce. Although the internet was intended to free the world from one singular authority, it is now dominated by a few giants who set the pace. The freedom it once afforded has disappeared.

Dominated by a few

Steve Ballmer, former CEO at Microsoft, warned that this scale achieved by just a few players would be dangerous and have an impact on the use of the internet.[14] He explained how data and algorithms match publishers, who want to sell ads, to advertisers, who want to buy them. The more inventory publishers possess, the more people bid for ad spots. As a result, prices rise and the publisher makes more money.

Scale invites more scale. The more players you have on the market, the more people will want to join. However, if only one company benefits from this scale, value will eventually be transferred from publishers and advertisers into the ecosystem of data and algorithms. Over time, this would lead to one person essentially controlling all ads, with the ability to determine how much individual businesses are worth. This is where the internet went wrong. Rather than removing the singular authority, it led to the institution of a new singular authority.

Instead of trying to bring people together and build a community, companies like Facebook have gathered data on people in order to divide them. Social media is not really a type of media. It is the fabric of our society. Using algorithms, Facebook can segment individuals into clusters of people who think alike and share similar interests and beliefs. These groups represent valuable data that they can sell to advertisers for targeted marketing. The algorithms that connect millions of people are designed for marketing and commercial purposes, playing with people's emotions to get the response they want. They're not made to create lasting connections.

Reduced to our primal emotions

In our ever more connected world and fast-paced society, communications need to happen quickly. Now we are even shown the estimated reading time of articles as we keep scrolling down the endless newsfeed. This speed causes us to fall back on our basic emotions: fear, aggression and lust (or instant gratification). I like to call this our reptile brain. Marketing algorithms are particularly suited to these primitive emotions. We no longer make decisions like we used to, looking at the long-term vision, making sacrifices and toughing it out for future gain. That was our rational brain. In a fast-paced world, our reptile brain takes over from the rational brain. Our reptile brain responds to the three basic emotions of fear, aggression and lust.

The Cambridge Analytica scandal in 2016, surrounding the US elections and the Brexit referendum, was a result of companies playing on these primal emotions. Alexander Nix, then CEO of Cambridge Analytica, used data provided by Facebook to identify people's biggest fears. It is incredibly difficult to discover what someone's dream is, because people often don't know exactly what their dream is themselves. Fears, on the other hand, are easy to detect. Nix used these fears to unite people against a single enemy: "the establishment". During the 2016 US election campaign, Cambridge Analytica shared around 40,000-50,000 different messages in Trump's name every day.[15] These messages contained different content targeted to each voter – playing on the fears identified using their data – to unite them against their common enemy.

In April 2016, I was part of a line-up of keynote speakers aiming to inspire Dutch entrepreneurs and show them the benefits of big data and AI. The event was organised by a large Dutch bank; the setting was an international tennis tournament in Rotterdam. In between the rehearsal and the actual keynote, for about four hours, the other speakers and myself were made to feel comfortable in a luxurious lounge. One of the other speakers was Alexander Nix. At first, when we were introduced, his name didn't really ring a bell. Of course I knew that his company, Cambridge Analytica, had been involved in the US elections and Brexit, but I wasn't really aware of all the details and the true impact.

I don't know whether it was the long and seemingly never-ending four hours or the wine that came with lunch that led to us talking, but I became fascinated (and disgusted in equal measure) by what he was telling me. He showed no emotion as he explained what he did with steel-cold precision, fuelled by my questions.

Now I remember. It wasn't the wine, it was what was served at lunch (Dutch *bitterballen* and milk) that broke the ice and got us talking.

Big data and AI can be used to create the good, the bad and the ugly. Regardless of how beautiful it was from a purely scientific point of view, what Nix revealed to me contained no good at all. It was technology and psychology merging into a form of augmented intelligence that allowed Cambridge Analytica to pull the strings of millions of individuals. During that conversation, I saw that my "magic formula" – c2MxEi (connect to many and engage individuals) – could also be used for the bad, and the ugly.

Social media is designed to be a place of instant reward. It is the new social fabric of our world, which is based on our most primitive reptile brain. Social media groups people into clusters, which have accidentally become echo chambers. By conversing with like-minded people, your ideas aren't challenged but instead cemented. Rather than benefiting from a global vision, people are exposed to a reduced reality. As a result, the internet is being used to sow discord. The alt-right has used social media for years to sow fear of the establishment. The platform social media has provided us is not giving the ordinary man a place to air his views, but rather is using the ordinary man as a mouthpiece, stoking confrontation and presenting an alternative to the controlled offline world. Online happenings can rapidly influence events offline. It may even lead to civil war.

In January 2021, Donald Trump's supporters stormed the Capitol, just as Congress was sitting down to confirm Joe Biden's victory, in an attempt to overturn the results of the 2020 presidential elections. Donald Trump claimed that the election was a fraud and called on his supporters to head to the Capitol and protest. That is what they did, united by their shared enemy – the establishment – and empowered by the voice they found on social media. In the aftermath, Twitter and Facebook temporarily suspended Donald Trump's accounts due to the risk of inciting violence. A few days later, Twitter decided to permanently suspend his account. Social networks and their algorithms have long been blamed for spreading misinformation and fake news while fuelling radical behaviour. The riots at the Capitol only prompted more questions. Was social media to blame for the riots? Did Twitter take too little action too late or did it overstep? Is suspending an account an infringement of our fundamental human right to free speech?

Closing the divide between online and offline

Social media has made us feel like we are the centre of the world and that, as a result, we can do whatever we want there. Nevertheless, the divide between our online and offline universes is narrowing. Long gone are the days when we had to dial up to the internet. Remember that awful screeching sound you had to endure as your computer took a few minutes to connect to the server, thus disconnecting your landline phone? Instead of purposefully accessing the internet, we can now conduct a simple Google search with the tap of a button or even by using our voice. This notion of "connecting" to the internet is unknown to young people who have grown up as a connected generation, always online.

In 2015 at the World Economic Forum in Davos, Eric Schmidt, Google's Chairman and ex-CEO, sent shock waves around the room when he said: "The Internet will disappear."[16] What he meant was that the internet would become so integrated into our lives, so seamless to use, that we would no longer regard it as a thing. He explained: "There will be so many IP addresses … so many devices, sensors, things that you are wearing, things that you are interacting with that you won't even sense it. It will be part of your presence all the time. Imagine you walk into a room, and the room is dynamic. And with your permission and all of that, you are interacting with the things going on in the room."

The internet is now a fundamental component of our lives. The EU is even examining the implementation of a new human right – the right to disconnect.[17] There is an expectation nowadays that we are always connected, always reachable. The internet is so integrated into our everyday lives that we have transformed from homo sapiens into OMO sapiens (online merged with offline). If you really think about it, can you identify where your online life ends and your offline life begins? Although you may be spending time with friends and family in person, your phone is likely within arm's reach, with the possibility to hop back online within seconds of a notification sounding. It's no longer about making the choice to connect once or twice a day. We are always connected.

Uncontrolled online threats are seeping offline

2020 accentuated our new status as OMO sapiens. In many cases, the police would have jailed people if they did what they do online in real life. And yet, our online world often seeps into our offline world. Ideas spread online before they jump offline like a fireball that devastates reality. The events at the Capitol are a perfect example. Nobody tries to stop these trends when they are small and seemingly insignificant. By the time they do act, it is often too late.

In 2020, governments were forced to take action in an attempt to halt the coronavirus pandemic. Many countries went into lockdown and took various measures to limit people's activities to stop the spread of the virus. Schools, shops and theatres were forced to close down, the government imposed a set number of social contacts and face masks became compulsory in many public places. In the face of this virus, governments took action. However, little action is taken online to stop the spread of incendiary messages, radical ideas and harmful comments. The way in which we tackle online viruses is a far cry from the measures governments took in 2020 to stop coronavirus in its tracks.

Many people, including politicians, warn that social media presents a serious threat to democracy. And it does. But how can we solve this problem? We can't ask social networks to change their algorithms, because that wouldn't really tackle the heart of the problem. So what if we tried to change the input into the algorithms, excluding some messages such as certain political ideas? This isn't an option either. This would be an infringement of free speech and thus also endanger democracy. We are trying to manage the new social fabric using rules that date back to Napoleon's time. It's just not possible.

The world seems to have been turned upside down. While liberals advocate for stricter rules on social media, conservatives fight to retain the right to free speech. Democracy is at stake, but we're stuck in a Catch 22. Social media poses a threat to democracy, but the solutions we could employ to alleviate that threat would also endanger democracy.

Socrates was a severe critic of democracy: how could the "uneducated and easily lead population" be entrusted to make decisions concerning the leadership of the country?[18] To him, it was like allowing people with no knowledge of seafaring to vote on who would captain the ship. Social media has further accentuated the political divide. It is now much easier for people to use their voice, or have their voice used as a mouthpiece for someone else's ideas. We have transitioned from a democracy to a mobocracy.

The internet was designed as a tool to connect people, to create international communities, to share knowledge. Social media and internet giants have made it primarily a place of commerce, with data as the commodity to be sold. In this way, they have sown discord that doesn't remain online but directly influences our offline worlds. A democratic system built on one central authority is not armed to deal with a hyperconnected world. Trying to stop the stream of data is like raising your hand to stop a tsunami. We didn't realise it before, but social media has been working in the shadows to steal the internet from under our very noses. Our rational brains have been replaced with reptile brains, attempting to manage the godlike technology we have been gifted using rules from a bygone era.

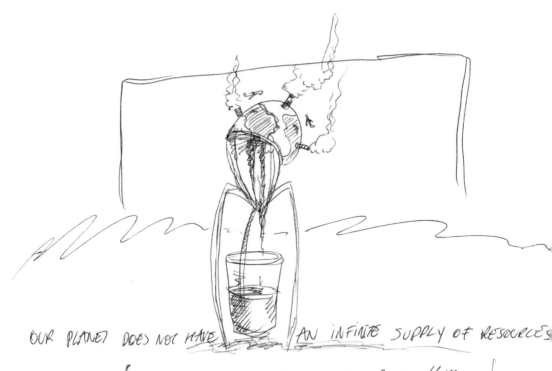

OUR PLANET DOES NOT HAVE AN INFINITE SUPPLY OF RESOURCES

Covid-19 also clearly exposed a fund problem with the economic model that we have maintained for so long. In our quest for profit, we forgot about another very important P: the planet.
The economic model that we applied for decades is no longer tenable; it has come to an end.

We cannot continue with a system that is based on constant growth, thus equally increasing consumption, in a world with limited resources. Every year, Earth overshoot Day, the day on which we have exhausted Earth's normal resources for the year, arrives sooner....

3. Our planet does not have an infinite supply of resources

COVID-19 also clearly exposed a third problem with the economic model that we have maintained for so long. In our quest for profit, we forgot about another very important P: the planet. The economic model that we have applied for centuries is no longer tenable; it has come to an end. We cannot continue with a system that is based on constant growth, thus equalling increasing consumption, in a world with limited resources. Every year, Earth Overshoot Day, the day on which we have exhausted Earth's natural resources for the year, creeps forward.

2020 gave our planet a brief breath of fresh air. In 2019, Earth Overshoot Day was on 29th July. By bringing the world to a standstill, the pandemic pushed that day back by 24 days in 2020 to 22nd August, the same position as fifteen years earlier.[19] Nevertheless, in less than eight months, with large portions of the world in lockdown, we used more resources than the Earth could regenerate in one year. There is one silver lining: COVID-19 showed us that it is possible to change our habits. We thought it couldn't be done, but it can. We can consume less and push back that day. It's just about making the change.

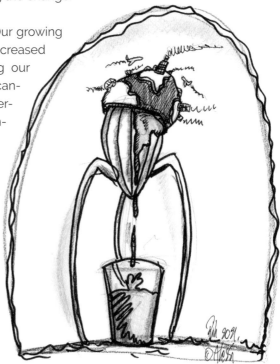

We cannot keep overconsuming. Our growing population and the consequent increased use of natural resources is eating our planet to the core. Our economy cannot be healthy if we place the ownership of natural resources, the planet's resources, into the hands of a few. Why should corporate entities be allowed to make a profit from natural resources such as oil, wind, water and sunlight? An economic model in which companies can make money off the back of the planet's resources is not sustainable.

By launching The Great Reset, the World Economic Forum has welcomed this time for change.

GREAT RESET HERE

Through their initiative, they hope to "offer insights to help inform all those determining the future state of global relations, the direction of national economies, the priorities of societies, the nature of business models and the management of a global commons".[20] We know that what we are doing is no good, we know that we need to change, but at the moment we have not come up with an alternative. Here's our opportunity. Klaus Schwab, founder and executive chairman of the World Economic Forum, said: "The pandemic represents a rare but narrow window of opportunity to reflect, reimagine and reset our world."

COVID–19 has presented us with a rare opportunity

The global economy is fragile. On 23rd March 2021, the *Ever Given*, a container ship as long as the Empire State Building is high, ran aground in the Suez Canal, completely blocking one of the busiest shipping channels in the world.[21] Roughly 30% of global shipping container volumes travel through the Suez Canal, equating to about 12% of global trade of goods. As a result, the blockage caused an estimated loss of $9.6 billion a day to the global economy[22]. The ship was stuck for almost a week and some 369 ships were left stranded, waiting to pass through the canal. One boat directly affected around 12% of the global economy.[23] For every minute that that ship was stuck, roughly $6.7 million dollars were lost. That doesn't even taken into account any consequent effects. It begs the question: what are we doing? Why are we producing goods in one place just to put them into a container on a ship for transit to the consumer? Is it worth the small saving we make on the product's price?

So if COVID-19 wasn't the tipping point, but just the torch that allowed us to see in the dark, what was? When did our economic model become obsolete? The Maya predicted that the end of the world was on the 21st December 2012. Perhaps they were right. Perhaps the world as we knew it came to an end in 2012. There was no massive explosion, no apocalypse, no dramatic event that signalled the end of the world, but perhaps there was an imperceptible shift. We cannot continue on the same path.

We know that our economy is obsolete and yet we haven't changed. Wouldn't it just be easier to continue doing the same thing we have always done and hope that things work out? To freeze the dinosaur? Change isn't supposed to be easy.

COVID-19 has given us an opportunity to find the alternative, to chart a new course, but we need to stop looking at the problem through the lens of the old economy. To quote Albert Einstein: "We can't solve problems by using the same kind of thinking we used when we created them." That's why we currently see no alternative. We're still looking at the economy as if it were linear, a reduced reality built on processes, values and procedures. We cannot imagine a new economic model through the lens of the old one.

"Rarely are opportunities presented to you in a perfect way. In a nice little box with a yellow bow on top. 'Here, open it, it's perfect. You'll love it.' Opportunities – the good ones – are messy, confusing, hard to recognize. They're risky.
They challenge you."

Susan Wojcicki, CEO of YouTube

This is the realisation that should have dawned on us much earlier, before COVID-19, perhaps in 2012, perhaps before or after. Whenever the tipping point truly happened, what we needed was chaos. Chaos to open our eyes to the true reality, not our assumed reality. COVID-19 has given us that chaos, an opportunity to get out of the rat race and reimagine.

It certainly won't be easy. It will be devastating, it will be dark, it may even get bloody. But is there any alternative if we want to wipe the slate clean and move forward to the future?

SURF's UP

Whether you are a manager or not, most people feel the need to get away from
the daily grind from time to time (I do it by the way, but then again that's for me).
Perhaps you'd like to go to Nazaré in Portugal, not necessarily to enjoy the sun,
sea and sand (although that is also an option).

Personally, I would recommend Nazaré as a spot to watch the crazy
surfers who gather here from all over the globe because it is
known as the place to catch the biggest waves in the world. There
you can find the best, and then the most insane surfers.

I've already said it but I'll warn you again: surfers are
more than slightly NUTS. That is exactly why you should watch
them. Our companies could use some more crazy people at the
helm. Leaders who think differently and dare to seek out the
insane ways to surf. The world in short you can energy you anyway but
surf became a wild, savage and unpredictable as the genius norm in
Nazaré. Instead of lucky in place, you need to seek them out, still
like those crazy surfers. In should you need to developed surfer's
mindset.

A SURFER'S MINDSET

3

Survival

"Change almost never fails because it's too early.
It almost always fails because it's too late."
SETH GODIN

---

featuring:
surfing
boiling red ocean
an ever-widening divide
contrasting customers
empowered people
the flywheel
heart

Surf's up

Whether you're a manager or not, most people feel the need to get away from the daily grind from time to time. Perhaps you'd like to go to Nazaré in Portugal, not necessarily to enjoy the sun, sea and sand (although that's also an option).

Personally, I would recommend Nazaré as a spot to watch the crazy surfers who flock there from all over the globe because it is known as the place to catch the biggest waves in the world. There you can find the best, and thus the most insane, surfers.

I've already said it but I'll warn you again: surfers are more than slightly nuts. That's exactly why you should watch them. Our companies could use some more crazy people at the helm. Leaders who think different-ly and dare to seek out the wildest waves to surf. The world in which you are steering your company has become just as wild, savage and unpredictable as the gigantic waves in Nazaré. Instead of hiding in fear, you need to seek them out, just like those crazy surfers. In short, you need to develop a surfer's mindset.

To be or not to be (William Shakespeare)

Surfers get a kick out of enormous waves and you should too. Nazaré is holy ground for surfers. It is the battleground of trial and error, of flirting with the risk of horrendous accidents, of seeking the thrill of finding and conquering the biggest waves out there. In order to surf a 24-metre high wave, you need to go at it full throttle and not second-guess yourself. That's exactly what the crazy but marvellous Rodrigo Koxa did in November 2017. You can watch his incredible feat on YouTube. He makes it look surprisingly easy.

The story goes that this Brazilian surfer had a dream the night before. It may not be true, but it's a beautiful story nonetheless.

"I had an amazing dream the night before, where I was talking to myself, 'You gotta go straight down. You gotta go straight down.' I didn't really know what it meant. But I figured somebody was talking to me. When I got my wave, I let go of the rope, I started to use my rail to angle towards the shoulder, but then realized, if I used my rail, I'd never get deep. And then I remembered: 'go straight down.' When I said it, I remembered my dream. I turned and I almost fell, but then I got my feet again and went super-fast. I've never had a big wave like that where I didn't use the rail at all. Just went straight down. It was amazing."[24]

It's probably best we don't ask ourselves what might have happened if his dream hadn't "informed" him what to do and he had tried to "use the rail", as surfers tend to do. A less fortunate surfer, Andrew Cotton, tried just that on the same day and ended up breaking his back. Koxa had also suffered a serious injury just three years prior, but he recovered, got back on the board and broke records.

To be or not to be. The right choice often only looks like the right choice in hindsight. That's when we tell the story, about a dream that inspired our choice, the one that ended up being the right choice. Surfing is far from risk-free. Entrepreneurs need to be aware of this risk.

A surfer's mindset

As you sit on that beach in Nazaré, soaking up the atmosphere, the warm rays of sun, the salty sea air, pay attention to a few things while you watch those surfers:

1. Surfers never give up on their dream to ride the biggest wave. Once they've found the biggest, they're ready for the next one, an even bigger wave, to pop up. Their constant hunger for the biggest, greatest and most difficult wave hangs in the air. It's contagious.

2. In order to catch a big one, you need to find the very start of the swell. Then you need to work very hard to follow it and get on top just as the mountain of water becomes a wave. If you miss that initial swell, you're definitely too late and if you try to get on top of it, it's life threatening. You haven't gained the necessary speed and you're going to be flattened.

3. Once a surfer has started the descent down a monstrous wave, there's no turning back. The slightest hesitation or hint of fear can be the difference between life and death. To surf that gigantic wave you need a hell of a lot of courage. "Straight down" is the only way to go.

4. Those who surf the biggest waves need to have the right skills to be able to handle it.

What about you? What have you observed? Perhaps you just wanted a few days' rest in Portugal. Why should you think like a surfer? It's simple. The digital upheaval we are now experiencing was never the tsunami we dubbed it to be. We never learnt to surf it, because we tend to shy away from dangerous and unpredictable tasks. We lied to ourselves. The rise of digital came in waves, big waves, with surfers on top. Daredevils riding the waves. We called it the digital tsunami. It sounds better for those who missed the wave. We called the surfers disruptors. It diminishes their status.

The Great Wave

Many of us are still swimming in the calm of the ocean. Waiting. We missed the waves. Perhaps we didn't see them, perhaps we saw them too late or perhaps we didn't have the courage to catch them. Perhaps we thought it was too soon or too dangerous. Perhaps we wanted to wait and see what other people were doing first. Whatever we thought, that's how we ended up waiting and not practising. Some companies did. They surfed that first primitive wave – the internet. Before we tentatively started building our first websites, companies like Booking.com, Google and Amazon had already started to conquer the scene. Remember, that was back in 1995. After that came the next big wave – social media – in 2005. We thought that this was of little consequence to companies, thinking it was just a toy for young people. Then we realised that they had managed to reach four billion people. Around 2012, we saw the rise of everything mobile and the way in which platforms were changing the world order. But we stayed still, out there in the calm ocean, treading water and waiting. Look around you. All of the waves are now coming one after the other. The gigantic one has already passed the crucial point and tonnes of water are beating down on us. We didn't even learn how to surf. We treaded water and waited, as the wave of algorithms, big data, AI and robotisation towered over us. It was the wave of new ecosystems that created these new superpowers.

Now there is no going back. Any separation between different types of industries will be swept away, mass production will become mass personalisation. It's a world where online and offline will become one and thus disappear.

The Great Wave and You

It's coming. You're not too late, not yet at least, but your window of opportunity is closing rapidly. Grab that surfboard, take a deep breath and get started. I know that you haven't learnt how to surf. It's a shame. But I have good news.

In this book, I'm going to teach you how you can avoid surfing alone. In fact, I'm going to tell you that you can't go it alone. Ecosystems are the solution. But if you're not already on the job and trying to stand on that surfboard, you'll never get there.

Later I will also tell you what you can start doing NOW to prepare to join such an ecosystem. Let me give you one clue in the meantime: data. Focus on it. Don't lose any information. Start NOW.

Surfing is fun

So let's all head to Nazaré to sit on the beach, watch the surfers and learn from them. You now have to become one as well. You need to become just as crazy as Rodrigo Koxa, because you have no other option than to tame that big wave.

Become a surfer, dude.

I wrote this passage, this story about surfers, before COVID-19 swept into our lives. Life seemed simple then. Learn to surf and everything would be fine. COVID-19 didn't see it the same way.

The wake-up call

The year 2020 served a purpose. It woke us up to the fact that our assumptions had presented us with a perception of reality that wasn't true. Our assumptions had been blinding us to the real happenings in the world. 2020, the year in which a global pandemic brought the world to a standstill, opened our eyes to the truth, to the ever-widening divide between what we perceived to be true and what actually was true.

It is now crystal clear that the old economy is dead. Remember in chapter one I talked about jumping off the train? Well, now's the time to do that. Jump off the old economic train so that you can have the opportunity to build something new. Don't be fooled; it's going to be a rough ride.

Perhaps you're not convinced that the old economy is dead. We have already explored three key reasons why the old economy cannot continue: changes in communications, the internet being stolen and the overconsumption of our planet's finite resources. However, we've only just scratched the surface.

Why companies didn't really develop their Day After Tomorrow

Business leaders have given me many excuses for not developing their Day After Tomorrow. Even companies that realised that their existing business model would no longer be relevant beyond 2030 didn't really put enough time, money, resources and talent into developing potential future revenue streams. Here are some of the reasons why:

1. We have no time. All of our people are so busy doing their jobs, generating money and trying to cope with the demand of customers, competition and internal issues, that we do not have the time to develop our Day After Tomorrow. We'll do it one day, but right now we don't have the time.

2. It is quite impossible to rebuild a plane while it is still in the air. We have to admit, we tried to convince each other that it could be done, but we knew better. We simply couldn't take the risk of letting the plane crash and we didn't have the opportunity to ground the plane for a few weeks. It's nice in theory, but it will never happen.

3. Why would we risk rebuilding our plane now? We are still making money doing the good old stuff. Developing something new would just burn through money. It would eat today's profits for something that we can't even know for sure will bring us money in the end. Where is the ROI?

4. If we develop something for the future, how can we know that we aren't there too soon in a market that's not ready yet? Let's wait and see. Then we'll R and D (Rob and Deploy) like we always do.

5. We are stuck in our own processes and procedures, scorecards and KPIs, organisation and structure. They keep us boxed in. We can't change.

Companies set their goals for the next five, ten, twenty years; goals that are supposed to realise their dream. But a goal is a dream killed by a timeline. You cannot plan for or design the unknown. The only way to realise that dream is to get moving, right now, and keep going for as long as it takes.

The old economy

The old economy was based on a blue ocean strategy, focused on constant growth and increased shareholder value. Companies sought to identify a target market, a new group of consumers they could sell their product to, perhaps customers in a different geographical location. The whole economy was based on new and more. But there's a limit to how many new markets we can find, how many new geographies there are in the world and how often we can market a supposedly "innovative" product as a must-have to consumers. The truth is that there are no blue oceans, no new markets left. The blue ocean strategy for the economy can no longer exist.

Our old economy was based on constant growth in a world with finite resources. It was like a red giant, growing and growing so much and so fast that it swallowed up everything around it. In its quest for growth, its true raison d'être was forgotten. As resources dwindled, the race to snatch them up intensified. The giant grew faster and faster. If this were to continue, our economy would eventually implode like a red giant, leaving us with nothing but a black hole. We have to avoid that happening.

If there's no blue ocean strategy, then what is there? How can companies continue to sell their goods and services to customers? If we're not looking for new target markets, how can we stand out from the competition? I'm going to tell you the cold hard truth: industries of the past cannot compete with the new data-driven companies that are sweeping the market focused on customer experience. What is coming is a giant, bloody, BOILing* red ocean.

We know that the future of the automotive industry is going to be ACES (autonomous, connected, electric and sharing). The automotive industry is going to melt down into a red ocean of mobility and, even further still, into a red ocean for society. It won't be about producing cars to get us from point A to point B, but about smart travel, smart utilities, smart society and so much more. New technologies are overthrowing the industries of the past to create new segments that respond to real customer frustrations. The transformation triggered by new technologies is so big that no existing industry can face it alone. We'll need partners, like the automotive industry in chapter one.

Time – the new currency

Given that one industry alone will no longer be able to respond to the needs and expectations of society, companies will need to effect drastic change. Consumers will no longer search for a car, but for an experience that suits their needs. Existing industries are going to melt down into something that doesn't exist yet - the red ocean. In the red ocean, everyone will compete with everyone, not just competitors in their industry. The key here is to create alliances, build partnerships and work together, rather than competing. By fostering networks with other players, companies will be able to work together to create ecosystems within the red ocean. These ecosystems will have the capacity to respond to changing expectations.

Not only are new technologies overthrowing traditional industries, they are also providing the world with new tools, such as artificial intelligence, big data, robotisation and automation. These new technologies boil down to data, data and more data. Data is going to be an essential

---

* BOIL = Blurring Of Industry Lines

facet of all future business. But again, there are no new blue oceans, no new markets to do research on, to collect data on. As a result, all companies will be chasing the same data about the same people. Without data, you will be left behind. Now, companies use data to show consumers adverts that are targeted to them. In the future, data will be used to hyper-personalise the customer experience.

Mary Barra made a very good point. Time is our ultimate source of value. If we can reclaim the time we spend on all those mundane tasks, the time we waste commuting, the time that seems to fly away on so many different tasks, we will be able to devote more time to the things that matter to us: family, friends, self-care, hobbies, you name it! Companies will use data to make the time their customers spend with them worthwhile. They will aim to create wellbeing for their customers by using their time well and adding worth to that time. Customers are at the centre of their own universe, so the only thing that companies will be able to offer is value, time well spent, wellbeing. Companies can't use fear or aggressive tactics. That's not creating wellbeing. That's wasting valuable time. Companies will all have the same aim of adding value, generating wellbeing for their customers and, as a result, they will all melt down into the same red ocean.

The fact that ecosystems already exist is the final nail in the coffin of the old economy that embodied the blue ocean strategy. Many of the big data-driven companies that dominate the current economic landscape are closed ecosystems. Tesla, for example, is not an automotive company. It's an ecosystem, where everything from the superchargers to the batteries to the cars themselves are manufactured within the Tesla system. This is what their "competitors" failed to understand. Traditional automotive companies saw Tesla as a traditional competitor. To them, Elon Musk was a newbie with grand ideas that would eventually go belly up and fail. The problem is that they misidentified their enemy. Tesla is not an automotive company, it is an ecosystem.

Human behaviour is unpredictable

No company can compete with an ecosystem on their own. Customers tend to be very loyal to a particular brand. You could say that they choose a brand to partner with for life. Does the Apple versus Samsung debate ring a bell?

When the iPhone came out, I was using a Blackberry – and I enjoyed it – but there came a time when the Blackberry felt like a dinosaur, so I made the switch. But not to an iPhone. I chose a Microsoft phone. I liked it because it had the same interface as my computer and because it was an open system.

However, I couldn't stay with Microsoft for long because there were too few apps on the App Store. It simply wasn't big enough, so companies didn't want to invest in making their app available there. The chicken and the egg: there aren't enough users so companies won't invest but the app store can't grow and attract more users if companies don't invest.

In the end, I went for a Google phone. I didn't want to be locked in by Apple to only use their apps, their devices, their accessories. And I certainly didn't want to be forced to buy the latest model again and again and again because they discontinued support for earlier models. That's not making me central. That's not making me your best friend. That's locking me in.

However, in order for a customer to stick with that brand, they need to experience the value in doing so. But companies cannot compete with ecosystems. Ecosystems will always be able to offer better value (in the broad sense of the word, not just financial) to their customers. Customers won't choose a brand partner for life, they will choose an ecosystem to be their partner.

It's clear that the old economy is dead. Ole Peters, a theoretical physicist in the United Kingdom, pointed out that the biggest mistake of modern economic theory is that it is based on the principle of "ergodicity".[25] Rather than being based on actual human behaviour, it is based on the average of all possible outcomes. Wealth inequality is the perfect example of this. A few people possess a personal wealth of millions or billions of dollars, while many others barely make enough to get by, living from pay cheque to pay cheque. However, if you calculate the average, the wealth of the lucky few will severely distort the average, making it seem like the average person earns much more than they actually do. This is the problem with modern economic theory. It doesn't take into account how one anomaly can skew the average, nor does it take into account human behaviour. Humans don't make decisions based on rational thought process; they make decisions based on their emotions, feelings and experiences.

For centuries, the economy has been based on growth, stakeholder value and, as a result, profit. But in the quest for more and more profit, companies have forgotten the other two Ps: people and planet.

In a so-called effort to care for the planet, and combat climate change, it seems that we've forgotten about the planet and reverted to the P for profit. The Emissions Trading System effectively allows companies to earn money by selling free CO_2 rights that they were allocated.[26] The limited number of emissions allowances ensures that these rights remain of value. As a result of the ETS system, some of the biggest polluters are earning money by selling off a part of their emissions allowance. The quest for profit has overtaken the importance of people and planet yet again.

The disruptors

The old economy is dead, but does that mean that the new economy will be governed by the likes of Amazon, Facebook and Uber? There is general fear among the population about the impact of new technologies: how many jobs will be lost? How will technology be used to infringe upon our private lives? Will artificial intelligence create its own army to destroy humankind? The questions about the future are endless. Scientists, tech geeks and researchers have tried to alleviate these fears by proving what technology can do, but the truth is that the power of new technology has been abused. That's why people are afraid.

The first lockdowns imposed in response to the global pandemic were life-changing for everyone. Non-essential shops were forced to close their doors, workers had to adapt to a new working-from-home situation, often overnight, and schools were closed. Customers who were used to hitting the local shops to get the items they wanted and needed were stuck. How were they supposed to entertain their children who couldn't go to school, while also trying to work in a new impromptu home office? Customers had no choice, even those who had shied away from e-commerce in the past. They were forced to turn to Amazon and similar sites to get the items they needed and wanted. The resulting increase in demand led to Amazon's algorithms raising prices across the board. Rather than employing human values of compassion and empathy in the face of rising unemployment and financial insecurity for many families, the algorithms saw increased demand and lower competition and sought to reap the financial rewards.

Amazon is a disruptor. It disrupted the retail industry just as Uber disrupted the taxi industry. Uber "stole" an existing business model and exploited the weaknesses using data. Uber created a FEAST interface: Fast, Easy, Accessible, Simple, Tempting. Gone was the hassle of calling a taxi company; the simple click of a button in an app was all that was needed to order a taxi. No more worrying about finding a taxi number, no unease speaking on the phone, no interrupting your conversation with friends to order a taxi. Simple, quick, easy. Uber managed to disrupt a regulated industry. Their drivers didn't require a special taxi licence, just a car and a driving licence.

Uber succeeded in making the old taxi industry look ugly and cumbersome. Their FEAST interface drew users to their platform, but instead of turning it into something good, they created something bad. Uber claimed to reduce the number of cars on the road, putting more people into fewer cars. However, a Transport & Environment survey[27] showed that the growth of services like Uber has led to more traffic and thus increased pollution and carbon emissions. That's not the only negative effect of Uber. Uber drivers receive pitifully low pay, data is abused and gender discrimination is a repeated occurrence. Not only have passengers accused drivers of sexual abuse, Travis Kalanick, Uber's CEO, nicknamed his company "Boober" because of all the women he could now pick up. In 2014, Emil Michael, Uber's VP, was recorded saying that Uber should "dig up dirt" on reporters[28] after Sarah Lacy, founder of tech website PandoDaily, called Uber out for sexist behaviour[29] following an ad campaign in Lyon aimed at matching male passengers with sexually attractive female drivers.

It's no wonder that the general public is fearful of what the new technologies of the future may bring. Companies like Uber and Amazon have exploited data and workers to maximise shareholder value. They created closed ecosystems that were in fact just a digital copy of companies in the old economy. They claimed to be customer-centric, by offering a FEAST interface and providing quick and easy service (one-click purchase and next-day delivery come to mind). But the rise of this type of morally questionable company in Silicon Valley has led to the development of a new phrase: "asshole culture". Anyone who has been to San Francisco will be familiar with that vibe you get as you walk around. It's a slightly hippie, cool, laid-back surfer feeling mixed with a gold-digger mindset and a hint of "we don't give a fuck about the world". But the laid-back, hippie attitude can easily blind you to the dark underground of what's really going on.

The old economy was unfair. Jeff Bezos, Elon Musk, Jack Ma and many others have all come to dominate the world with old money. How is it possible for Musk to be so rich when his companies aren't even turning a profit? They created a digital twin of the old business model. They used the TREE principle: Technology first, Red ocean strategy, Engaged people, Ecosystem economy. But their idea of an ecosystem is not the same as ours. These disruptors used old customer frustrations to create interfaces that would drag us in to their world. The old economy was about making choices: operational excellence or product leadership or customer intimacy. Digital players changed this by using the power of digital to create FEAST. We perceived this as customer-centricity but we were being used to gather data. The more data they collected, the more they were able to use customers as a free marketing department. They created the sharing economy and then blew it apart. Uber became a dark evil company feeding on the old world but not making a profit. Online retailers, such as Amazon, are just copies of post-order companies with one big difference: they're digitised. They were clever. They used the frustrations of the old world to create their own closed ecosystems, digital twins of millions of old-form companies. They employed their own red ocean strategy.

Let's turn the tide

We can use this. We can do unto the disruptors as they have done unto us. We can turn the system around and truly put the customer at the heart of our work. But how? How can we turn the tide? How can we use their world to build a better world for tomorrow?

First, we need to use digital. That's not to say that we should copy their systems, but we are going to need digital technologies to build the new economy. We have to understand and use (but not abuse) the power of big data, robotisation and artificial intelligence to zoom in on small but honest data. We can create humanisation where they created customer frustration. We can focus on augmented intelligence, using our intrinsic emotional intelligence to add a human touch to the capacities of AI. Digital will help us with our second point of action: identifying and responding to customer frustration.

As customers, we fell in love with the solutions that the likes of Amazon and Uber provided. They were Fast, Easy, Accessible, Simple and Tempting. But they forgot the most important human factor: HEART. Until Uber came along, nobody noticed that the taxi industry was rubbish. The first rides I took with Uber in San Francisco felt like a revelation. It was as if

we were pirates partaking in a new secret society. But the cracks soon started to form as the platform's spell of enchantment wore off for drivers and passengers alike. They had succeeded in creating a FEAST interface, which led customers to believe that it was all about them, that they were the centre of the universe. Instead, customers were being used for marketing, infrastructure and data mining.

True customer engagement has to come with HEART: Honest, Ethical, Authentic, Responsible/Responsive and Transparent. Customers want services that are transparent, so that they can clearly understand who earns the money we spend. Customers want services that are responsible to people and planet and responsive to their needs. We are now in a consumer economy, but we are going to create small local smart ecosystems. Smart because we use technology, but also smart as in good for people and planet. Ecosystems will be driven by data and strong partnerships, because no company can go it alone. We will use the TREE principle – Technology first, Red ocean strategy, Engaged customers and Ecosystem economy – but we will do it with HEART.

TREE is the formula for exponential growth. We live in two worlds: the real world and its digital twin. In 2007, when the iPhone was launched, we logged onto the digital world once or twice a day. Now we are constantly present. There is no more parallel world. We are living in the Matrix. Travel brochures no longer talk about the sights that will take your breath away; instead they offer a selection of the most "instagrammable" spots to visit during your trip. People try so hard to take the perfect selfie that selfie deaths have now become a real problem. Whether we like it or not, we live in an online-offline world.

Different, yet the same

Mary Barra said that the next ten years would bring more change than the last 50, but don't be fooled if the change isn't visible. The day after tomorrow *is* going to be different. It's going to be so different you'll feel like your world's been turned upside down. However, on the surface things may look the same and this superficial similarity may be confusing.

Back in the 1960s and 1970s, we expected that the world would look completely different by the year 2000. We expected flying saucers, trains in the air and futuristic-looking buildings. Instead, we have skyscrapers and aeroplanes that look much like they did in the '60s. Nevertheless, the world has changed. It's not what we see, but what we don't see – the invisible element, the internet – that has turned the world on its head. Further change is coming, even if cars continue to look more or less the same as they do now. COVID-19 exposed the fact that our world was already undergoing change; it might have even accelerated that change. What you do about it is down to you.

Now, when I speak to companies, I like to start by asking them two questions. First, if you could have any business superpower, what would it be? Two answers dominate: being able to read our customers' minds and being able to predict the future. Second question: what would your kryptonite be? Just one answer prevails here: being blind.

Whatever your answers to these questions, now answer this one: what about your business model? Does it enhance your superpower or does it embody your kryptonite? Do you really know your customer or do they all look the same? Do you know the people behind your personas? Are they real or just a figment of your imagination?

New, scaled, impersonal

We call tools like facial recognition, data exchange and surveillance new, but in reality they're not that new. When I go to my favourite local restaurant, I'm watched by my waiter and I like being watched. If not, I don't feel like the centre of the universe. I want the waiter to be on the ball in customer relationship management. If I give them information, I want them to remember that information and not to have to ask time and time again. I've never asked for the right to be forgotten, because I want there to be data exchange between us. It's not about the food, the décor, the music; it's about whether the happening is customer-centric.

How often can we say that we have this sort of interaction now? You certainly won't get it at the local branch of a fast-food chain. The problem is that, in order to grow, companies scaled the existing model. When they scaled, it became about sending not listening.

For the last 50 years, we have been living in the ice age of customer engagement – we had no other option – but the next ten years will be drastically different. When scaling our companies, we tried to reduce the happening to a process. By making it a process, each customer became a number, not a real person, because you can't build a process for every customer. The customer became a result of the process rather than the origin of species. By definition, the process thus became more important than the customer.

By scaling, we stopped listening to our customers. It wasn't a purposeful decision; we just didn't have the toolkit to listen to them. And why would we listen to our customers if the process is more important? We developed personas in their stead, but that's how we became blind. Companies turned from outside-in, driven by customers, to inside-out, driven by processes.

What happens when you become an outside-in company is that your concept may no longer be in tune with customers and the outside world. That's what happened to Kodak, Nokia, taxis, the automotive industry and many others in the last 50 years. The next ten years are set to change even further so we need to be alert.

Due to our locked-in process, the gap between what our customers want and what they get is growing. Due to the fact that we can't listen, because of our process, we're not even aware that we're no longer in tune with the unhappy customer. Here's the danger. Our brain uses those processes, which means that we don't need to change all the time, to gradually update our picture of reality when the gap between what is and what we perceive becomes big enough. As long as those changes are small, our brain's minute updates work. It's incremental innovation. However, if the outside world changes very fast, the gap between our perceived reality and the true reality can quickly grow so large that it's too late. The danger comes when you're not aware that you're no longer in tune with your customer.

"If the rate of change on the outside exceeds the rate of change on the inside, the end is near."

Jack Welch

A red ocean of frustrated customers

We're living in a red ocean of frustrated customers, sped up by the divine instrument – our phones – that put us at the centre of our universe. We used that phone to start to connect. We created a digital twin under the flat earth. This digital twin makes it possible for us to find idle capacity in the non-digital world. With all that power and potential, we can suddenly see where we can make shortcuts between the dots.

Imagine if every waiter in your favourite restaurant were half-robot half-human. When that restaurant scaled, they developed 1,000 restaurants around the globe with the same concept: half-robot half-human waiters. Every evening, every customer interaction with a waiter is data; it's a small data interaction. But if every waiter around the globe serves 30 customers in an evening, you could connect all that small data, from every customer of every waiter in every restaurant, to make big data. Imagine if a collective brain was fed by all of those waiters in real time, processed that data into information in real time and sent it back to every waiter in real time. Instead of each waiter improving evening by evening, taking a long time to become anywhere near as good as a human, we can speed that up by feeding each waiter with the information collected by all the other waiters.

That's the power of combining small data to create big data which you can use to create artificial intelligence, a collective brain. That brain can use the small data of the happening to do clever stuff for each individual customer. Without data, when we scaled the happening we lost that one-on-one connection. Now, thanks to data, we can recreate the personal experience. Data is the key ingredient to making the OMO world human.

Bridging the gap

The world isn't flat any more; we're in the multi-dimensional world where online has merged with offline. As the old world dies, the new world shifts away and the gap between the two grows. As a company, the longer you stay in the old, the harder it will be for you to take the leap to the other side. Moreover, the other side is uncertain, so you may try to keep one foot in the old while you send one foot to the new. But you don't know where you'll land.

When my daughters were young, they did ballet. As they practised their techniques, my grandmother used to say "Oh sweetie, you're going to split yourself open." That's how I feel when I look at companies. The longer you wait, the greater the leap will be and the more you'll be forced to do the splits. Companies want to do both, but it's either one or the other. If you try to have a foot in both the old and the new world, your foot in the old will lose ground as the earth around it dies while your foot in the new will be on uncertain footing as the earth there hasn't yet developed.

"Don't see things as they are, but see them as they can become."

Cinderella

Your choices are simple. Either you stay in the old world, eating the remains of the old business model and survive for another five, ten or perhaps fifteen years. Or you leave the old and dare to go for new ground, where you can write your future.

CUSTOMER-centricity

If we know one thing about the future of business, it's that the customer will be forefront and centre. Companies are no longer the flower that bees – or customers – swarm to. Now the customer is the flower, surrounded by the buzzing cacophony of companies. Extreme customer-centricity must be at the heart of how we do business. So how do we do this? We need to know our customer – not just what they like

and dislike, but also how they're feeling, what's important to them. We need to go beyond fulfilling their basic needs to understanding and offering what would truly be of value. Let's take Emily as an example CUSTOMER.

Emily is **connected**. Before the coronavirus pandemic, we were already living in a digital world. If anything, COVID-19 accentuated our status as OMO sapiens. Facebook saw a surge in global users and we all quickly experienced Zoom fatigue. Emily is living in an online-offline world, with information readily available at her fingertips. But Emily is **confused**. There's too much choice, too much speed, too much change. Unbeknownst to Emily, her **crocodile** brain has taken over to cope with the onslaught of content, content and more content. Companies aim to build an engaged community through clear and captivating communication, but customers are left connected and confused, guided by their primitive emotions: lust, aggression and fear.

Emily is **urban**. The global population is largely concentrated in dense urban areas, a small space at the service of thousands or millions of people. Paris is seen as the city of love and lights by visitors, but residents can quickly forget that charm when stuck in the rat race, crowded in the metro like sardines in a can. Anne Hidalgo, the mayor of Paris, wants to change this reality and make Paris a fifteen-minute city, where everything you need – work, home, gym, shops, restaurants – can be accessed by bicycle in fifteen minutes or less.[30] She is also planning to create more green spaces, including an extensive wooded park around the Eiffel Tower. With so many residents calling for a better lifestyle, Paris is not the only city envisioning a change of environment for people and planet. Cities must be the leaders of change for a more responsible future. Urban residents, like Emily, crave balance between work and personal life among other things. But, at the same time, Emily seeks **imbalance**. She had a dream, a goal for the next five, ten, or twenty years of her life. Perhaps she got the job, the partner, the house, the kids or whatever it was she wanted. However, the routine and predictable rhythm soon turn into the daily grind from which she wants to escape. A holiday in a faraway place may provide that escape, that change she so desperately needs, or perhaps Emily experiences a so-called mid-life crisis to shake up the daily rituals. Whatever it may be, Emily then returns to a steady rhythm. The more Emily wants balance (or stability) in her life, the more she feels unbalanced. Nevertheless, Emily needs unbalance in order to make progress, to move forward. It's a confusing paradox that we all live with. It's a constant shift from stable to unstable, from settled to unsettled, from balanced to unbalanced. At the end of the day, Emily is **unsatisfied**. She wants and deserves more. When buying her favourite products, she doesn't want a simple transaction, she wants an experience.

Emily is **self-centred**. She is driven by her needs and desires. The internet has given us a digital twin of the real world. It gives us a different sense of freedom, where we feel like we can do whatever we want. There are no police, little-to-no social norms, no accountability. Scrolling, sharing and subscribing have been added to our regular vocabulary and activities. This sense of self-importance is also seeping offline into the real world, as the divide between the two closes rapidly. Emily may be self-centred but she is also **sympathetic**. She believes in **solidarity** with people less fortunate than herself, with living beings placed in danger, with causes that mean something to her. Despite being more self-centred, customers believe in **sustainability** and solidarity.

Emily is **tribal**. She has a tribe made up of family and friends she knows in real-life, as well people she has met, or follows, online. Emily trusts her tribe. If someone she knows and trusts recommends a brand, she is more likely to try it. This tribe, our community, is essential for our mental health, but they're not always harmless. Think *Lord of the Flies*. The hostilities that the group of boys in the book dealt with are not dissimilar to the conspiracy theories and flame wars that now spread from our online to our offline world. Just like the boys in the book, we are reverting to our primitive emotions, our crocodile brains. It's stoking tension, leading to civil wars, a mobocracy. Being part of a tribe, Emily is **tempted**, constantly. Person A is using said hair product, Person B is reading said book, Person C is playing said game… and they're all raving about it! Our online world is teeming with information, reviews and recommendations. When faced with our tribe's favourite items, we can't help but be tempted to join in or face the FOMO (fear of missing out).

Emily is **on demand**. One of our crocodile emotions is lust, or instant gratification. We want what we want when we want it. That's why Amazon with their next-day delivery and Netflix with their abundance of TV series and films have become so popular. No longer do you spend your evening flipping between channels to find something interesting to watch; you can just catch the next episode, or two, or three, or more, of your favourite show on Netflix. In our modern fast-paced society, everything needs to happen quickly at the click of a button. But with this speed and abundance of choice comes overwhelm. Emily is **overwhelmed**. How much time have you spent perusing Netflix, or a variety of streaming services, for something new to watch? How often do you hesitate and check as many different websites as you can before making a purchase? With so much available on demand, the customer is overwhelmed.

Emily is **mindful**. As a result of speed and digitisation, Emily now needs to make a conscious decision to practise mindfulness. She may practise yoga and meditation, or take walks in nature listening to birdsong and the leaves rustling in the trees. Instead of fast food, she may now be following the trend for slow food, an eating experience about nourishing the body rather than just giving it fuel like a car. As Emily attempts to be more mindful, she also has her **mind full**. There is a multitude of information filling her head: things to remember, things to check out, things that must absolutely be done as soon as possible. As our minds get fuller and fuller, the world has come up with a trend to iron out our living spaces: minimalism. For many people, however, minimalism can be an impossible task in a society that has become materialistic. This discord of opposing forces means that customers like Emily are trying to be mindful while their minds are full.

Emily is **ethical**. Or perhaps **emotional**. The rise of internet giants in the last few decades has led to customers making purchasing decisions based on price and speed of service. However, customers have come to realise that one key component is missing: the human touch. Customers want an **experience**, an **escape**, the type of service that only small local businesses can provide. And, on top of that, they can feel good for supporting small businesses, individuals, rather than lining the pockets of people who are already billionaires. Thanks to platforms like Instagram, Emily can see whether the companies she likes align with her values. What sort of projects do they support? How are they working on improving their brand and offering their customers more value? Does their messaging resonate? Emily's emotional response to your brand is what we should now be tracking as a new KPI: measuring sentiment.

Finally, Emily is **radical**. She wants to know that your brand upholds the same values as she does. There is no more grey zone; everything is black and white. Are you racist or anti-racist? Are you serious about change or just projecting an image of change? In the wake of major events, consumers are adamant that the companies they give their hard-earned cash to, or the influencers they support by following them, are in line with their values. At the height of the Black Lives Matter movement in 2020, just after George Floyd was killed by police, many customers turned away from companies that did not play an active role in supporting the movement. Vocabulary is crucial. Whether you talk about George Floyd's death or George Floyd's murder, you are taking sides. Perhaps involuntarily, but it matters to Emily. If you remain silent, because you don't want to make your business "political", you're taking a side. This matters to Emily. Did you donate to an anti-racist cause, without doing the work to effect real change? It matters to Emily. If you fail to be vocal and transparent on issues that are important to your customers, and prove that you are effecting the change within your company, customer numbers will plummet. In the eyes of customers, companies and influencers have a platform that they must use.

Otherwise, what right do they have to that platform? Being neutral is no longer an option. Pick a side.

Are you really customer-centric?

Customer-centricity is a key part of my keynotes. It's quite simply impossible to future-proof your company nowadays without putting the customer front and centre. Nevertheless, companies often tell me that I don't need to talk to them about customer-centricity, because they already know about it, they already do it. "Don't worry Rik, we already treat our customers like our best friends." I would love to believe that, I really would, and in some cases it might even be true, but in most cases it's not – despite the company's best intentions. Let's do a quick test. How do you talk about your customers? Do you use phrases like: hunting customers; locking customers in; keeping customers happy (at minimum cost); maximising the value of customers? If you do, you might want to take a second look, because I for one don't want to be your best friend if you treat me like that.

By definition, your company can't treat customers like they are your best friend. You don't charge your best friends for what you do for them. Customer-centricity is not about friendship; it's about exceeding the terms of engagement.

The problem often lies in a misunderstanding of the term, which may indicate the need for new terminology without the old connotations. Although new terminology tends to be rejected, I think we need to find a way to wash clean the existing terminology that has been tainted by the definitions of the old world.

Think about what you call the people who purchase your goods or services: do you call them customers or consumers? How does the word you use influence how you see that person? For me, when we use the word customer, we tend to think of the transaction: that person is paying for that good or service. The word consumer is somewhat broader, but it still reduces the person to a being that consumes and nothing more. Maybe we should just talk about people, because that's what we are. We're not defined by a single instant, such as one in which we make a purchase; we're defined by millions of instances that make us all unique.

So I'm still going to use the words customer and consumer – we can't just sweep all vocabulary aside – but I want to be clear that what I mean is something more.

Empowered people give and receive

Perhaps we could label what I mean with the phrase *empowered people*: people who buy your product/service, use your app, act as your sensors, network, infrastructure and so much more. Empowered people are not just people who made a purchase, they are a part of what you do. They are empowered because they choose to use your application and they get something out of using it. They are empowered because they simultaneously contribute to your platform by sharing their data.

When we open an app like Waze, data is gathered from us. Waze didn't invest in setting up new sensors, they used what already existed: us and our smartphones. Whenever we use the app, we activate our sensor and share our location. Spotify works on a similar model, but instead of location they collect data about our music tastes. They can know what kind of mood we're in thanks to the type of music we're listening to. You'd never share your location with Spotify (unless they partnered with Waze) because there's no point. If you can't see the benefit in sharing your data, you won't do it.

When we use an app like Spotify or Waze, we share our data in return for the use of the platform. We benefit by being able to use the platform and they benefit by being able to gather our data. In turn, our data can be used to make the platform better for us. It can also be improved for use by other companies.

Boosting the power of connection

As human beings, we are connected. We're connected digitally but, and sometimes we forget this, we are also connected with other humans. When we use a platform, we not only offer the platform our data, we also offer them our connections. By empowering people on your platform, most importantly giving them something valuable in return, you will find that you save on other areas of investment. Empowered people become your infrastructure, your quality controllers, your marketing and sales departments and so on. In short, the platform and the user benefit from each other.

The users of your platform can be used as a powerful tool, but beware of abusing them. People boost our platform because they feel empowered and engaged and, most importantly, because they want to be involved. That's the crux. In the old world, when companies thought about customer engagement, all they could see were the dollar signs rolling up and up and up. Customer engagement used to be a costly endeavour. However, the digital world has once again given us the tools to overcome this hurdle. The more you engage your customer in the digital space, the more they will want to be your infrastructure, your sensors, your marketing representatives.

By users for users

A good example of this is user-generated content. On Spotify, anyone can share their music with other people and grow their community. In other words, individuals can share their music on the same platform as renowned names such as Prince. Wouldn't you feel empowered? By allowing people to upload their own content, you are also creating more content, which in turn leads to more data, more marketing, a better platform and more engagement. When it comes down to basics, the more you scale empowering people, the less expensive it will become.

This is crucial; it's the economic rationale of an ecosystem. The more you scale, the lower the costs. You just need to get the flywheel turning. And to get the flywheel turning, you need to speak to the CUSTOMER.

A brief reminder

C   connected, confused
U   urban, unbalanced, unsatisfied, uncertain
S   self-centred, sympathetic, solidarity, sustainability
T   tribal, tempted
O   on demand, overwhelmed
M   mindful, mind full
E   ethical, ecological, engaged, empowered
R   radical

When Uber entered the market, their goal was not to disrupt existing industries. They wanted to use the power of an empowered customer. They wanted to make them a part of the company and they used the advent of smartphones and apps to do that. If you look at many of the big companies that we label disruptors – Spotify, Amazon, Uber, Airbnb – we can see that their breakthrough came around 2010-2012. They were the first ones to get moving in the new space, thus disrupting companies that could have done the same but didn't see it coming. Their goal was the customer, a person who could serve them in more ways than just as buyers of their product/service. Their aim was to know their customer as well as possible, because the better they knew them, the better they could serve them and the more they would engage them.

That's why I don't like the term *disruption*. It's not about disruption, but rather about tapping into untapped potential.

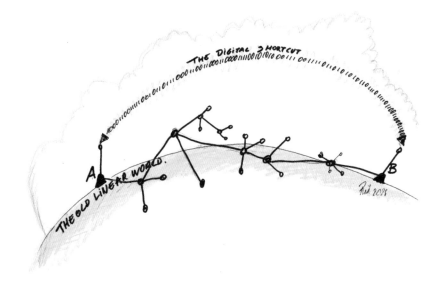

The digital space added a new dimension to our space, just like the Dutch artist Escher (1898-1972) does in his paintings. In his work, we can get lost in the staircases which seem to be going up yet down. And companies have been doing the same thing. Digital has given us the power to fly – we no longer need to travel by road, or find a route that bypasses those towering mountains in front of us. We have the power to fly over those mountains, soaring among the clouds and looking at the landscape spread out around us. What are our customers' frustrations? How can we tap into them and create something valuable? Every company can become an ecosystem if you can just find that untapped potential.

Tap into that potential

Ecosystems are capable of solving society's complex problems, tapping into existing potential in the non-digital world and responding to the individual. Ecosystems can look very different, but underneath they all have the same building blocks: people. If people are unwilling to share their data with your ecosystem, your ecosystem won't work. The question is thus: in what situations, when and why, would people be willing to share their data?

In recent years, perhaps in the light of documentaries such as the ones available on Netflix, people are becoming more and more aware of their data – what data they produce and how it may be used. This might sound awful, but it's true nonetheless: we used to be naïve about our data. We shared it left, right and centre without much care. However, we – as individuals – are the owners of our data. Legislation is changing, and will change, in an effort to protect people and empower them as owners of their data. Companies will thus go from owning data to accessing it and they will only be able to access it if people grant them that access.

This is another element of empowered people. Being empowered is also having the power to govern your own data and grant access to certain entities if you believe that sharing your data with them will bring you value, if you will get something in return for opening that door. In order to show people your worth as an ecosystem, so that they trust you with their data, you need to operate with HEART (Honest, Ethical, Authentic, Responsible/Responsive and Transparent).

From superficial data to real data

We found ourselves in this red ocean, the BOILing red ocean of blurred industry lines, because we scaled. We took the customer experience, the happening, and turned it into one-directional communication. As our profit margins grew, we listened less to the customer and they became frustrated. It's the blue ocean paradox. By adopting a blue ocean strategy – searching for new markets – we created a red ocean of frustrated customers. On top of that, we didn't know what we had created, because there was no part of our business model that was designed to sense what was going on in the outside world. We didn't know when, why or how people were using our product/service. All we could count on were sales records.

In the music industry, we can see a clear progression of truly listening to the customer and thus of empowering people. CD producers could track sales of their product and perhaps where these sales were happening, but they didn't know who was using those CDs or when, where or why. iTunes was a step up: they knew who was buying what, but they didn't know when, where or why people were listening to that purchased content. Spotify has gone further still. Spotify can tell what our mood is because it knows what we listen to at certain times, they can tell what device we're using and, like iTunes, they know what music we like. These three media show us a clear progression of data collection. It's a data game.

Spotify has empowered people who are willing to share their data to get useful recommendations. At this point you might be saying "But Rik, why have we seen a surge in the number of LPs being sold then?" The answer is fairly simple. We are going back to LPs because we want the feel of the original. Like many people, I use both. Either I share my data and get something in return with Spotify or I opt for the feel of the music. I get something different from each medium. With Spotify I get ease of use; with LPs I get the experience.

Spotify was dubbed a disruptor in the music industry. Now, even artists who initially shied away from the platform have joined the data game, to reach more people through personalised recommendations. To me, it's not about disruption, but Spotify did disrupt the industry – it pushed it to reinvent itself with the changing times. Business has long been about B2B and B2C, but it's now turning into P2P – platform to people. Whether it's the platform interacting with business or private individuals, we're all people. We all want to get something out of the platform. We participate because it gives us something in return.

THE SPOTIFY MODEL.
Rik 2021

Return on investment

I can hear your objections, your questions, resounding in my head as I write. Here's the next one we need to address: "Rik, where's the money?" You're right, the platform isn't always a money-making machine. In a smart city, the platform certainly isn't going to make money by charging users. It's about their wellbeing. Nevertheless, the idea of a platform is that the user doesn't just benefit from it, they also work for it (although it shouldn't feel like work). Users are your most powerful marketing, sales department, infrastructure, network and producers of data. Users also often pay to benefit from the platform (just think Spotify).

In a traditional business model, you have to invest in all these services. You pay out large sums of money for marketing campaigns, you pay the salaries of thousands of sales representatives. You pay these representatives to work for you, and they do, but they don't share data. They don't relay data they pick up during their communications back to the company. They might share the highlights, the problems that really stand out, but that's it and it's not enough. It's enough to make you comfortably numb to what's happening in the real world. You have all the sensors you need available to you but you don't use them. It's like picking up a hot cup of coffee and letting your fingers burn, because the data relay isn't there.

Not only do users act as your sensors in ways your sales representatives don't, they also act as your sales department. In reality, you don't need a sales department if you have empowered customers.

At this point, I hope that the penny has dropped, that you see how empowered people can do as much for your company, and perhaps more, than you can do for them. You may even be saying "How stupid are we? Why didn't we see this before?" But you're not stupid. You did what you needed to do to survive in the old world. For the last few decades, and especially since the launch of the iPhone, the old world has been dying out. The problem is that companies have been eating the remains of the old, surviving on what's left but food is quickly running out. Soon, you will be faced with low-hanging fruit that you can't reach if you don't develop the tools you need to be able to grab it.

Don't just create an illusion, create the digital dimension

It's like the illusion of a third dimension that you see when you look at Escher's paintings. It looks like those stairs are never-ending, but it's impossible to build stairs that go on and on and on – it's impossible to survive on the remains of the old indefinitely. Many companies live in a two-dimensional flat world, having created the illusion of the third-dimensional digital space. But they're not really using that space. To illustrate my meaning, we can just look at websites. Many companies have developed websites – a digital version of their shop window if you will – in their "attempt" to keep up with the changing times. But this is just digitising the old, it's not utilising the power of digital.

THE PARADOX OF PERFECTION VS IMPERFECTION

A recurring paradox in this book, which I'm just going to address right now, is how I refer to companies like Spotify, Uber, Tesla and so on. As with everything, they all have their positive aspects and their negative ones, and we can learn from both.

IMPERFECTION MAKES ME PERFECT

Spotify is a company. On the one hand, we get the benefits of the platform, but on the other, they are selling their insights into our music tastes to record companies. As a result, record companies start developing music based on our tastes. Netflix is doing the same thing; identifying what we like and producing series they know we'll love. It's kind of scary, but also like a self-fulfilling prophecy in which you can predict the prophecy you are going to self-fulfil. It's also contrary to learning through trial and error, because trial and error doesn't exist any more. In the end, you are just producing products that you know are going to work with so many people. As a company, you may be sitting up in your seat, saying, "Yes this is the way to go, producing products we know people will love." But on the other side, as a person, it's just producing another fog, reinforcing what we know, only getting what you already knew you wanted to get. Where's the element of surprise? The thrill of finding something new, exciting, different?

In the end, if you think about it, it's a vicious circle that will get smaller and smaller over time. If an artist goes to a record company, they'll already know what type of artist they need so they'll try to squeeze them into that box because they know there's an audience for that box. This has been the case for a long time, but if we're not careful it will become even more so. That's the paradox – we need human input.

The human touch is what makes an ecosystem, on top of all the other building blocks. An ecosystem still has that element of human imperfection, which is what we're largely missing now. Imperfection, a lack of synchronicity and unity is what makes it human. The human touch is what we miss and what we will miss in our interaction with companies. We don't want something smooth and calculated. Perhaps this is one of the advantages of the pandemic, when we are constantly connected to digital even more so than before. Perhaps this will show us that all things digital, which run smoothly and perfectly, are simply not enough.

The paradox is there. On the one hand, we need to raise the bar, to get closer to perfection. But on the other, we need to allow room for human imperfection to make it even better. However, beware: it should not lead to *making* imperfection; you cannot make it, because by definition it wouldn't be imperfect. It needs to remain a happening, something natural. In every real happening, there's that element of imperfection, serendipity, unpredictability – the elements that allow for surprise. Perfection is boring and there's no excuse for being boring.

We don't like people because they're perfect; we like them because they're almost perfect. It's like a relationship. If every day were perfect and your partner always knew exactly what was going on in your head, it would drive you nuts. If your partner constantly asked you what you wanted, it would drive you nuts. You want your partner to know you, what's in your head, but not wholly and completely. You want them to not make too many mistakes, but without any mistakes the relationship would be utterly boring. A relationship is a dynamic balance, just like the one you want to create with your customers. Collecting data across the board, not just what you think you might need, will give you the ingredients you need to surprise people. A good relationship doesn't become rigid, it's not about knowing exactly what the other likes and doesn't like. If it did, it'd be losing its soul, its fire. It's the same for companies. If another company comes along and offers that surprise, that novelty, you'll lose your customer. That's why you need an ecosystem, which has all the data, sensors, short feedback loops and other building blocks you need to be able to be responsive.

I think there's room for another type of Spotify. When they first set out, they were like pirates. However, over time, if you become more like the navy than like pirates, you leave room for new pirates. The solution is to make pirates a part of your company, to allow for constant piracy in your ecosystem. It's difficult. Most companies, in one way or another, become the navy in the end. By allowing piracy within your ecosystem, rather than trying to squeeze everything into formulae, you are contributing to the survival of the ecosystem.

Business with HEART

"A customer is the most important visitor on our premises, he is not dependent on us. We are dependent on him. He is not an interruption in our work. He is the purpose of it. He is not an outsider in our business. He is part of it. We are not doing him a favour by serving him. He is doing us a favour by giving us an opportunity to do so."

Mahatma Gandhi

Honest, Ethical, Authentic, Responsible/Responsive and Transparent (HEART) practices are essential to help us overcome the abuse that has wreaked havoc with the digital canvas of society. We have all been influenced by it. Fake news has become so widespread that it's almost impossible to trace it back to the source. In the third season of *Casa de Papel*, the robbers released state secrets to the media and online in order to blackmail the authorities. In response, the government flooded social and traditional networks with similar but fake news to drown out the truth. In a world where so much information is being published on a daily basis, the truth is easily pushed aside. Instead of generating further transparency, large-scale technology has led to a complete lack of transparency. The solution doesn't lie in working to identify what's fake and what's not fake. Any attempts to do this can just be turned around and used to tag you as the enemy. The new economy is unfair, even more so than the old, and we can't be blind to that if we want to turn things on their head.

The solution lies in bringing the economy back to more local systems, helping us create a more transparent and understandable society. This is the antidote. We need to use technology to downscale communications, to be completely open and transparent about our message. The new world will be about finding that delicate balance between freedom and equality. Freedom is not absolute. Absolute freedom leads to deepening inequality, with wealth concentrated in the hands of a few. Absolute equality, on the other hand, is a communist system, which in turn leads to a total lack of freedom. Instead of absolute freedom or absolute equality, we need to find a middle ground, a delicate balance of the two.

Customers are frustrated. The Ubers of this world have "stolen" the good (technology), made the old look ugly (e.g. taxi industry) and created the bad (abusing technology for their own gain, forgetting about people). We can take back the good, avoid the ugly and get rid of the bad. We can use their holy trinity of big data, artificial intelligence and robotisation to focus on small but honest data. We can develop augmented intelligence, making the most of the best humans have to offer. We can create FEAST interfaces that bring HEART to our business, focusing on what's best for people and planet. This is how we can create real customer engagement. Using ecosystems, we can bring the good from the old normal and infuse it into the new normal.

The red ocean ahead of us is going to be challenging, it will be rough. You will need to adopt a surfer mindset in order to ride the waves. If you are still standing on that beach when the tsunami hits, you will disappear. Trying to stick things out with the same old processes may give you a few more years but that's it. You would be like a beach chair company focused on operational excellence – more chairs, cheaper chairs, less space between chairs etc. – instead of surveying your surroundings and seeing the big wave coming toward you. Don't be the person stuck on the beach, be the surfer. See the wave as a new challenge to tackle and go with it.

This may all sound scary but we're lucky. 2020 has offered us a golden opportunity to break into the paradigm that we had created. We were unable to stop it and so we kept putting out those chairs. But 2020 drilled a wormhole into that paradigm. The pandemic brought the whole world, the global economy, to a halt. It created chaos, a chance for us to make a change. The effect of our economy imploding by itself, like a red giant, would have been thousands of times worse. It would have been devastating. We have been given an opportunity to avoid that happening. In ten years, we will be able to say one of two things: either we grabbed that opportunity or we missed it.

"When one door closes another door opens; but we so often look so long and so regretfully upon the closed door, that we do not see the ones which open for us."
Alexander Graham Bell

THE OLD NORMAL — THE NEW NORMAL

THE TWILIGHT ZONE

THE TWILIGHT TWENTIES

For years, I have stood on stages around and
then we are now in the twilight zone.
needs, but doesn't want to hear.

the world telling people
it is what the audience

The twilight zone is that messy period between the end of the old normal
and the beginning of the new normal. In the twilight zone, the old continues
to toil to survive while the new sweep in to take their place, with no
certainty of the truth of the old.

In my talks i explained that the twilight zone would be dark →
and terrifying

4

Storm

"The old world is dying,
and the new world struggles to be born:
now is the time of monsters."
ANTONIO GRAMSCI

---

featuring:
comforting old ways
the horrific twilight twenties
tipping point
changing climates
moving people
urban but local
the unknown

In 2017, I was on stage at a large event about "the future of automotive". It was in one of those cities in Germany where the whole canvas of society is based on that one industry. It's a place where they believe that that industry will be there for eternity, whatever eternity may be.

THE OLD WORLD

THE NEW WORLD

NOW is THE TIME OF MONSTERS

I was asked to shake, rattle and roll. "Wake them up, don't be too soft on them" was the message. Little did I know that the next speaker would be the CEO of the car manufacturer that was the city's lifeline and the main sponsor of the event. Little did I know that the whole set was being designed as a sales pitch for all the CEOs and press representatives in the large audience to keep them buying internal combustion engine cars for their employees, to show them that this industry was stronger than ever.

I did not know. I just did my thing: proving that the future would be ACES, that we had passed the point of no return, that my grandson would live in a world with zero emissions, zero accidents and zero ownership. I made fun of my Tesla, said I was a lunatic who had paid a shitload of money for a battery, two washing machine engines and a large iPad on wheels. I joked that it was not even a car. The audience laughed. How funny, even a Tesla driver admits that it is not a car. Then I paused. "It is a different breed," I said. "It is a vehicle from the future. I wouldn't call it a car, because when I get to drive a car now, I feel like I am in *Back to the Future*, being thrown back into the '80s."

It was only when the CEO of that premium brand took to the stage that I realised I had been tricked. I had been framed as the antichrist in a church of petrolheads. The more radical I made my talk, the easier it was for him to use the fear and confusion I had sown to comfort people. He was their North Star; what I had said would never happen. He gave reason after reason to prove that what I had been talking about was no more than the naïve dream of "an alternative San Francisco surfer dude". It was anything but realistic. He used all the arguments that we can still find alive and kicking on social media today: children dying in cobalt mines in Congo, the pollution caused by electricity production, limited battery life, the problem of recycling batteries, the lack of charging stations, blackouts in the electricity network and so on. He presented all the spectacular innovations and technologies his brand would release between now and 2025, using them to show that they were way ahead of the pack. He announced that, one day, diesel engines would purify the air rather than pollute it. He ended his speech with: "Tesla will be broke by the end of the year. It will be nothing more than a small footnote in the history of the automotive industry, like the DeLorean from *Back to the Future*." He added: "Electric and autonomous will never happen, not in five years, not in ten years, not in fifteen years. It will never happen."

Less than ten days before this event, I had been to San Francisco where I visited a company called ChargePoint, which designs and distributes charging stations and software to charge electric cars. I was lucky to hear one of their early investors and board members explain the business case for electric cars in a clear and convincing manner (he was an ex-GE Capital executive, early Tesla investor and member of the Advisory Board for the Bay Area based innovation centre of the German brand I was speaking for today). It took him no more than five minutes to present the case for electric cars, using nothing other than crystal clear facts, figures and business rationale to make his point with a fascinating interactive numbers game. I was hooked.

I was in San Francisco with a European investment fund. That same evening, management held an unplanned board meeting in the restaurant. They decided to invest in Tesla and ChargePoint, both as a company and private investor. I spoke to the CEO of that fund on the phone not that long ago and I can assure you that he doesn't regret the decision he made that night. Not one bit.

The five-minute speech I heard that day was one of the most impressive pitches I have ever seen. Afterwards, I remembered the whole flow of reasoning, as well as the numbers. I recall writing it down in my Moleskine on the bus back to the hotel later that night. I was 1001% sure that it would happen, regardless of what anyone else said.

I learnt a few things that day, at that event in a city in Southern Germany. I realised that the old world would not die without a bloody fight and that the new would have to fight mercilessly to conquer the old. I realised that I needed to make my speeches even more shocking. It was after that event that I started using the surfer mindset analogy. Wearing this great T-shirt,[*] "This is not a tsunami, it's just a great wave", became my new stage gimmick.

On the train ride home, I made new slides introducing the Maya calendar and the concept of the Twilight Twenties: the zone between the dying old normal and the emerging new normal that will soon be born. How could I have known back in 2017 that the Twilight Twenties would kick off with a bang – the implosion we know as COVID-19?

Skip forward to February 2021. The same German brand that said "It would never happen" now claims to be a pioneer in electric vehicles, a thought leader for people and planet in the business. They announced dozens of new electric models to come in the next couple of years. Jaguar announced they would stop producing combustion engines by 2025, even for Land Rover. The Twilight Zone for the automotive industry seems to have taken less than five years. Or at least, that's what traditional car manufacturers are hoping. I don't think so. I think this was just the first battle. There are plenty more to come.

---

* The Great Wave by Hokusai - T-shirt bought at the Met Store in New York

We all know the Kodak story and the phrase "Get Kodaked or Uber-ise". They must have been shared thousands of times, but it still seems like most companies have not listened. Far too many companies are waiting to get Kodaked or have no idea what Uberisation is all about.

It's like driving a car on icy roads: if your car loses grip and you need to avoid an obstacle, don't look at it; otherwise your hands will follow your eyes and you will crash. Looking away from the obstacle might save you. Use the Kodak example to know what you need to avoid, so that you no longer have to look at whatever dark shadow might come along to disrupt your business.

In short: Kodak was killed by Kodak.

Companies and their leaders seem to excel in finding rational reasons to convince themselves to do nothing or, in other words, to do the same as they have been doing for the last few decades. When I mention Kodak or Uber, they always have an excuse: there is no business case; Kodak couldn't have done anything anyway; we are not Uber. What if, instead of giving excuses, we look for what we can learn?

Digital photography was invented at Kodak. It could have been spectacular, but they made one big mistake. They had fallen in love with their almost perfect solution: the film roll. A hundred years of engineering had resulted in what we could dub one of the best products on the planet. But that was the problem: it was the perfect solution to a problem/need that wasn't that important after all.

Most companies fall in love with their solution and will even change the definition of the problem to fit the solution, rather than adapting the solution to better solve the problem. But if a company is too in love with their perfect solution, they may forget about the very problem it was originally designed to solve. They won't even try to unearth problems that customers themselves were unaware of (remember the Steve Jobs quote?).

It seems that Kodak thought that a perfect, high-quality reproduction of reality is what people were looking for. However, what if the real problem was capturing a moment in time in a picture that you could share with others? Even Kodak seems to have been fooled by their own marketing, which was centred on the belief that what people wanted was a perfect reproduction of a happening frozen in a frame.

When Kodak had digital photography (and the patents) in the palm of their hands, they could have made it a worldwide success and conquered a brand-new market, if only they hadn't been blinded by their love for their solution, locked in by risk management, KPIs and ROI statements.

Digital photography wasn't high quality. It was actually, and still is, very low quality. But it has another advantage: instant reward. With digital, you don't have to wait until you've finished the film roll to take it to the shop to get it developed, then wait to pick it up. You can see and share the photo instantly.

From a photographer's point of view, it was a joke. Nevertheless, I remember taking all of my Canon gear and a small Sony digital camera with me on holiday to Spain and falling in love with that crappy Sony.

I was a photography afficionado; I knew the different types of film, the different tonalities of Kodak, Agfa and Fuji, the difference between 400 Asa and 100 Asa, I handpicked the specific paper needed to print the pictures myself. But all of that technical quality suddenly seemed of no importance when I returned from a trip to the beach with my wife and two daughters and could look at the pictures we had taken that same day on my laptop that evening. If Kodak had had the guts or the curiosity to look at how digital solved a very real problem, they could have experienced the same thrills my family and I experienced that week in Spain in 1995.

That week, I also inadvertently did some marketing for Sony. Every time I took that digital camera to the beach, people came up to us and asked me what it was. It was like a magnet. People from throughout Europe, who had never had an interest in photography before, were suddenly fascinated. I'm convinced I was a patient zero that week, spreading the virus of digital photography. (Yes, I know this is an unfortunate analogy to use in COVID-19 times, but it gets the point across.)

Was there a business case for digital photography? No, not if you compared Kodak's product with what the competition had. But the problem is that traditional business models do just that – focus on the competition rather than the customer. If Kodak had looked at what the customer wanted (even though they didn't know it yet), they would have realised that digital photography opened a whole new market.

Was Kodak doomed anyway? No. Kodak could have identified the changes occurring in society and reinvented their business model to make the most of it. They could have developed the digital market. Yes, it would have eaten into their existing business model, but why not do that instead of letting someone else do it for you? They could have been the driving force to create a world where both film rolls and digital photography have their place: the first for the experience and the latter for the ease of use.

We're no Uber. Indeed, Uber came from outside the industry just like Sony. But that doesn't mean you can't Uberise. It's not an excuse you can use to not even try to write new scripts and pretend that nothing's going on. When I met Uri Levine, one of the founders of Waze, at a conference, he was wearing a T-shirt that summarises exactly what the crux of Uberisation is: "Fall in love with the problem, not the solution." Have the curiosity, the courage, the passion to look outside of your industry, outside of your process, five-year plans and KPI's, outside of your solution, to find out what the customer really wants/needs. Then fall in love with that problem.

The Twilight Twenties

For years, I have stood on stages around the world telling people that we are now in the Twilight Zone. It's what the audience needs, but doesn't want to hear.

The Twilight Zone is that murky period between the end of the old normal and the beginning of the new normal. In the Twilight Zone, the old continue to toil to survive while the new swoop in to take their place, with no compassion for the trials of old.

In my talks, I explained that the Twilight Zone would be dark and terrifying. I predicted a bloody merciless battle to survive. I spoke of the monsters we might find there – that just because something is different we're afraid and thus dub it a monster. There will no doubt be monsters with bad intentions, but there will probably also be those with good intentions. However, some monsters are just ugly, inside and out.

I told business leaders that there was no point wasting time or energy trying to stave off the new and preserve the old. Instead, they must devote their time and energy to understanding the physics and natural forces that govern the new world. They need to use this knowledge and energy to prepare themselves for the new world, a world that doesn't yet exist but that soon will, around 2030 perhaps.

There were always businesses that said "But 2030 is so far away, we don't need to worry about that yet". Think about it though. 2030 is just around the corner. It's much closer than the financial crisis of 2008. Just think about how much your life and work have changed in that short period of time?

I needed to get drastic. I needed a shock statement, to wake them up to reality. So I told them that the Maya were right. The Maya calendar ended on the 21st December 2012. Doomsayers dubbed it the end of the world, survivalists prepared for the long-predicted apocalypse. Yet we woke up on 22nd December 2012, breathed a sigh of relief and laughed at those doomsayers, because the world was still there. We could continue with business as usual. (You never know, perhaps the doomsayers were unhappy that the prediction didn't come true.)

So I said that the Maya were right. The world as we knew it ended in 2012. The world kept spinning so fast, life speeding by, that we didn't even realise we had passed the tipping point. So many forces that had been accumulating for years eventually came together to push the world from the old into the new. There was no turning back. But many of us didn't even notice as, on the surface, life sped on.

So what changed? What caused this tipping point? Communication. The way in which we, as people, connect, manage, communicate and interact with the world, each other, companies, brands, products and services changed. It was a slow burn, but we reached the end of the wick. Companies that didn't adapt were doomed to die out, just like the dinosaurs. It wasn't because they weren't big enough or strong enough (the dinosaurs were certainly large beasts), but because the environment around them had changed so drastically. They were completely out of sync with clients and thus utterly irrelevant. The dinosaurs had time, but not much. Time to adapt to the new environment around them. They had a dark decade to change their DNA.

Well, here we are again. Companies haven't necessarily died out yet, but the clock is ticking. It's a hard message to share. I could see that business leaders thought that they still had time, time to get started in 2025 and everything would work out. Plenty of time even. But that's the catch. Companies often claim to be forward-thinking, when in reality they love to stand still and wait.

I was born in 1963. I am officially a late "boomer". I only started to realise that most of the forces of this perfect imperfect storm were caused by humans when I became a grandfather. I realised that our generation either helped it on its way for some short-term comfort in return, or just turned a blind eye and pretended not to notice because we have comfortable lives. I suddenly realised that one day, Nout, Line and Sam (my grandchildren) might ask me "How could you?" as in "How could you do this?" as in "How could you do nothing about it?"

Here we are. We're in the Twilight Twenties. There are many great forces that could, and probably will, turn our world upside down. I'll mention just a few here (otherwise my book would be the length of an encyclopaedia). Let's see if you're ready to weather the storm.

Climate change

It's been more than 30 years since scientists sounded the alarm about global warming, since we found out what greenhouse gas emissions were doing to the planet's atmosphere. We cannot deny that our planet is warming up, as increased gases in the atmosphere trap the sun's heat and make us feel like we're in a greenhouse.

COVID-19 dominated the headlines in 2020, but do you remember the other major news stories? Wildfires, hurricanes, melting permafrost... The Australian bushfire season resulted in 46 million acres of burnt land.[31] Homes were destroyed, animals lost their habitats, food sources and, in many cases, lives. The smoke spread as far as Chile and Argentina. On the West Coast of the United States, 2020 was the worst recorded wildfire season they had every experienced, while in the Atlantic the hurricane season broke records with 30 named storms.[32] Meanwhile, as the permafrost continued to melt dramatically, much earlier than scientists had predicted, research also found that twice as much carbon dioxide and methane were being released into the atmosphere as expected.[33]

DIGITAL DISRUPTION?

Some may say that every man is an island. If climate change has taught us anything, it's that that's just not true. We cannot deny our collective human impact on the planet. We are responsible for burning fossil fuels and greenhouse gas emissions and we are responsible for destroying the ecosystems that help the planet regulate itself, from deforestation to changed land use. The ice caps are melting and sea levels are rising. Coastal areas may soon be flooded if we don't reverse the tide. Our food supplies could also be affected, as harsh weather conditions make it harder to cultivate crops. In fact, I say that this "may" happen or "could" happen, but it is inevitable if nothing changes.

The problem is that climate change, or global warming, has been growing gradually. Climate deniers had a following because the changes weren't clear. There is no denying it any longer, and we are dangerously close to the point of no return. Under the Paris Agreement, 196 governments pledged to limit global warming to 1.5-2°C above pre-industrial levels.[34] However, little has been done to achieve that and models show that we will reach 3°C by 2100 if we continue on our current trajectory.[35] It's no longer way off in the future. Our children could live to see this happen… and suffer the consequences.

More than half of all carbon dioxide emissions have occurred since we found out what global warming was in 1988.[36] Only now are people starting to wake up. Is it too late? Let's hope not. However, even if all companies became carbon zero right now (which, let's face it, isn't going to happen overnight), the planet would still suffer from our indifference of the past. Nevertheless, the truth is that if we don't act now, businesses won't survive. We have been selfish, racing to be the biggest and the best with little regard for the consequences, acting like teenagers who've been awarded their freedom.

Social climate

Of course there are sceptics. On the one hand, we have climate activists with their buzzwords and slogans: eco-friendly, zero-waste, carbon-neutral, clean energy. On the other hand, we have climate deniers, who refuse to believe global warming is even an issue. In the middle, we have everybody else, from those who refuse to do their part "because one person can't make a difference" to those who make some effort to make their lifestyle more environmentally friendly. This is what makes for healthy society: debate. However, as the planet's climate has changed, technology has simultaneously transformed our social climate.

The internet has become a space where we feel like we have the freedom and anonymity to say what we want, when we want, how we want. What is more, algorithms designed to connect us with like-minded people and ideas only serve to confirm our ideas, not challenge them, however wrong they might be. Radical ideas, from white supremacy to conspiracy theories, are spreading like wildfires across the web. In the 21st century, when many people believe themselves to be open-minded, we realise that we are only as open-minded as the algorithms allow us to be.

As OMO sapiens, our online and offline worlds are blending in more ways than one. Children who used to be bullied only at school and could find solace at home are now subject to a constant onslaught of hurtful comments on social media. Trolls surf social media feeds and find any reason they can to criticise influencers, seemingly forgetting that they are real people. Protests are now organised online and sometimes livestreamed by participants. This is leading to the "gamification" of real-life events, with online spectators commenting on and encouraging the livestreamer to do certain things.[37] In March 2019, the shootings in the first mosque in Christchurch, New Zealand were livestreamed from a camera on the shooter's head.

There's an old saying: if a tree falls in the forest and there's no one around to hear it, does it make a sound? The new version is something like: if something happens and you didn't post it on social media, did it really happen? Does making your relationship "Facebook official" ring a bell? Social media companies are engaged in a race for our attention and they know how to get us hooked:[38] autoplay the next video (YouTube), ping notifications from your groups (Facebook), tally the number of consecutive days you have maintained communication with a friend (Snapchat). Technology has transformed our social relationships, from matching us with like-minded opinions to encouraging us to have certain conversations.

The climate is changing, both for planet and society. COVID-19 gave the planet a brief respite, but that won't be enough to turn back the clock. For society, on the other hand, the pandemic put its foot on the accelerator of our evolution into OMO sapiens. Instant messaging has turned us into an instant society, where we no longer take the trouble to choose precisely who we want to talk to and what we want to say. We say the first thing that pops into our head. Such mindless activity can be like a hurricane, destroying everything in its path. The transformation of the last 30 years has been extraordinary. Who knows what's next?

Migration

Migration is in our nature. It's embedded in who we are. Our species, homo sapiens, evolved thanks to migration. However, in recent years, migration has become a top concern for voters in many Western countries. In the United Kingdom, many fear immigration from Eastern Europe. In the United States, they fear immigration from South America. These are not unique cases, but they depict the surge in populist policies, from the UK referendum on membership of the EU to the election of Donald Trump and his promise of a wall. Thanks to social media, algorithms and growing differences in society, messages are spreading far and wide to incite fear of "the other".

Migration can be a choice or a necessity. During World War One, my grandfather and his sisters were sent away to three different places in the Netherlands. He was nine years old, placed with a rich farming family where he learnt to read and write. When he went home after the war, his city had been burnt to the ground and he was sent to the coal mines. He was only fourteen. Just 20 years later, at the start of World War Two, their memories of World War One led the whole town to seek shelter in France. My father was three years old. They walked the 100km to France in three days. When they returned home after three weeks, their tiny house had been plundered by the Germans.

Refugees are forced to leave their homeland. They flee conflict, persecution or violence. It was after the Second World War, in response to the flock of refugees fleeing Europe, that the 1951 Refugee Convention was implemented to protect refugees by according them universal rights.[39] Now, war continues to force people away from everything they know and love. It's often not until they come to our shores that we sit up and take notice. Even then, we tend to overlook the reasons for their flight.

Another type of forced migration is climate migration, which we can imagine will surge in coming years. According to the Intergovernmental Panel on Climate Change, sea levels are expected to rise between 26 and 77 centimetres by 2100 if we keep global warming to 1.5°C above pre-industrial levels.[40] As a result, many are being forced to leave their homes as they are claimed by the sea, become flooded more often or are at particular risk of other natural disasters such as hurricanes. We call them natural disasters, but we have turned them into human-enhanced natural disasters.

However, migration can also be a choice, made mainly for economic reasons. In the hope of a better life elsewhere, people may choose to emigrate to live "the American Dream" and perhaps send money home to support their family that has stayed behind. The effects of migration can be both positive and negative. Highly skilled migrants, who fill shortages for doctors, nurses, teachers, are often welcomed with open arms in the West, which is also facing the challenge of an ageing population. However, skilled migration from developing economies leads to brain drain in those countries – the very brains who are needed to help the economy grow at its full potential. Low skilled migrants, on the other hand, are often not welcomed. They are blamed for stealing jobs from native workers. However, these jobs may have become obsolete (perhaps as a result of automation) or may be tasks that natives no longer want to perform (i.e. fruit picking).

In 2020, 59% of the global population were active users of the internet.[41] Can we expect there to be a rise in migration as more people get access to the internet, as more people see how people in developed countries live? Will more people develop a dream of a better life elsewhere?

Social migration (aka. Social mobility)

Migration doesn't necessarily involve crossing borders, or even moving at all. It can be about moving in society, a phenomenon known as "social mobility". Studies show that countries with greater income inequality are less responsive to social mobility.[42] As a result, children born into poor families often have far fewer prospects than children born into rich families. "It's about who you know, not what you know." This saying is an unfortunate reality for many from low-income neighbourhoods who lack the education and connections to rise from their position, even if they have the drive to do so. They feel stuck, hopeless, maybe even resentful of those who have opportunities thrown at them.

The social divide between the rich and the poor, or the super-rich and the average person, is severely detrimental to wellbeing. According to the World Economic Forum, in the United States, "The top 1% of income earners in 2018 earned 158% more than in 1979, in comparison to just 24% for the bottom 90%."[43] Rather than focusing on national GDP or economic growth, greater income equality is an objective that would allow people to fulfil their potential, feel motivated and cherish their role in society.

Nevertheless, income equality is far off the agenda. Gentrification, for example, has been hailed as a sign of progress in our cities, giving run-down neighbourhoods a facelift by encouraging fresh investment, new businesses and new, often college-educated, residents. However, on the flip side, existing residents may be forced to leave their neighbourhood as housing prices soar and their familiar businesses disappear. Some research shows that a few residents may stay and benefit from the positive effects of gentrification, but other studies indicate that these poorer residents, disproportionately people of colour, are forced out.[44]

On the surface, society has changed dramatically in the last century. Imagine your great-great-great-grandparents coming into your home now. What luxury to have central heating, running water and electricity! Don't even get them started on that coffee machine, the television, the fridge-freezer and your various technological devices. In your great-great-great-grandparents' eyes, you might as well be living in a castle. In 1920, just over a hundred years ago, only 35% of American households had a landline phone.[45] In 2019, 96% of Americans had a mobile phone, including 81% who had a smartphone.[46] Innovation after innovation, improvement after improvement, has transformed our lifestyle completely. But as our living conditions improve, our expectations swell and we become more and more unsatisfied.

My grandparents, my father's mother and father, were born in 1905. They witnessed the first cars on the muddy streets where they lived in those tiny houses that were built to house the labourers of Flemish textile mills. When I watch *Peaky Blinders* on Netflix, I'm reminded of those streets. My grandparents barely had any schooling and started working at a very young age in the same mill as their parents. They saw the first planes fly over their town. They survived two World Wars on the European battlefield called Flanders. Their town was burned to the ground twice in less than 25 years. My father was born just before the Second World War, in a house that was no bigger than four by four metres with only half a second floor. They had a hole in a plank above a hole in the ground for a toilet. My grandparents saw the first man on the moon. They witnessed their grandson become a managing director in the same mill where their parents had been labourers with no rights and no education. They saw the first PCs and even the birth of the internet. But it was only in the 1950s that they saw the sea for the first time. They never owned a car or a phone. They never set foot on a plane, never slept a night in a hotel and never went to a restaurant just the two of them. We lived on the same planet for over 30 years. I remember them being at peace with life. Me, on the other hand, I grew up in the '60s and '70s and it seems that "I can't get no satisfaction". It's just never enough. How come?

Reality television shows allow us to see how the other half lives. (The other half? Who coined that phrase? It should be the 1%). Social media platforms show us the highlights of other people's lives. It's not surprising that we feel jealous or depressed when scrolling through the glossy, photoshopped snapshots. This image of the "elite" is tempting. If you only had enough food for one meal a day, how would you feel seeing influencers share shots of their "instagrammable" dishes at expensive restaurants? The working class want a voice, and the middle class have to choose. Will they sidle up to the "elite", trying to elevate themselves, or will they support those who are cast aside by society?

Social media is empowering the ordinary person, it's giving them a voice they never felt like they had before. I lived in the Netherlands for several years. For anyone who knows the Netherlands, you understand the feeling of an open, free society where people from all walks of life are welcomed. You wouldn't expect there to be riots in the Netherlands of all places, but in January 2021 that's what happened. People took to the streets, empowered by the platform they had found on social media, to protest, to voice their frustrations at COVID-19, restrictions and the system. They rallied against the elite upper class, who they saw as wanting to run the world and silence the lower ranks of society. We may wish to believe that class is no longer an issue nowadays, but that's just not the case.

The impact of technology is far from over. Automation is going to replace certain jobs, often manual jobs, but none of us know how far automation will be able to go. What we do know is that the workforce will have to be empowered to learn new skills that will enable them to work alongside robots and automated technologies. If they're not, social divides risk deepening even further. Who knows what the repercussions might be?

Urban living

In modern times, more than half of the global population lives in an urban environment. By 2050, estimates predict that up to 70% of people worldwide could live in a city.[47] This migration (yes, another form of migration) from rural to urban areas has put a lot of strain on existing infrastructure, which must adapt to a growing number of residents. Instead of thriving, our cities are surviving. We must now reconsider our way of living, just as generations of our ancestors did before us.

With a global population expected to hit 11 billion,[48] we face a dilemma. How can we ensure sufficient food and energy for everyone while also preserving our planet and its natural resources (what's left of them, at least)? Urban spaces need to adapt. Ideas are sprouting up left, right and centre: living walls, rooftop gardens, vertical agriculture. Awareness of the importance of green open space for our mental health is also growing. Built in the 1930s as an elevated railway to prevent traffic accidents on the streets below, the New York High Line was the main freight route into the city. However, as trains were replaced by trucks, it fell into disrepair by the 1980s and there were calls for it to be demolished. Others wanted to make it a public space and that's how the High Line, a former eyesore, was transformed into a 1.45 mile long park. It was reappropriated for the public good and now plays host to numerous cultural events, including art displays and performances.[49]

Let's imagine a worst case scenario: we allow urban areas to keep growing and growing. People are forced to commute several hours to get to their work, the closest supermarket, the nearest park. There are regular power cuts, because there's not enough energy, and food is in short supply. More and more people suffer from asthma and lung cancer because of pollution. Is this a future you want to see? Agriculture, mobility and energy are just some of the key challenges that must be tackled to reinvent the cities of tomorrow. I can't imagine what's to come, but I certainly hope it's not like the scenario I described above.

Urban community

Through our migration from rural zones to urban areas, we have lost our beloved sense of community. It can be maintained to some extent: perhaps you still have a local baker, butcher or market. You may be well acquainted with your hairdresser. But living in a city is not like living in a small village where everyone knows your name. So we artificially create our communities, whether in real life or online. Instead of a geographical nature, our online communities are made up of people who share the same passions as ourselves: video games, books, baking, new technology. Whatever your interest, you can find like-minded people online.

Emmett Shear, the CEO of Twitch (an online video streaming platform), is a strong advocate of the communities we build online. Twitch is a platform for gamers to livestream themselves playing games while other people watch and comment. This shared form of entertainment can be compared to our earliest entertainment: sharing stories around a campfire. With the advent of television and radio, we became passive spectators of entertainment that was broadcast at us, basically one-way communication. We felt lonely. Online communities, on the other hand, allow us to foster human connections with others who share similar interests.[50]

Social media is an interconnected network, thriving with different communities, but there are no rules on how we should behave.[51] Although unspoken, there are basic social norms in real life which guide our interactions with others. We instinctively know how we should act whether in a bar or a library or at work. In the online world, however, there is no such structure. LinkedIn is a professional social network, but even there people are trying to figure it out: should I be strictly professional or let my personality shine through? As a result of this lack of structure, time spent on social media can be like a lottery. You may feel happy and inspired, or downtrodden and upset. Other people's actions can have a considerable impact on our mental state. We're still figuring out how to generate the most good from our online communities. We have to wait and see what will happen as the online world merges further with the offline world.

Pandemic

In 2005, a programming oversight generated a pandemic on the popular MMORPG (massively multiplayer online role-playing game) *World of Warcraft*.[52] The final boss of a new raid, Zul'Gurub, cast the point-draining spell "Corrupted Blood" on players. It was highly contagious but disappeared when players left the raid. Players' pets, on the other hand, were forgotten by the program. Once they left the raid, players were recontaminated by their pets and the virus spread across the virtual world. In the ensuing chaos, cities were littered with cadavers and players reacted. Some didn't care, others let curiosity get the better of them, some fled cities out of fear and certain healers took to the frontline to heal others.

Epidemiologists developed a keen interest in the *World of Warcraft* pandemic, to study the way in which the virus spread and how it changed human behaviour. The parallels with the real-life coronavirus pandemic are astonishing. We all reacted differently: from those who denied the very existence of COVID-19 to those who were so fearful they shut themselves inside. We witnessed the very worst in people who rejected all restrictions and the very best in those who heroically sought to care for and help others. Some friendships were strengthened while others were shattered (their friends may not have reacted as they expected, turning out not to be the person they believed them to be). Our morals were put to the test.

This pandemic is unlikely to be a one-off situation. Indeed it wasn't the first. In the 1300s, up to 200 million people died of the bubonic plague.[53] Between 1918 and 1920, around 50 million people died from the Spanish flu.[54] In recent decades, we have dealt with numerous epidemics which we were fortunate to contain to a certain extent: Ebola, Zika, SARS, HIV/AIDS. Scientists and policymakers around the world are preparing for future epidemics as well as biological warfare and other invisible agents which could ravage both population and economy.

Nevertheless, very few people saw COVID-19 coming. I know I didn't. I wasn't the only one, given the shortages in face masks and other personal protective equipment at the beginning of the pandemic. Globalisation turned out to be the perfect breeding ground for the virus to spread quickly. It hopped from one place to another through global supply chains and international travel. Does this interconnected network remind you of anything? Of course, the internet. The internet is just as fertile a breeding ground for viruses, malware and fake news. In 2020, the first person died as a result of a cyberattack when hospital computers were shut down in Dusseldorf.[55] I wouldn't be surprised if more were to come.

A crystal ball

The upheaval in our lifestyles as a result of technology and human activity is astounding. Nobody could have predicted all of the consequences, good and bad, pandemic or no pandemic. Of course, COVID-19 accelerated the digital transformation and changed the nature of human relationships, but change was already afoot long before the pandemic. Just look around you; look at the smartphone in your hand, the computer in front of you. No one knows what's next. Will there be another pandemic? Another iPhone moment? Another internet moment? Who knows?

We still keep talking about going back to the old normal, life before COVID. But I've already told you: that system was already broken. There is no going back. That door has closed. There is now a new world waiting in front of us, full of monstrous uncertainty and unknowns. It will be terrifying. It will be exciting. Grab that surfboard!

Hope and a new toolkit

This book is not designed to be a comprehensive list of all the problems humanity is facing, nor does it aim to bring a ready-made solution. This chapter is simply a taste of some of the problems we are facing: climate change, a changing social climate, growing population, pandemics, income inequality and migration. There are so many issues before us that all seem to be impossible to solve. Each issue comes with its own set of variables, but they also influence each other. Climate change, for instance, has an impact on migration, forcing people from areas that are no longer hospitable. This is just a single example of how variables can also play off each other and become a double variable.

It's like the weather, which is very complex to predict. Now we are capable of creating a fairly accurate weather forecast for the next five days. Meteorologists look at a range of potential scenarios, then go through a process of elimination based on historical data to mark the scenarios that are the least likely to come about. That's also how artificial intelligence works, using a process of elimination to identify something: it's not a dog, it's not a donut… it's this.

If we are able to predict the weather, which implies a very complex set of variables, we must be able to find solutions to the problems we are facing. With ecosystem thinking, data, data and more data, I hope that we will be able to solve these issues. Einstein once said: "We cannot solve our problems with the same level of thinking that created them." In the same way, we cannot solve these problems using the knowledge, mindset and tools that we used to create them. These problems were all created by humans, directly or indirectly. We are the plague.

The dawn of new and more advanced technology is providing us with a host of opportunities to turn this around. I hope it won't be a Pandora's box, but rather a box of tremendous opportunities.

CHERNOBYL

1986. Saturday 26th April.
In the Ukraine Soviet
Socialist Republic, at
the Chernobyl Power
plant approximately
130 km north of
Kiev, operators are
preparing to carry

out an

electrical test of an reactor n. The test has already been delayed by about 11 hours, following a request from Kiev's electrical grid controller for the output to be ~~somewhat~~ maintained in order to cop with peak evening electricity demand. Once the go ahead for the test is given, operators aim to determine for how long the core of the reactor could be kept cool in the event of a ~~main~~ electrical outage. In their inch established procedure, the set allows decreasing the power output of the reactor in order to perform the test.

5

Resilience

featuring:
the core has exploded
the insurance teacher
starting fragile
controlling risk
the art of illusion
pattern addiction
computing power

Chernobyl

1986. Saturday 26th April. In the Ukrainian Soviet Socialist Republic, at the Chernobyl Power Plant approximately 130km north of Kiev, operators are preparing to carry out an electrical test on reactor four. The test has already been delayed by about eleven hours, following a request from Kiev's electrical grid controller for the output to be maintained in order to cope with peak evening electricity demand. Once the go ahead for the test is given, operators aim to determine for how long the core of the reactor could be kept cool in the event of a mains electrical outage. In line with established procedure, they set about decreasing the power output of the reactor in order to perform the test.

1:20am. The test is well underway. Operators follow the instructions they have been given. Not everything is as planned. Reactor power dropped rapidly to a near-shutdown state, far below the power needed to carry out the test. After partly bringing the power back up, control-room personnel continue the test.

1:24am. An explosion. Followed by a second explosion. From the confines of the control room, operators struggle to figure out what has happened as alarm bells ring out across the room. Under orders from the chief operator, personnel continue following procedure, unsure of what has happened.

A younger operator runs into the room. "It's exploded. The core has exploded."

Everyone stares at him in shock, but the chief operator dismisses him. "That's impossible, the core can't explode."

Operators continue to follow procedure, pumping water to cool the core. The core that no longer exists.[56] [57]

The mistakes of Chernobyl

What happened at Chernobyl on 26th April 1986 was horrific, terrifying and largely avoidable. You may have preferred my invitation to go and sit on a beach in Portugal and watch surfers brave the danger in order to ride the biggest wave, but life's not all about sun, sea and sand. Get ready for some dreaded viewing. In fact, do it now. Put down this book. Go sit on the sofa and watch the TV series *Chernobyl*. It makes for terrifying viewing. I'll see you when you get back.

Finished? Okay, well I hope you won't have nightmares now. Or maybe I do. Maybe you needed to be shaken awake to the dangers of continuing business as usual. Don't think that I asked you to go and watch *Chernobyl* just for some history lesson. No, we have a lot to learn from Chernobyl, about what went wrong and what is going wrong for many of our companies. Watching this series is a necessary evil in order to understand why we need ecosystems and what could happen if we are not (part of) an ecosystem.

Perhaps you were already drawing parallels between the happenings at Chernobyl and your workplace during the very first episode. If you were, it might be better to just start running as far and as fast as you can right now. However, if it's your company or you are in charge, you need to start doing something about it right now. Maybe it's not too late.

Exactly what went wrong in Chernobyl, the disastrous result of a combination of conditions and human error, only becomes evident in the last instalment of the five-episode series. However, that first blood-curdling episode leaves no room for confusion: a seemingly efficiently organised system can fail completely if something unexpected happens. Simply adjusting rules and procedures that serve to keep the system going is completely insufficient when disaster strikes. In one fell swoop, institutional power became institutional impotence.

In the first episode, we are already shown the facts. An explosion shook the whole complex. In the control room, they knew that something had gone horribly wrong, but they didn't know exactly what. That was a riddle. The manager in charge tried to give instructions that should help, in vain. They tried all sorts of procedures to solve the problem, but they didn't even know what the problem was. They guessed. They assumed. They made decisions based on assumptions because they didn't have the information and didn't know how to go about collecting it. Even if they did have the information, they wouldn't have known what to do with it because there are no set procedures that could process this information. The algorithms are fixed. In the control room, they adjust the procedures they know and are trained in. They don't solve anything and later we find out that they've made it worse. And it could have been even worse.

The crucial scene in that first episode is the part where the supervising manager orders that the core be cooled and one of the operators, who had actually gone to see what was really going on, came in white as a sheet and said "The core has exploded." The manager's reaction is curt, powerful and borders on delusion: "The core can't explode."

What happened to Nokia?

One of the most common reasons managers give me to explain why they're not making changes is "Why fix something that isn't broken?" It's true. There's no point in fixing something that isn't broken. But are you 100% sure that it's not broken? Or is what you think isn't broken actually broken? In the end, at Chernobyl, they didn't know that their procedures were broken. It wasn't about not knowing what you don't know; it was a case of not wanting to know what you know.

IPHONE is just A NICHE

Do you remember that mobile phone brand called Nokia? I'm sure you do. Who didn't have one of those early Nokia phones, like the Nokia 3210, in their pocket? In 1998, Nokia was the bestselling mobile phone brand on the market. Between 1995 and 1999, Nokia saw its operating profits surge from $1 billion to $4 billion. However, all that was lost in the space of just a few years. In 2007, Steve Jobs introduced the iPhone, but it took Nokia a devastating three years to launch a so-called "iPhone killer". By then, it was too late. The launch of their "iPhone killer" only served as free marketing for the real thing. Between the launch of the iPhone in 2007 and 2013, Nokia lost roughly 90% of its market value.[58]

During a press conference in 2016 to announce Microsoft's acquisition of Nokia, Nokia's CEO Stephen Elop said: "We didn't do anything wrong but somehow we lost." He was right. Everyone in the company did their job, but the system failed. The system was so well structured, so perfect in its own universe that it was wholly incapable of responding to sudden and unexpected changes in its environment. Individuals can try what they want, but if the survival of the system has become more important than its original purpose, their efforts will be in vain.

Timo Vuori, assistant professor in strategic management at Aalto University, and Quy Huy, professor of strategy at INSEAD, Singapore, carried out a qualitative study to understand Nokia's rapid demise from its position as a pioneering technology giant. They published their results in the 2015 paper "Distributed Attention and Shared Emotions in the Innovation Process: How Nokia Lost the Smartphone Battle". After interviewing 76 Nokia managers, engineers and external experts, they concluded that the culture at the company was the main cause: an inside-out, top-down culture driven by rigid processes, assumptions and fear.

"Together, organizational attention structures and historical factors generated various types of shared fear among top and middle managers. Top managers were afraid of external competitors and shareholders, while middle managers were mainly afraid of internal groups, including superiors and peers. Top managers' externally focused fear led them to exert pressure on middle managers without fully revealing the severity of the external threats and to interpret middle managers' communications in biased ways. Middle managers' internally focused fear reduced their tendency to share negative information with top managers, leading top managers to develop an overly optimistic perception of their organization's technological capabilities and neglect long-term investments in developing innovation."[59]

The Chernobyl Syndrome

Nokia suffered from what I like to call "The Chernobyl Syndrome". Nokia ignored the reality. When the iPhone launched, Nokia's CEO Olli-Pekka Kallasvuo brushed it off as a "niche" product.[60] Despite all the evidence, he couldn't see, or refused to see the reality, just like the chief engineer in that control room at Chernobyl. I can't even imagine how many times this same scene has played out in boardrooms across the globe.

Let's go back to our example of the automotive industry. When Tesla threw its hat in the ring, many traditional car companies dismissed it as a competitor. They denied the idea that the future of automotive would be ACES (autonomous, connected, electric, shared). They even denied that it would be electric. Now, they are finally starting to wake up from their slumber in the safe, familiar environment of the past. They have been feeding on the leftovers of their old business models. When they finally start to get the cogs of change turning, to prepare for the Day After Tomorrow, they'll be two days too late.

These types of companies turn a blind eye to the changes around them. At most, they'll evolve from a Company 1.0 to a Company 2.0, where all processes and procedures are set in stone and where innovation is defined as more operational excellence. Some companies, however, are more in tune with the happenings of today. They are 3.0. Some are even forward thinking, looking ahead to tomorrow. They are 4.0. Nevertheless, very few companies are truly prepared for the unexpected happenings of the Day After Tomorrow. These companies are 5.0. They're companies like Apple or Tesla. Companies that were slow at starting to engage the wheels of change are in deep shit. COVID-19 launched us into a 5.0 environment.

Culture eats strategy for breakfast

What happened at Chernobyl was the result of a number of devastating characteristics that defined its culture. I sincerely hope you don't recognise any of these in your immediate surroundings. Chernobyl was ruled by:

STRATEGY FOR BREAKFAST

- One directional, top-down communication. Decisions came from the top and travelled downstream. All communication flowed in one direction. Senior managers took their instructions from the authorities, middle managers took instructions form senior management and operational managers took instructions from middle management. All each one needed to do was listen, obey and carry out instructions, regardless of what those instructions actually meant, whether they were truly useful or not. (In the case of Chernobyl, it turns out that they weren't.)

- Strictly driven, rigid processes and procedures. Real decisions weren't made that day. Nobody was supposed to actually think. All they needed to do was follow processes and procedures that were previously defined. There was no room for any alternatives, no room for the "impossible". Reactor four exploding was "impossible". It didn't fit any of the scripts they had been given, so they continued using the procedures they had received, procedures that had no bearing on reality.

- Management through fear. Operators were afraid to tell the truth to middle management, middle management was afraid to tell the truth to senior management and senior management was afraid to tell the truth to the authorities. When anyone dared speak up (as we saw the operator do in the series), they were shut down, told they were overreacting. They felt threatened, thus perpetuating the culture of fear.

- Inside-out thinking based on assumptions. Management never even considered the real cause behind what was happening for three reasons: first, the core exploding was completely "impossible"; second, information from the outside coming in had no means of travelling upstream due to one-directional top-down communication; and third, the fear of breaking the rules and telling the inconvenient truth.

The management processes at Chernobyl can be likened to those used at many different companies. These processes are rigid structures of hierarchy that struggle to adapt to change. Chernobyl is the perfect example of a solid system that failed to deal with the unexpected. Be honest. Were you expecting COVID-19? Was your company prepared to deal with the consequences? The virus had, and is still having, devastating effects on people, companies and governments who are scrambling to respond. Now, more than ever, we need dynamic companies that are empowered to ride the waves.

The digital transformation was already well underway before COVID-19. Now, however, it is hurtling forward at lightning speed. The challenge for leaders is to understand how to cope with these exponential changes that are leading to new, more aggressive and diverse competition. COVID-19 swept away all old world barriers and is driving the digital revolution forward. This isn't just a great wave, it's a tsunami that will wipe out all stragglers. The post-COVID-19 world will make or break companies, organisations and countries. Leaders need to shape this new world. Leaders need to be CHIEFs; they need to show Connection, Humility, Integrity, Empathy and Forgiveness.

The only way to do this is to focus on cultural change. Companies and governments must connect to and empower their employees, citizens and customers. They need to be aware of their emotions and state of mind. They need to empower everyone to use their voice, to share both their ideas and their concerns. In the words of Ken Robinson, international education adviser: *"The role of a creative leader is not to have all the ideas; it's to create a culture where everyone can have ideas and feel that they're valued."*

Creating a culture that is based on listening, learning and harnessing individual passions and talents is key to building a dynamic company that can move with the times. Empowering employees, so that they can realise their full potential, is the greatest strength a company can have. That's how companies can turn external threats into opportunities.

Rephrasing the question

As I mentioned earlier, in the wake of COVID-19 I was no longer being asked to talk about the Day After Tomorrow. Instead I was asked to talk about "How to build an ecosystem that is agile and responsive". One of the requests for this type of workshop came from an insurance company. As I prepared my talk, I dove deep into their business model and realised that insurance companies are an interesting starting point when you want to understand ecosystems, agility and responsiveness. However, the question is not how to build agile and responsive ecosystems. Ecosystems are both agile and responsive by definition. The question is: how do you build an ecosystem?

Through my research, I discovered that the insurance business itself would help me explain to the insurance business how to build an ecosystem and why:

1. Insurance companies have possessed the basic DNA of an ecosystem company since they were first created.

2. Insurance companies have built a business model based on the unexpected.

Companies that are able to thrive and grow stronger on the unpredictable seem to have cracked the magic formula for eternal business life. It is crucial to understand that secret if we want to build sustainable companies that can thrive and grow throughout the Twilight Twenties.

In the beginning, there was the VOC[61]

To find the origin of ecosystem-based companies that have seemingly found the key to eternal business life, we need to travel back to the Netherlands in the 17th century. During the Little Ice Age, the Dutch were suffering from bad harvests due to the difficult weather conditions. As a result, many people were starving. In many parts, people had boats that they used for fishing. However, they thought: what if there were grain, food somewhere else, that we could bring back here to feed people? If there's food somewhere and hungry people elsewhere, there's business. That's when they travelled to the Far East, finding valuable goods such as sugar and spices. As a result, the VOC (the Dutch East India company) was founded in 1602. They bought goods in the Far East, transported them across the ocean and sold them in the Netherlands. Amsterdam and Rotterdam became the centre of the modern world and the VOC became the first global company. It was more valuable than Apple, Google, Facebook and Amazon put together if you account for inflation in the 21st century.

The VOC was a trading company. Or that's how it started at least. They made a very profitable business out of importing precious goods from the Far East to be sold on the European market. By 1669, the VOC was the richest private company the world had ever seen. It had over 150 merchant ships, 40 war ships, 50,000 employees, a private army of 10,000 soldiers and a dividend payment of 40% on the original investment.

However, there was one big problem. The small ships and the rather primitive navigation tools were rather vulnerable during their long voyages on the open seas, when faced with storms, typhoons, pirates and exotic diseases that killed whole crews. In 1688, Evert van Heijningen started insuring the ships and their cargo against these disasters. Three centuries later, although the VOC no longer lives on, their original business model does. The VOC itself grew into Aon, one of the oldest insurance companies in the world. Did Evert van Heijningen discover the elixir of eternal business life? Is the legend of the antifragile not a legend after all?

First fragile, then robust

Nassim Nicholas Taleb is a name known by almost everyone in the business world nowadays. He wrote *The Black Swan*, about the existence and potential impact of unexpected and disruptive events, in 2007 and *Antifragile*, about things that benefit from shocks, disasters, stress, uncertainty, risk and disorder, in 2012. Many of us probably read those books when they were topping the bestseller lists.

However, many of us read them and continued business as before with no changes at all. Schools, universities and companies continued training and rewarding managers who built what Taleb dubbed "robust" companies. No company wants to be fragile or vulnerable. Being robust is a much more attractive option, designed to be good at managing risk and making the future predictable (through concepts such as predictive maintenance and predictive customer behaviour).

I know all about these types of companies. I ran robust businesses for over 20 years and I was damn good at it. We created a dangerous illusion that we were in control of everything. We thought that we could just continue performing those strange rituals we know as processes, procedures, balanced scorecards, management, control sheets and KPIs in the Holy Church of Management stuffed with facts, figures, checklists and predictive features.

Every business model has four basic components: input – algorithm – desired output – the environment in which it operates. (Let me just step in here to shine a light through that dark cloud surrounding the word "algorithm". Many people just switch off as soon as they hear it. But an algorithm is simply a methodical tool used to make calculations and decisions and resolve problems. An algorithm is simply a set of steps to be followed to reach an answer.)

Fragile

When the first Dutch boat sailed from Amster-dam to India in the late 16th century, the business model was extremely fragile. Goods that were bought were the **input**; the buying process, voyage, storage and sale of goods were the **algorithm**; the goods that were sold were the **output**. The desired outcome was to maximise the difference between the original cost of the goods and the sales price with minimal operating costs. They started with one boat at a time, one load of goods at a time. The input was highly variable, as was the operating algorithm that allowed them to maximise the output. Those first boats were also heavily dependent on the unknown and utterly unmanageable context. The biggest risk was the journey across the seas. If that one ship went down, it was the end. That risk could strike at any moment. Many ships were lost in those early years. They were pioneers in a very risky business. Whether they made a profit or not varied. We can clearly recognise the analogy with a tech start-up here.

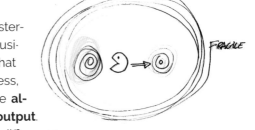

Companies that are just starting out on their journey are fragile. They don't yet know what kind of algorithm, or business model, they will need. They don't yet know what kind of data they'll have to cope with. And they don't yet know what the output of that unknown data processed through that unknown algorithm will be. Using data from the enormous existing data lake, start-ups have to try to format an algorithm and, at the same time, some sort of output. They don't know what data they'll need, what they're going to do with it nor what the output will be. They may have a dream of what it could be, but they don't know. As a result, the data lake is undefined, the algorithm (or business model) is undefined and the output is undefined. This makes for a fragile company and a very fragile business model. That's why around 90% of start-ups don't make it past the first three years. If the input isn't there, or the input is overwhelming, or the algorithm can't cope with the input or provide the desired output, the company fails.

	Input	Algorithm	Output	Environment
fragile	unmanaged small data	simple and agile	unmanaged	high risk

Robust

The solution for those early traders in that very risky business was simple: scale the business, control the environment and minimise the risk to maximise the output. That was the VOC's secret for decades. They started to control the environment, scaling the algorithms by imposing processes and procedures to be followed, implementing management and control systems to make sure that the rules were being obeyed. In this way they maximised their desired output and grew bigger and bigger and stronger and stronger. Their knowledge about their environment even helped them to manage and minimise the risks of the open seas. They avoided stormy seasons, sailed in convoys and protected the merchant ships from pirates with war ships and an army. (This explains their 150 merchant ships, 40 war ships, 50,000 employees, 10,000-strong army and dividend payment of 40% on the original investment.)

Robust companies are very attractive and seem to benefit from eternal life. This VOC model is still the blueprint for many companies worldwide. They have a complex but rigid algorithm. It's a process to find out what data you need, what you want the outcome to be, and what the algorithm is that enables all of that to happen. Once companies find that magic formula, many of them make the natural "mistake" of rendering the algorithm rigid. Any change in the algorithm may be risky and risk is something that should be avoided. So the only manageable factor is the input.

	Input	Algorithm	Output	Environment
fragile	unmanaged small data	simple and agile	unmanaged	high risk
robust	managed larger data set	rigid and complex	managed	minimised risk

However, minimising risk is not enough. The unexpected is by definition unexpected. It can't be predicted and thus can't be measured and can't be managed. When an unexpected typhoon hit early in the season and destroyed a convoy, disaster would strike: the input data would turn into chaos, the algorithm would be unable to handle the data and the result would be a fiasco.

Companies make forecasts for the years to come, already planning what they expect the output to be. With a rigid algorithm that they can't change, and a future plan in mind, the only thing they can do is try to influence the input. This is what makes a company robust. It works, as long as you can control the input. However, sometimes it is not possible for us to control the input. The environment may change so substantially that your business model is no longer valid. The pandemic is once again an example of that. The data lake changed so quickly, so far beyond our control, that the algorithm was no longer valid.

Take me for example. Before March 2020, I used to give keynote speeches across the globe. I had a full calendar awaiting me. Then, as countries locked down, event after event was cancelled. My previously full calendar quickly went blank. The environment around me had changed. I couldn't control the input, so I had to change my business model, quickly. I had to adapt so that I could give my keynotes virtually, while also adapting to the corresponding changing demands of my audience.

One of the most common misconceptions in many companies is that we can manage risk. To manage risk, we manage the input. We see the world in a certain way, with our lenses, and that's where we gather the data we use about the market. By having a restricted set of perspectives, we create a robust organisation. Robust companies are built to survive but they're only valuable as long as you can control the input. As soon as the input changes, the system breaks, your algorithm is no longer valid, and the desired outcome no longer exists. If you live by the outcome, your desired outcome, you break. That damage is beyond repair.

Being robust is not the answer to being fragile. Instead of trying to control and minimise risk, companies need to build a model based on the unpredictable.

The legend of the antifragile

Nassim Nicholas Taleb wrote about a legend: antifragile companies. A third breed alongside the fragile and the robust. They're companies that thrive on the unexpected like people grow muscles in their body by working them so hard that the fibres in the muscles break and grow back stronger when they heal.

These mythical companies became as mythical as giants, dwarves, elves and the holy grail. Taleb became the Tolkien of business books. Antifragile companies were like the mythical serpentine water monster in Greek and Roman mythology, a creature with multiple heads that guarded the gates to the underworld. According to the myth, for every head that was cut off, Hydra grew back two.

It's a hell of a story, but who builds a business model based on a legend? Business leaders kept on building and running the same old robust companies with the same old metrics and the same old management tools. They told themselves that they needed to be more agile and used the buzz to cut out the cost of middle management. They told themselves that being agile was about being able to predict the future. That was an illusion. Even though the threats mentioned before, like pandemics, were known to exist and to be potentially devastating for business, the number of businesses that were ready to grow an extra head were close to zero. In fact, I know of none.

Why do companies ignore chaos? The problem lies in the belief that management is about control and that chaos is uncontrollable by definition. Managers prefer a clean model that represents a version of reality rather than reality itself.

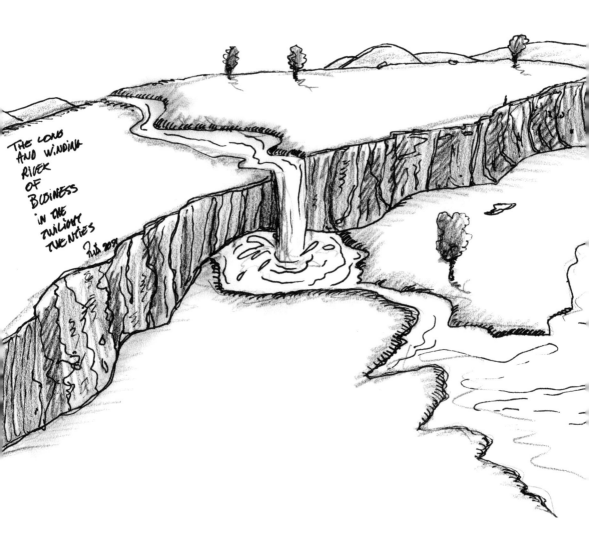

THE LONG
AND WINDING
RIVER
OF
BUSINESS
IN THE
TWILIGHT
TWENTIES

FRAGILE

Imagine if you were to give a child a pile of 100 blocks of Lego and ask them to build a solid house; the best house wins. The first house won't be amazing; it may be very fragile. But the trick is to break it apart and rebuild it, getting better by doing it over and over again. At a certain point, that child may find their optimal house, win the prize and stick with that model as long as it wins. The house becomes a plan that they stick to. Why would they bother trying to create something new if their plan already wins?

RIGID

Every time you give that child the same 100 blocks, they will follow the plan and build the same house. If you change a few blocks, that probably won't be a problem as long as they're not the crucial ones. However, give that child only 80 blocks and they may panic and not build a house at all. Give that child 120 blocks and they probably won't use the extra blocks to build a different kind of house because it's too risky. They might just build an extension.

Imagine that you were to give them more and more advanced blocks and pieces. The child probably won't use them because their method works; they're still winning. But think of what would happen if a new child came into play, using the blocks to make a way better house and win. The first child, who followed the plan, wouldn't be capable of adapting fast enough to do better than the new child, because they haven't trained with the new blocks at all.

But imagine what would happen if the child kept breaking the house down and rebuilding it relentlessly, over and over again, no matter the number or type of blocks. They may not win every time, but in the end they will be the better builder.

That is antifragile. That's the genetic algorithm.

Yes, I am giving you an example of a child playing with Lego, but just think about how this relates to your model. If you break that house apart time and time again, you're taking risk after risk after risk, but you keep getting better. There is no such thing as digital disruption. Companies don't get disrupted by digital. They get killed by avoiding risk.

My suggestion: implement a chaos monkey, someone or something to keep you on your toes. It's not easy to do when things are going well, but you have to implement it, at least theoretically. If the car company I took to San Francisco in Chapter 1 had sent in the chaos monkey on a regular basis, they would have noticed the changes in the environment. But I had to drag them away from their daily business for them to realise it.

Reductionism brings order – until reality sets in

I like to compare robust organisations with the amazing sketches by Escher. Escher's sketches create impossible universes that are so clean, harmonious and elaborate that your eyes and mind accept the obvious. In his work *Waterfall* (1961), Escher depicts a three-storey tower in which water seems to stream upwards toward a waterfall, running upwards again in an endless cycle.

The key to understanding Escher's world can be found in one of my favourite books of all time, *Gödel, Escher, Bach: an Eternal Golden Braid* by Douglas R. Hofstadter (1979). Reading it is like fighting with mathematics, art, philosophy, music and more for 800 pages. I know most people need to read it a couple of times to understand what it is actually about, so let me keep it simple here. Escher's sketches are about what

a sketch really is: a reduction of reality. A sketch is two dimensional. The third dimension is suggested and, as such, is an illusion. To make the illusionary third dimension, Escher plays tricks with your mind. Look at his work *Waterfall* and focus on what is wrong with the pillars. Notice how Escher turns depth into height and height into depth.

This illusionary reductionism of the unpredictable world out there is exactly what robust companies do. They turn chaos into an illusion that can be managed and make sure we all believe that the water is running upstream. That perfect illusionary world is broken once the extra dimension of reality kicks in and we realise we are being fooled. We are not fooled by randomness, but by the illusion that we can control it.

Analysing antifragile DNA

While researching this book, I discovered another business model based on the predictable, which is Dutch as well. This is no coincidence. This business model is the lottery.

The lottery was invented in the Low Countries. In the 17th century, it was fairly standard practice to organise lotteries in the Netherlands. They were a popular and more painless form of taxation. The Dutch *Staatsloterij* [state lottery] is the longest running lottery in the world.[62]

The business models used by insurance companies and the lottery have survived many devastating changes in society between the 17th and the 21st centuries. When we are able to unravel the DNA of their business model, we may be able to crack the magic formula to build antifragile companies that are future-proof.

DNA Ingredient #1 – Fate is not a variable

The word lottery is derived from the Dutch noun "lot" which simply means "fate". It is no wonder that both the lottery and insurance business were developed in the Netherlands in the 17th century and that it is a direct result of their attitude toward fate.

This is a business book, so I have no intention of walking the slippery slope of religion and the differences between Catholicism, Lutheranism and Calvinism. One thing, however, is fairly clear: on average, the Dutch of the 17th century believed strongly in a notion that can be best described as "predestination", but is also known as "the paradox of free will". Once you accept your fate as something that is predestined, and the fact that fate can't be changed or influenced, you are completely free to act and build a life, society and business in which fate is a given fact. Bad luck or good luck doesn't exist. You don't know fear. The sky is the limit.

This notion of predestination is one of the driving forces that explains why the Dutch were so dominant in the 17th century and why the VOC is still the most valuable company of all time.

→ Accept that risk cannot be managed.

DNA Ingredient #2 – Large numbers

In 1688, Evert van Heijningen had a brilliant idea to develop a simple business model that would solve the third method used to deal with good or bad luck: the acceptance of fate. Fate can be devastating for the individual, but it is just a calculated risk for a large group of individuals.

What if all boat owners paid a fairly limited amount of money into a communal pot? Nobody knew, nobody could predict who would lose their boat. However, Evert just needed to know the average number of boats that would be lost during a trip to the Far East. He then needed to calculate the value of the boats that would get lost and spread that amount of money across the participants. They all contributed to the platform with the guarantee of being compensated for their loss if that were their fate. If one man's boat was lost, the money you and others had paid in to the scheme was given to him to cover the losses. If your boat was lost, the money was given to you.

There's more. The insurance company only worked with large contextual data, with no interest in managing or changing or influencing the data. It accepted the chaos out there and turned it into a business.

→ Collect data like crazy.

DNA Ingredient #3 – The output is an optimisation

If you want to build a company that can survive the most devastating events and get even stronger by accepting fate as a given in the algorithm rather than something to be minimised or managed, you have to rephrase the output of the business model. If you dive deep into the original insurance algorithm, you will see that this is a very complex exercise designed to optimise the delicate balance between the calculated risk, the number of participants, the reasonable amount of money they contribute and the money in the bank in case of payment of a claim. Only by optimising this delicate balance can you make sure that the company will survive even the worst disasters.

In this case, profit is not the desired outcome. If the algorithm only tried to maximise profit, it would have to minimise fate. That was the exact problem faced by the robust VOC, which led to replacement with the antifragile insurance model. Profit is a side effect of the algorithm, but not the desired outcome itself.

→ The output is not a number, it is an optimised balance.

DNA Ingredient #4 – Genetic algorithms

When the desired outcome is an optimisation rather than a single number and when the input is big data, the algorithm in between the two by definition cannot be large. Traditional algorithms are fixed. The input data are collected to fit the algorithm that turns them into a result. Robust management is about trying to influence the data so that the algorithm produces a better result. In robust organisations, the algorithm isn't changed. It's risky because the outcome would be unknown. Fragile companies are not in control of the data. Given that they want the outcome to produce a maximised result, they adapt the algorithm and hope for the best. Robust companies have turned the algorithm into a rigid machine and control the data to feed the engine. The engine, however, is built for the expected and is not capable of dealing with the unexpected.

Genetic algorithms are capable of generating high-quality solutions for optimisation. In an antifragile company, the data set is large and might even be chaotic. Every environment is chaotic and any model of that reality is a reduction of the complexity. The algorithm changes in line with the data input. The more data, the more the machine knows and learns and is able to adapt to keep that delicate optimisation running.

Soon after starting to insure the VOC fleet in 1688, the large quantity of data started to define the algorithms to optimise the delicate balance in the ecosystem. Not every ship had to pay the same amount of money for an ever growing number of reasons: season, age of the ship, type of ship, accompaniment by guards or not, reputation of the crew and the owner, etc. Over the years, insurance companies became experts in genetic algorithms.

→ Let the data design the algorithm.

DNA Ingredient #5 – Be a platform

The only way to build genetic algorithms is to become a platform: minimise the fixed assets in the algorithm in between the large data set and the optimised outcome. Excess assets will be a barrier to designing genetic algorithms. Assets are infrastructure and should be detached from the machine that runs your model. The more virtual a machine is, the more it is no more than an algorithm, the better it will be for your company. Make sure that the outcome of the platform is not a single number. Platforms must find an optimised balance. If you want to make money, create applications built on top of the platform. That is where the money comes from.

The original insurance company, back in 1688, needed no ships, no warehouses, no goods. It didn't need to store, buy or sell. It needed no crew or army. The only thing Evert needed was a clever algorithm that optimised calculated versus claimed risk. He didn't even need money, because the money was collected from the participants for the participants. The insurance company developed products. Every signed policy was an application on top of the platform. Many new applications were developed. Policies for the ship, the goods, the warehouse, the crew and so on.

→ Be just a genetic algorithm. Nothing more.

Antifragile DNA

The magic formula for antifragile companies compared with fragile and robust companies seems to look something like this:

	Input	Algorithm	Output	Environment
fragile	unmanaged small data	simple and agile	unmanaged	high risk
robust	managed larger data set	rigid and complex	managed	minimised risk
antifragile	unmanaged big data	genetic	optimum	fate is embedded

Feed a genetic engine with unmanaged big data to optimise the balance and make sure that the company can survive any unexpected devastating happening. It's no wonder that *the antifragile* was a legend. No company can ever live up to that. It is simply impossible.

Not every company can become "just a platform". Not every company can collect big data. Not every company can create genetic algorithms. The answer is more than just building an antifragile company. The answer lies in building an ecosystem.

Ecosystems are the answer

Now that we have unravelled the various ingredients embedded in the DNA of an antifragile company, it's clear that this is not something that one company running one business model can do. It's not a linear business model. Even the insurance company is not antifragile as such. It needs the assets, it needs the data, it needs the context and it plays a role in the context as an essential element in the ecosystem. That's what it's about: building an ecosystem.

Over the years, the VOC transformed from a linear business model into an ecosystem for good reason. Traders were under the constant threat of losing their ships and cargo at sea. The traditional supply chain of supplier – transport – stock – sales was too vulnerable. A chain is only as strong as its weakest link and the weak link in the VOC was the voyage at sea. When a ship was lost, the trader, the wholesaler, the retailer or the supplier could go bankrupt. It could affect traders throughout the supply chain.

Consequently, traders started to work together to absorb those risks and value chains were replaced by an ecosystem in which they all worked together. This made the VOC the biggest company that ever existed. To this day, the Dutch are highly cooperative. Ecosystems replace classic supply chains, in particular in sectors where fate plays an important role and the danger of the unexpected is ever present, such as in agriculture.

Ecosystems, however, are strange. They are a fixed and variable set of elements which create a delicate balance between all those elements to create an optimal result. Until 1688, even the growing ecosystem that replaced the traditional supply chains was still too vulnerable. The balance was still too fragile as the weakest link could still damage the ecosystem. The more elements there were in an ecosystem, the more complex the algorithm, but the greater the balance between the elements. With more diverse elements, the algorithm becomes even more complex, but it's better for the balance.

It's like the balance in the food chain in the ocean. Sea urchins feed on kelp, but if left to themselves the sea urchins would eat so much kelp and breed so fast that all the kelp would be eaten, leaving the urchins with a foodless desert and they would die. The kelp ecosystem needs a third species so that it can survive for centuries: the sea otter. The otter can eat up to 1,500 urchins per day, thus maintaining the balance between kelp and urchins.

The insurance company was to the VOC what the sea otter was to the kelp ecosystem: the final element needed to balance the ecosystem.

Adapting to change

Despite what they might say, or desperately try to believe, companies don't constantly react to change. Instead, they rely on patterns – trends that they see in the outside world which cause them to react only once the change is substantial enough. Then they change the pattern. This is a workable option in a slow-changing environment. This is what companies have been able to do for hundreds of years, operating in a robust way, incrementally making changes to adapt to the slow-changing market.

In a fast-changing environment, this slow, incremental change is not an option. If you change your patterns every five to ten years, you have a problem. It's no coincidence that I'm saying this now, when the environment is reinventing itself at an unforeseen speed. Technology is driving change faster than ever before, so the gap between our business models and the reality of the environment keeps growing bigger. This was already happening before COVID-19, but the pandemic has taken the speed of change to another level.

That gap, between your business model and reality, is a goldmine for new companies to edge in and find their place in the changing market. Technology is driving the change, but it is also your toolkit to ride the change. Before, we didn't close the gap because we didn't have the tools. Technology has given us those tools, the tools that will allow us to be more agile, more reactive to change and allow us to change faster. If you can use those tools, if you can put all the elements you need in place, you can become more capable of adjusting your algorithm, or business model, in response to the changing data lake. Rather than aiming for your desired outcome, you can find the optimised outcome. You can use technology to transform your company from a robust company into an antifragile one.

Humans vs computers

Computer programmers have long puzzled over the travelling sales-person problem, which asks the question: given a list of cities and the distances between each pair of cities, what is the shortest possible route that visits each city exactly once and returns to the origin city? In theory, you could say that this is easy enough to solve; just calculate the shortest trip. And you'd be right. However, the challenge lies in the number of cities, the number of variables you have to take into account in order to solve the problem. If you have ten cities, there are more than 300,000 possibilities. With fifteen cities, this surges to more than 87 billion.[63] To date, programmers have been unable to devise an al-gorithm that solves every travelling salesperson algorithm. The closest they have managed to get is an approximation algorithm which allows them to devise a route at most 50% longer than the best possible result.

Needless to say, although given time humans would probably be able to find a fairly good solution to this problem, the larger the number of cities, the longer it would take them to calculate a good solution, and even longer to create an optimal solution. Computers, and their com-puting power, are the solution. Computers are the key to optimisation.

Genetic algorithms correct themselves when the input changes and are perfect for optimisation. Genetic algorithms are used to predict weather and crops. Growing crops is all about an optimal balance be-tween sunlight, water and minerals. As humans, we can only do our best, estimating the amount of water and minerals we need to give to our plants, trying to place them in the best spot so they can benefit from the sunlight they need. This is what companies will have to do in the future. They will need to find the best balance for their customers.

The data pool will become unpredictable and unmanageable. The en-vironment is changing so quickly that by the time we update our tradi-tional processes and procedures, the new ones are already outdated. We know that in the next five, ten or twenty years there will be changes beyond our imagination. Nobody can predict what's to come. The changes over the last few decades have already been dramatic; who knows what will come next? Genetic algorithms will help build companies that are able to adapt to the environment, thus allowing them to outrun the competition the very moment the environment changes.

In a recent interview, I was asked what my definition of a smart city was. I had no time to prepare my answer, but the first thing that came to mind was a city not run by people, but by an algorithm. A smart city would be a city focused on the wellbeing of its inhabitants. The problem is that everyone has a different definition of wellbeing. My own definition of wellbeing changes throughout the course of a day. How then can we create a city that generates wellbeing for all of its citizens, despite their diverse definitions of the concept? That's why we need genetic algorithms that can optimise our range of collective and changing desires, creating an optimal idea of wellbeing for the city.

The more sensors you have out in the world, the more lenses you have to look through, the better you will be able to gather data from that perfect storm. If you try to input that data into a robust algorithm, you will break the algorithm. The genetic algorithm will be able to cope, using the data to devise an optimal outcome and constantly re-evaluating the data lake to continuously optimise the outcome further.

A dynamic balance

Running a business is all about finding a delicate balance between a multitude of paradoxes. Good leadership is a balance of control versus empowerment; good teamwork is a balance of tasks versus relationships.[64] On a personal level, we all struggle with work-life balance. It's a constant battle to achieve a dynamic balance between these two opposing elements that are both conflicting and complementary. We have already discussed this type of balance earlier in this book, with the balance between freedom and equality. We cannot have absolute freedom, for we would not be equal. We cannot have absolute equality, for we would not be free.

Every company wants a magic formula for the next ten years. That simply doesn't exist. Once this period of instability is over, we're going to come out on the other side in a new world. We won't be able to reuse the old balance of our old normal for the new normal of the future. We will need a new dynamic balance.

Companies ask me what the new silver bullet is. They want to know what they need to look like, how they need to prepare for 2030. The catch is that you can't plan for the future, knowing what is going to happen and designing a model for that. We don't know what the future will look like. The new silver bullet is the never normal, a constantly changing environment and your platform needs to be ready for constant adaptation. React to the changing environment out there using your sensors, network and platform. Feed off the new information.[65]

In the USSR, operators at the Chernobyl plant followed detailed scripts and everyone was trained to follow the script. Reactor four's core exploding was not in the script, so it didn't happen. Companies react the same way. They have a script, a ten-year forecast, and when happenings in the outside world don't fit with their script, they ignore them and pretend they don't exist. Until the change becomes so obvious you can't deny that it exists.

Building your future

Right now, you may be wondering how you can transform your business model, whether you need to drop everything and start again with a clean slate. The answer is no. Yes, you need to get rid of everything that made you a Chernobyl company. You need to release your company from the shackles and pare back your business model to the fundamental building blocks. With these building blocks you will then be able to creatively make new structures for a new paradigm.

In the Twilight Twenties, a zone of unexpected twists and turns, filled with constant and unexpected changes in the business environment, we need companies that don't try to control the chaos but instead use it to grow. Companies must dissect their current business model until only the naked resources remain. These resources will serve for the construction of a new reality. Use these resources to plot your building blocks and connect the dots on a new canvas that will make you anti-fragile: the ecosystem canvas.

one of the few times I really had to think about how to actually build an ecosystem was when I was ~~asked~~ asked to participate in a (design-thinking) workshop.

A hotel wanted to build a stronger connection with their customers, to turn them into engaged members with a different kind of relationship.

The workshop was being run by an intern, which says a lot about the company and the company culture. Senior managers would not leave much (such as myself), and the double meaning — actually experience in a workshop run by an intern. Believe me, this is no common occurrence.

Understand

"Prejudice is a burden that confuses the past,
threatens the future and renders
the present inaccessible."
MAYA ANGELOU

---

featuring:
curious thinking
sporting magic
inspiration in nature
comfortably numb
data, data, data
hot water
seagulls

One of the first times I really had to think about how to actually build an ecosystem was when I was asked to participate in a design-thinking workshop. A hotel wanted to build a stronger connection with their customers to turn them into engaged members with a different kind of relationship. The workshop was run by an intern, which says a lot about the company and company culture. Senior managers mixed with key users (such as myself) and the whole customer-centricity department in a workshop run by an intern. Believe me, this is no common occurrence.

For me, that workshop was an amazing experience for four reasons:

1. I was not running the workshop. I noticed how different the outcome would have been if I had been in the lead and that's the problem: I would have led the workshop, but she didn't – she facilitated. She made sure that we followed the steps carefully, using a framework to ensure that we created a free flow of ideas.

2. I found out how important it is to rethink how we define the "customer" when building an ecosystem, and the role of the company as the organiser of the ecosystem.

3. It was at that workshop that I started to think about the building blocks, dynamics, roles, functions and basic rules of an ecosystem.

4. It was at that workshop that I first thought about the power of curiosity.

As I watched the intern run the workshop, I realised that she managed to artfully balance a rigid framework with free-flowing content and I wanted to know how she did it, what her magic ingredient was. I offered her a ride home after the workshop. During that one-hour journey, we had one of those unexpected conversations that changes your course.

Only now do I realise how much of that conversation has stayed in my mind and evolved into slides, loops in my keynotes, blogs, ideas and concepts, many of which have become the foundations of this book and probably the next one.

Her magic ingredient was curiosity in its purest form. Not artificial, but real and authentic curiosity. I can't say that she gave me the insights, but she certainly facilitated them during the workshop, during the car journey and long after.

In the following weeks, I developed the concept of #NCS (Net Curiosity Score). I started to create slides and write about the building blocks like infrastructure (the framework of the workshop), "a happening" within that framework and how you can kill a happening by not using the input given by others.

I started to see curiosity as the antidote to assumptions, because assumptions that aren't challenged kill the happening and, as a matter of course, the customer relationship.

When she got out of my car, I grabbed my notepad and wrote:
· Curiosity.
· Do not question the loyalty of your customers, question how loyal you are to them.
· Customers: another definition.

Suddenly, all the pieces of the puzzle, which I didn't even know I needed, were falling into place. Suddenly, it all made sense.

Sporting magic

I'm sure that every sports fan can relate to the moment of intense awe that you experience when you watch a sportsperson do something absolutely remarkable, something that could be classed as an incredible feat of human engineering and training. Let's take tennis as an example. In 2006, David Foster Wallace wrote a profile about Roger Federer, detailing some of his astounding exploits that simply took Wallace's breath away.[66] He also mentioned the state in which his spouse found him afterwards, wide-eyed, surrounded by popcorn, in pure shock and awe. Some argue with Wallace's depiction of Federer's prowess in certain situations, but we can all concur that there are particular sporting moments that leave us speechless.

The accomplishments of our favourite sportspeople are fairly easy to measure in terms of medals, tournament wins and world rankings. However, they're not the only ones who can achieve the sort of divine moment that leaves us gaping in awe. Highly successful companies, which seem to be batting the competition out of the park, can also inspire that kind of feeling. When we look at the likes of Google, Amazon, Netflix, Spotify and Apple, we become more in tune with our own business environment and struggles. Their achievements cause us to dream and realise that we are not, nor will we ever be, like them.

Our actions influence the outside world, and the outside world influences our actions. What came first, the chicken or the egg? When Steve Jobs launched the Apple iPhone to market, was he making a product created as a result of the market or did the product influence the market? Was the iPhone the chicken or the egg? I think it's a combination. Jobs noticed happenings in the outside world and developed a product that combined understanding of those happenings and new features that would influence the outside world in turn. The iPhone wasn't the root cause of changes in the market; it wasn't patient zero. It wasn't even the first smartphone. But at Apple, they noticed that there were things going on in the outside world that they could influence and accelerate.

Elon Musk had a similar realisation. Tesla already existed when he started investing in it. Tesla wasn't even the first to come up with the electric car. That was Toyota before the dawn of the new millennium. But Toyota tried to bring out a new product too quickly and their new "innovative" product simply wasn't radical enough. They were the first hiccup. When Musk noticed that people's attitudes were changing and they were becoming more concerned about sustainability and the planet, he invested in Tesla and released cars that accelerated our awareness of human impact on the environment. He responded to happenings in the outside world and influenced them at the same time. Musk and Jobs didn't just respond to the changing context, they interacted with it.

The circular economy and ecosystems are not made equal

It's easy to think that I'm talking about the circular economy when I talk about ecosystems, but I'm not. An ecosystem only becomes sustainable (and, by its very nature, an ecosystem) if the energy it produces is used within the ecosystem. It must not just be used to "feed" the ecosystem and make it sustainable, but also to help it grow. The problem with traditional business models is fairly straightforward: they produce something different to what they input as raw materials. Traditional business models are linear and one-directional; growth takes up energy and resources.

Circular models, on the other hand, have only aimed to "close the circle". They try to make the end of the line feed the beginning. Materials are not wasted at the end of the line, they become the new materials. This type of cradle-to-cradle solution is probably the best we could hope for in a flat, one-dimensional world, but we tend to forget all the extra external energy these systems need to absorb in order to close that circle. Circular systems reduce reality, leaving one or more variables out of their formula.

One doesn't need to transform from linear to circular. A circle is still a line that breaks at the weakest link and there is always a weakest link. One needs to transform into a network of connected dots. The future of our planet is in ecosystems.

Thinking back to that carpet company I managed fifteen years ago, at the dawn of the technological revolution, I remember us wanting to create carpet made completely of recycled materials. It could be done, but it was painful to see just how much energy was needed, the chemistry required to make it happen and, as a result, just how bad it was for people and planet. Recycled carpet, in those days, would require all of that harm just to be able to tell the public that we could make 100% recycled carpet. My management team and I wanted to do more than what we called Green MBS (marketing bullshit). The term "greenwash-

THE GREENWASHING MACHINE

ing" didn't even exist back then. We didn't want to use claims like "We recycle fishnets and turn them into carpet fibres to save the ocean" or "We take back your old carpet and use it to make new carpet" if these processes weren't truly beneficial to the environment. It was possible to fulfil these claims, but the industry that lay between those raw materials and new carpets was dirty. We tried to figure it out, to make the process truly clean, but we couldn't find a solution. Back then, in 2005, I guess a truly beneficial solution was out of the question. Tools such as the Internet of Things and networks, artificial intelligence and big data didn't exist yet – we were still living on the flat earth and the extra dimension was on its way.

Do I claim that the ecosystems I set out in this book are able to have zero impact on the planet? Yes, I do. And they can, but there's a massive *but*. Building an ecosystem is not simple. Ecosystems are not born as ecosystems, it's not something that can happen overnight – building an ecosystem takes a lot of time, money and energy before it can become a true ecosystem that is fully up and running and following the rules of an ecosystem. Perhaps most companies would benefit from becoming part of an ecosystem as a starting point, a kickstart to speed up the process of becoming an ecosystem and learning about it.

ReGen Villages – an example of an ecosystem that combines nature, society and technology

Let's take ReGen Villages as an example. ReGen Villages is an eco-village, a platform, a brain powered by artificial intelligence that runs a sustainable city.[67] It needs data. The more data it is fed, the better the brain will be able to create a village that is fully sustainable, with no need for external resources to provide food, water, energy or waste. It would only use the natural resources that are in abundance, such as rain, wind and sun. It also needs people who are empowered as a community (going off the grid) and engaged (contributing to the city's ecosystem by letting themselves be guided by the artificial intelligence that runs the city).

ReGen Villages is the perfect example of an ecosystem, as it combines all the required building blocks. It has the infrastructure: the buildings, greenhouses, aquaponic growing systems and so much more. It has the sensors, the data sources, which collect and send data back to the central brain through networks. It has the applications, not just digital but tangible, that connect the central brain back to people. People can participate through a blockchain-enabled app and they receive food that is grown within their ReGen Village ecosystem. The applications make all that data collection valuable for people at an individual level. That's the key here. ReGen Villages run on data. They combine the best of mother nature and the best of technology to learn and improve year on year. There are no winners or losers here. Everyone chooses how they want to participate in the community to make it work for them. By making everyone feel happy, empowered, engaged and fulfilled, by optimising the systems that provide food, water and energy, by improving waste-to-resource management, ReGen Villages fulfil the very reason behind an ecosystem: its survival.

I met one of the founders, James Ehrlich, a couple of times at Stanford University and we still exchange messages on LinkedIn. When looking at Ehrlich, I saw a very clever guy who shared his dream with business leaders around me in order to absorb the spirit of that magical place we call The Valley. Stanford is one of those places you have to visit and stories like Ehrlich's are about the new Stanford, the Stanford that cares for people and planet.

Nevertheless, I guess that most of the people who listened to Ehrlich thought that he was just sharing a dream and nothing more. He talked about his son, his source of inspiration, and how he wanted to create a better world for him. The first time I saw Ehrlich, his wife and son were there too. He also shared his other sources of inspiration: the hidden networks of a forest, how every node is a sensor and a connector, how all nodes create a gigantic brain with no central authority. I noticed how he struggled to make the link to the idea behind ReGen Villages clear. I tried to figure it out myself, so that I could help the people around me better understand ReGen Villages. I guess that we can trace the origins of this book back to that lecture theatre in Stanford as well, where we sat much like high-school students listening to a passionate, yet slightly nutty, professor.

At a TEDx event in Klagenfurt, Ehrlich explained how the idea came to him when he visited Versailles where, within two weeks, about 20 eco-friendly homes had been built with electric vehicles whizzing between them.[68] He thought about how he could combine that with the concept of eco-villages. He imagined a place that was completely self-reliant, an off-grid community where everything you need to live a healthy life is on your doorstep. You buy or rent a house, pay an association fee and receive a basket of organic produce at your door every week. If you participate in the community through the blockchain-enabled app, your association fee is reduced. Ehrlich dreamed of building a community on organic arable land and making it more productive, in terms of water, energy and food, than simply arable land could ever be.

The political framework is replaced by an algorithm

Later, I was in Berlin with another group visiting the Smart City project, an initiative run by companies like Siemens. The young manager guiding us asked us: "In your opinion, what is a smart city?" I paused and thought, then I said: "A city that is not run by politicians, but by a genetic algorithm." The manager paused for a long time then said: "I have never looked at it like that and I didn't realise that's what I was working on, as it can be a pretty devastating thought, but I guess you're right." It is a devastating thought that I had not fully realised myself until I spoke those words.

I guess that's one of the big hurdles that stands in between the dream of ReGen Villages and that dream being realised. Perhaps we have to take into account the potential de-humanisation of building and running an ecosystem, with at its heart a brain that runs on 1s and 0s and people in the system having to "follow the orders" given by the brain. I want to come back to this later, when I write about the function of that central brain. We need to mix up our old way of thinking (and our terminology) to describe a new way of thinking.

It's not all blue skies, still waters and plain sailing

I make the same "mistake" when using words like "central". The "central" brain I refer to when talking about the components of an ecosystem is the centre of the dynamics, but it is not central as per the definition of a central authority. It is a distributed authority that gathers together all the dynamics of all the nodes, which are simultaneously sensors and connections. An ecosystem needs a "brain" like our body needs a brain to process all the data being collected by the nodes into information. It needs to activate that data, by giving feedback to the nodes to act on that information, collecting the resulting new data, processing it and giving fresh feedback. It's a constant feedback loop in which the central brain is fed and trained by the nodes and their data. As such, the brain is the collective of all the nodes and is not "dehumanised". It may even be more human than the best human. Humans just "follow orders" that are in fact their own. It is the ideal way to balance the me and the we to create a "perfect" society. In the end, that is what every society, in whatever shape or form, tries to accomplish: balancing the individual and the community, bridging the divide between freedom on one side and equality on the other.

The second problem when "building" an ecosystem is the actual building process. During this time, the ecosystem is not sustainable nor is it off the grid. It needs quite a lot of resources – materials and energy – to build the infrastructure it needs (unless it can "hack" or "reuse" existing building blocks). As a result, it may burn through a lot of money, or lots of energy, before it is actually up and running. Furthermore, artificial intelligence can only operate at full potential once it has been fed by big data and "matured". In order to feed it with big data, it needs to create applications (use cases) that collect data and are, by definition, immature because they are not yet based on enough data to be fully mature, fully optimised.

Will ReGen Villages work right from the outset? Probably not. Some applications may work well, others may fail big time and the system will most certainly not be sustainable immediately. There are too many unknown variables – sun, rain and wind. It may also take a few cycles before an off-grid food supply system and energy and water systems are fully sufficient.

Furthermore, ReGen Villages are not just an algorithm that you can use in any city. It requires specific buildings and specific urban planning in order to work (houses with solar panels, greenhouses with aquaponic culture, arable fields, community hubs etc.). In short, not only does it need the data to kickstart the effect of distributed wisdom, but it also needs to build new infrastructure. The images Ehrlich shared with us were tempting, the story was engaging, but the feeling in the room changed the second he had to refer to aspects of the "old economy".

The pilot ReGen village was to be built in the Netherlands, in Almere just 25 minutes east of Amsterdam. Ehrlich claimed that the land had been acquired and that they would be breaking ground in 2017. Four years later, nothing has happened yet. What went wrong and, most importantly, what can we learn?

1. ReGen Villages is not just about a smart city. It is about creating a new type of society, the first of its kind, the first of a new breed in an old society. They need permission not only to build the city, but also to create an off-grid community which is also off the political grid. That could be a deal breaker.

2. Nobody can predict the future, what's going to happen, because it's never been done before.

3. ReGen Villages need people to live there and become part of the learning organism, but it's a project that may fail and if it does, it could be catastrophic.

4. ReGen Villages needs money to build the infrastructure, so they are asking for investment from companies to be part of the infrastructure and participate in the ReGen ecosystem. But that's the point at which Ehrlich started talking in terms of the old economy and failed to engage companies.

The amount of money ReGen Villages is asking for in order to become a "ReGen Villages Partner" is quite substantial. It's natural that companies would question the ROI. What is in it for them? Why would they participate in a project that may never be given the authorisation, the go-ahead, that may never work, that may never have residents without some prediction as to the ROI? For the old economy, there is no ROI in this model. Could they use it for marketing or extra sales? Maybe, but there are better ways to create positive buzz around a company.

Only once companies realise that old industry lines are going to disappear, that the new economy is the ecosystem economy and that to build an ecosystem companies need to understand what it is, will they realise that the invitation to participate in this experiment may be just what they needed. By participating in this experiment, companies could get a kickstart in data; it may end up not being as expensive as it seems, a once-in-a-lifetime opportunity. ReGen Villages may provide them with the data and knowledge they need to become an ecosystem themselves. It may feed them with the information they're missing but need to build new use cases that are in tune with the society of the future, rather than the remains of the old.

Looking to nature for inspiration

When we think of the word "ecosystem", the first thing that tends to come to mind is the biological sense of the word, the way in which different living and non-living entities in nature interact. The Cambridge English Dictionary defines ecosystems as "all the plants, animals and people living together in an area considered together with their environment as a system of relationships".[69] When talking about ecosystems in the business world, we may be tempted to copy nature and apply its principles to our companies. I agree with this idea to a certain extent: we can learn from nature. However, we shouldn't build a company like nature builds her ecosystems.

Natural ecosystems are complicated and slow, with all elements in the ecosystem completely interconnected. If one element changes or disappears, the rest of the ecosystem suffers and must find a way to adapt to the change in order to survive. This adaptation often occurs slowly. Let's take the example of the dinosaurs again. The meteorite changed their environment, yet the dinosaurs were too slow to adapt to this change and thus didn't survive. In theory, we can learn a lot from nature's ecosystems, the way in which different entities are connected and the fluidity of the ecosystem in which every member is clear about their role. In practice, however, we cannot just imitate the natural world and hope for success.

Inspired ecosystems

In my opinion, this is the definition of an ecosystem: an organisation that is capable of detecting change in the context around it (people, society, environment) and interacting with that context. I call them smart ecosystems, because they need to be data-driven and sustainable. Companies need to be in tune with their environment. They need to know whether their actions will have an impact on the environment and if that impact will destroy the environment (perhaps not in the immediate future, nor in the next five to ten years, but ultimately). If your actions are leading to the destruction of the environment, then you are not interacting well with your environment.

Companies that are not in tune with the context are what I like to call "comfortably numb" (thanks go to Pink Floyd for this phrase). Companies that are deaf and blind to quite a lot of happenings are firmly rooted in their comfort zone. They'd rather not know what's going on than know. Being comfortably numb means that you don't collect data, new data, or all the data you could possibly get. Comfortably numb companies are robust. They limit what they want to know about the outside world. They limit the different perspectives available to them, restricting the lenses through which they can see the world.

The antidote is data. Data-driven organisations benefit from a range of touchpoints with different points of view. They are not afraid to capture lots of different data that they can use, process, learn from and do something with to become more in tune with the outside world. These types of organisations have guts. They have the guts to admit what they don't know and use that knowledge to learn. Leaving your comfortably numb state of mind takes guts, but it's necessary.

For me an ecosystem has to be smart. It has to be an organisation that is constantly learning, that is not numb but data-driven. As a result, the organisation is good for people and planet. This is what I mean by smart. Smart organisations don't eat the planet, stripping it of its resources. If they do eat the planet, they eat what they can from the environment but not one ounce more. They also give something back. In order to be good for the planet, you need data. If you don't collect data, you can pretend that you don't know that you're eating the environment. This is one of the reasons I don't like to compare human-made ecosystems with natural ecosystems. We can interact with and change the environment, nature can't. Natural ecosystems simply have to adapt to the environment.

In short, what I mean by ecosystem is a learning organisation that adapts to changes in the environment but is also capable of making changes to the environment in a smart way, driven by data.

The structure of an ecosystem

In order to imagine the structure of our smart ecosystem company or smart ecosystem city, I'd like you to think about your own body. Your body contains a lot of different elements and features with different functions. They're already there. You didn't design them or make them or plan for them to be there. They're just there. Your organs, blood vessels, muscles, nerves, bones and more are not there by your design. You're also not in control of them, they control themselves. These components are your infrastructure.

If I want to design a smart city, I'm often not going to start completely from scratch. I'm going to take an existing city with everything that implies (houses, streets, shops, transport etc.) and make it clever. Even if I did start from scratch, I would still need a lot of these elements. These elements make up the infrastructure. Infrastructure is always the basis of the ecosystem. It serves the ecosystem by being there, but doesn't serve any other function within the ecosystem. The first step to creating a smart ecosystem is to analyse what you already have and throw most of it into the box labelled infrastructure.

The next step is to think about what you could turn into a sensor. Let's go back to the body. You have sensors throughout your body. You have sensors in your hands which allow you to pick things up and identify danger. Say you pick up a cup. In that cup is boiling hot coffee. Your hand will tell your body that it's hot, warning it of the danger. If you do end up bringing that cup up to your lips (maybe it's so well insulated your hand doesn't feel the heat), you have sensors on your lips and your tongue that will warn you if the liquid is too hot, if it could burn your tongue. Sensors are crucial because they give us data about the outside world.

Once you've identified what you already have that is infrastructure, you can look at that infrastructure and figure out what you can turn into a sensor. You need data and to get data, you need sensors. So, what can I turn into a sensor to make my city smart? Every vehicle can become a sensor, as can every pedestrian through their mobile phones, as can traffic lights. Postal workers could also become sensors. Right now they travel the same route almost every day delivering post, but they could be so much more. How about an instant version of Google maps or Google street view? In Brazil, they attach sensors to seagulls to find illegal dumpsites. Seagulls are naturally drawn to dumpsites, so by following their flight paths you too can find those dumpsites. If you really think about it, and get creative, you can turn a lot of your infrastructure into sensors. The more sensors you have, the more data you will be rewarded with.

Companies can do this same exercise. Look at your old business model. What are the building blocks of that model? Without a doubt, you already have a lot that you can put in that box labelled infrastructure: factory, cars, employees, sales department, marketing department etc. Once you have identified those basic building blocks, your infrastructure, think about what you can turn into sensors. Perhaps some of them are already sensors, such as your marketing department, which very likely senses changing market trends. How can you make these existing sensors better? What do you do with the data they collect?

In future chapters, we will talk about how to optimise and minimise your infrastructure to keep your ecosystem as healthy as possible. Just like your body, you need to keep your infrastructure healthy. To do that, you need your brain. But first, we must continue with the key components of your ecosystem.

Your body has needs. If you're thirsty, your brain sends a signal to your hand to pick up a cup of water and drink. Your hand thus becomes an application. Your hands are both infrastructure and sensors that detect aspects of the outside world. However, when they interact with that outside world, they also become applications. Applications change both a part of my infrastructure and something in the outside world. Within a smart city, applications will change something within the city but also in the outside world, creating an interaction. Within a company, you have a sales team which interacts with the outside world and makes changes within the company, so they are an application.

If you don't use your applications as sensors, you're missing a trick. Imagine if your hand had no sensors and you had no warning that the liquid in your cup was hot. Imagine if in a smart city, you had no sensors on your public transport. You would learn nothing, you wouldn't know where the bottleneck areas of your city are or where the traffic jams are. In order to make something smart, you need to have as many sensors, or touchpoints, as you can.

However, collecting the data is not enough. You need to be able to process that data. Your hand has sensors which can detect heat, but without the brain they can't do anything with that information. Your hands themselves are not clever. They're stupid. Sensors are stupid. Your brain receives the raw data from your sensors and decides what to do with it. This is the most important part of the ecosystem: the central brain. If your brain decides to ignore the data about the boiling hot liquid, you could burn yourself. This is what I have previously called the Chernobyl syndrome. If we have no plan in place that allows us to notice that something is boiling hot, because it doesn't fit with our business model, then we're stuck in a Chernobyl state of mind.

Having sensors is crucial, but what you do with the data they collect is equally, if not more, important. If you put sensors on city buses, but the data captured isn't processed into information that adds value, what's the point of those sensors? If you have sensors on buses and traffic lights, but don't connect the data gathered by both touchpoints, what's the point? The brain needs to connect those sensors, putting the two data sets together to obtain enriched data (information) that can be sent back to the sensors so they can function better. If your sales representatives and suppliers bring you data, you can put those two sets of data together to get enriched data about the market. Your brain is the crucial component that can turn data into information. Enriched data is information. Once you have that information, you can send it back to the applications, which can put the information into action. These applications will also be sensors, which feed data back to the brain through short feedback loops.

We've talked about the different elements in the ecosystem – infrastructure, sensors, applications and the central brain – but these various elements are useless unless they communicate. Data needs to be able to travel from sensors and applications to the central brain and back. All these elements need to be connected, through the final key component: networks. Networks enable data to travel from sensors to the central brain where they are processed into information.

When we think of the word network, we often think of an internet connection, but a network is more than just an internet connection. A network is everything that makes data, and later information, travel through an ecosystem, smart city, smart company and my body. Without a network, this communication between elements doesn't happen. Networks connect all the dots. They connect the sensors in my hands with the sensors in my lips with the sensors in my eyes and so on. In a city, the network can also be made up of people. Postal workers, for example, can be both sensor and network.

The network needs to be efficient. If there is noise on the network, false information may be added to the data that travels to the central brain. If the network is slow, the data doesn't travel quickly enough to the central brain. In numb organisations, the network for certain types of data just doesn't exist. If your sales representative notices something, but you haven't created the appropriate channel for them to communicate that information, they can't send that information to the central brain. Networks are a crucial element, connecting all the parts of your organisation.

The building blocks

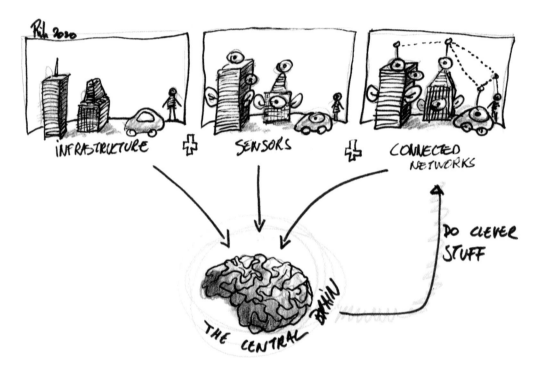

These are the building blocks of a smart ecosystem: infrastructure, sensors, applications, the network and the central brain.

The tangible elements – the things we can see and touch – are the **infrastructure**.

Some of that infrastructure is turned into **sensors** which collect data.

Applications make changes within the ecosystem and interact with the outside world.

For communication between the different elements of the ecosystem, we need **networks**.

Finally, the **central brain** processes all the data collected into useful information for the ecosystem.

These five elements make up a smart ecosystem. In future chapters, we will zoom further into each of these for better understanding.

CURIOSITY DID NOT KILL THE CAT.

#NCS

curiosity may have killed a few cats,
but it made the cat, as a species, smarter.
Curiosity certainly mean t kill companies;
it will be their key way to overcome their tipping point.

tipping point

Most companies started their business driven by curiosity.
It all starts with a problem that you're trying to solve.
It can be anything really: from trying to solve a problem
for the very first time (Microsoft and software for the masses)
to solving it just a whole lot better and more creatively
than existing solutions, just like WAZE or UBER and Spotify did.
They find a shortcut, or a completely new angle, then used
the power of the new world to offer something much cheaper, faster
and more convenient to users.

Ⓐ

Shortcut!

Ⓑ

7

Learn

"Listen with curiosity.
Speak with honesty. Act with integrity.
The greatest problem with communication is
we don't listen to understand. We listen to reply.
When we listen with curiosity, we don't listen
with the intent to reply. We listen
for what's behind the words."

ROY T. BENNETT

---

featuring:
curious cats
learning the world
first words
decreasing vision
ingrained bias
being like the small
optimisation

Why you should measure your organisation's Net Curiosity Score (NCS)

Curiosity may have killed a few cats, but it made the cat, as a species, survive. Curiosity certainly won't kill companies; it will be their life buoy to survive this tipping point.

Most companies started their business driven by curiosity. It all starts with a problem that you're trying to solve. It can be anything really: from solving a problem for the very first time (Microsoft and software for the masses) to solving it just a whole lot better and more creatively than existing solutions, just like Waze, Uber and Spotify did. They found a shortcut, or a completely new angle, then used the potential of the new world to offer something much cheaper, faster and more convenient to users. It can also be about solving a problem that nobody was aware of until you solved it. (I suppose when creating the touchscreen, Steve Jobs must have thought "Why would we need a keyboard if we have our fingers?")

In any case, passionate curiosity was the driving factor, the complete opposite of doing business based on assumptions, patterns, scripts and procedures.

Back to the beginning

When we are born, we usually start crying straight away. A strange environment, new sights, sounds, smells and sensations. It's a minefield of feelings with which we don't know how to cope. We've just been ripped from the safe and comfortable environment of our mother's womb and thrust into a whole new world. Luckily, when we are born, our senses are slightly numbed and designed to reach full sensitivity later. It's nature's way of preventing overload for babies' brains in those early days.

We don't spend our lives in hospital delivery rooms, but our environments program us with patterns that help us deal with different situations. If we do find ourselves in that delivery room again, for the birth of our own children perhaps, we have the patterns that help us recognise what is normal, what is expected, even though we are experiencing a multitude of sensations (excitement, hope, fear, longing, anxiety etc.). These patterns relieve some of the pressure on our brains. Babies don't have these filters. They receive more or less the same input as we do, but that information flows in unfiltered. It takes time for their brains to start developing links between all the different information their body's senses are picking up and sending to the brain.

Throughout our lives, we are unconsciously formatted with these patterns. Instead of having to formulate a fresh appropriate response in a variety of situations, the formula is often ingrained in us. Invited to dinner? Bring a bottle of wine or flowers or something else (of course this depends on social etiquette in that culture).*[70] Going to a job interview? Dress well, smile and give a firm handshake. We are not born with the knowledge that allows us to navigate social norms, geographical differences and problems of good versus bad. We learn these things as children; notably between birth and the ages of five or six.

Our patterns are wonderful tools to help us cope with what would otherwise be a continuous onslaught of information throughout our day. However, they also construct an alternative version of reality, which prevents us from perceiving true reality. If we can fit what is happening in the outside world with our patterns, it's like been there done that. We don't learn and develop new patterns. However, this routine of unconscious thought and action makes us long for escape, adventure and experiences that stimulate our brains, which are hungry for development. Other mammals have the same impulses. Elephants know that if they eat rotten fruit, they'll experience a sort of high (getting drunk) that will free them from the patterns for a little while.

The act of learning

When we learn to speak as a child, we go through various stages. First we imitate the sounds we hear around us, attempting to form the same sounds with our own mouths.[71] We start with vowel sounds such as *ooh* or *aah* before we begin adding consonants to the mix to make sounds like *dooh or maah*. This testing of sounds is a process of imitation, copying the sounds made by our mothers and fathers. After imitation, we proceed to trial and error. Every mother can't wait for the first time their baby says *mama*, so imagine your mother's reaction when you made a

---

* Culture is also something we learn during our early years and even as a foetus in our mother's womb. There is an Aboriginal community in Australia that doesn't use words like *left* or *right*, but uses the cardinal points instead (*north, south, east* and *west*). This has a profound impact on their perception of the world, giving them an excellent sense of direction. Their culture has trained them in this way; it's part of their patterns.

sound that came close to *maah*. As a baby, we notice these reactions. In this case, babies might see their mother's face lighting up as she interacts more with them and encourages them to make the sound again. The baby will note this as a positive result. (Babies are good at statistics.[72] They will mentally note how often certain sounds/words get the desired result or how often they hear a word around a certain object.) Through this process of trial and error, the baby will learn which sounds elicit a reaction. It's like a short feedback loop: make sound > notice reaction > reaction good? > continue making sound.

These statistics allow babies to start making connections. Babies excel at making connections between what they see and hear. If they repeatedly hear one word around a particular object, they will associate that word with that object. They are also incredible at learning new things. Research shows that we stop learning new sounds by the time we're teenagers. That's why it's often said that it's best to learn new languages as a child, because at a young age we still have the capacity to distinguish and learn the different sounds.

Notice that until now we have not yet mentioned grammar, also known as programmed learning, at all. Learning the rules comes after the stages of imitation and trial and error. Learning these new rules may also cause the child to seemingly take a step back. Where once they may have correctly said *we went to the park*, they might now say *we goed to the park*. When they learn these rules, in this case the fact that most verbs in the past tense take an *-ed* ending, they go through a new type of trial and error as they try to fit these rules into the language patterns they have already learnt.[73]

The importance of learning

Learning is about curiosity. There's always a driver, something that says what's in it for me, what's my reward. As a child, you learn to walk because you want to move faster, you want to be able to stand up to have a better overview of your environment and to free up your two hands for other purposes. Adults in particular only want to learn something new if they make the connection in their head that learning this new thing is worth the effort. In most cases, learning something new comes with a reward in the future, but not an immediate reward. We need to be convinced that this future reward will outweigh the reward of doing something that will have immediate effect. We are more likely to opt for instant gratification, such as a slice of chocolate cake to satisfy our craving, than stick to the habits that will help us achieve a long-term reward, such as being healthy. Behavioural scientists call this hyperbolic discounting.[74] The threat of obesity or heart attack is something distant that at the present time seems very low risk, whereas the slice of chocolate cake is a source of immediate reward. Therefore, we are more likely to choose the immediate reward, even though it has negative long-term consequences. When children learn, I think that they make these types of calculations inadvertently, automatically calculating the expected reward for the effort made.

In order to learn, we have to sacrifice. We sacrifice time and energy to learn something new, so we need to be sure that it's worth the effort. Nature hasn't built us to sacrifice anything for no reason. There's no point in wasting energy. In fact, nature has programmed us to be lazy. As hunter gatherers, we needed to save our energy where we could in case there was a shortage of food or we needed to be ready for a difficult hunt. This trait is ingrained in us.

An adult human brain accounts for only 2% of our body mass but consumes 20% of the glucose we burn. Children's brains, on the other hand, consume 50% of their glucose while infants' brains consume 60%.[75] As adults, we reduce the cognitive load on our brains by letting our patterns do the lion's share of the work. Research shows that memory is a dual process (system 1 and system 2).[76] System 1 is a more unconscious process which allows us to make fast automatic decisions but is prone to error. System 2 is a conscious thought process which takes time and effort but is more reliable. System 1 memory allows us to recall information that we have remembered, whereas system 2 allows us to apply critical thinking to our actions. When learning to drive, we will use system 2 to actively encode and analyse every action and the reason behind it. As we practise and improve, our movements become more habitual and what was once conscious thought and action becomes automatic. When something happens in the outside world that seemingly fits with our patterns, system 1 kicks in and

uses our patterns to respond. However, this may mean that we fail to notice something that we must actively and consciously think about.

Business learning

In business, as well as in our personal lives, we can learn from how children learn. Children don't opt directly for programmed learning (such as grammar rules); they go through the processes of imitation and trial and error. Companies, on the other hand, tend to skip to programmed learning. They program how their company works, how they interact with customers and the outside world and get started. This isn't necessarily bad in a slow-changing environment, but in a fast-changing one, where reality quickly splits away from your patterns, it's a sure-fire cause of death.

At the age of seven, after our most critical learning period, we don't suddenly tell ourselves we can stop learning because there's nothing left to learn. We don't think that we have learnt all we need in order to survive. Why then does this happen to companies? Companies tend to fall into the trap of thinking that their processes, systems and procedures will enable them to survive anything. That's not smart. Companies also attempt to define the outcome before gathering the data. As children, we don't learn new words knowing what we want to do with those words. We learn them and learn how to use them and why later. Being smart is about constant on/off interaction with the outside world, and nurturing passionate curiosity to create the systems and mechanisms that will allow you to learn continuously.

Trial and error learning is known in company speak as experimenting. It's about trying something, learning from errors and adjusting each time to gradually inch closer to the result you want to achieve. Imitation learning for a company is about identifying how you can mirror happenings in the outside world, at least to a certain extent. For both of these methods, you need plenty of sensors that are trained to be outside-in, to bring data from the outside world into your company. The more sensors, the better. The more outside-in, the better.

Nevertheless, we are not clean slates like newborn children. We have already established patterns. We need to maintain some of these – if not, our brains would overload with information – but we need to ensure that we operate on a minimum set of patterns which will allow us to glean and learn from new information in the environment. If you maintain too many patterns, they will determine how you interpret data rather than allowing you to truly learn. Say something happens once, twice, three times, four times. Your patterns will only pick up on something new, a change, that happens repeatedly, that is big enough to ring an alarm bell. But if your patterns manage your perception of the outside world, you won't notice the first or second time; you may only notice after it has happened a hundred times, but because of your patterns you perceive it to be the first time.

Agile learning is the capacity to quickly learn from experience and drop perceptions and assumptions that are no longer useful.[77] One of our most basic patterns is our mindset. Some have a fixed mindset, which equates to seeking success and avoiding failure at all costs. Those with a fixed mindset feel they have something to prove about their current ability and avoid leaving their comfort zone for fear of looking stupid. People with a growth mindset, on the other hand, are passionate about learning and see failure as evidence of effort and an opportunity for further growth. They are focused on their potential.[78]

Handling a large number of variables

Being smart is not just about curiosity and learning. You need to be able to do something with that curiosity. When we think in patterns, by definition we are reducing reality to the patterns, making an abstraction based on just a couple of dimensions that simplify the issue so that we can find a solution. We simplify it so that it becomes something we can manage, something we can cope with. We do this because the human brain is not that good at managing very complex equations, which are more of an optimisation than just an equation. What goes into running a company, a city or a country? Think of all the variables you need to take into account.

I ran a company. I was a managing director and I'm not afraid to admit that I wasn't capable of dealing with all the variables simultaneously. I relied on patterns. Patterns made my job *manageable*. In my business, I had to evaluate the cost of raw materials, fluctuating capacity in my production facilities, current and future market demand, the balance between the price of raw materials and the stock of finished or semi-finished products, the balance of cash flow and more. If you think about all the different variables, it's just mind-blowing. There were big decisions to make, but how could you make the right, or optimal, decision? Should I bring in a third shift of workers? There's too much work for the first two shifts, but if I bring in a third shift they won't be fully occupied so it will cost money but it will provide room for growth. There are so many what-if questions and statements like "If I do this, it will improve this but will cause this problem." It's like trying to gauge wind direction by licking and holding up your finger. If you get it right, well done, you're a good manager. But if it fails, it fails.

Our brains are not made to cope with all of this data, but what if our companies could be driven by data? Back in 2004/2005, I started to try this at my company with a very primitive form of artificial intelligence. We didn't want to be run by Excel files any more, analysing cost-benefit ratios across a number of variables and deciding to move our production facilities because it would bring the cost of a product down by one or two cents, before moving that production again next month because the prices changed. We didn't want to let systems run our interaction with our customers. It's not as simple as that. It's not as simple as we tend to make it.

Companies like Facebook have reduced people to sets of data, but people are more than data, they are people. Of course, they come with data but we can't reduce that data to understand people. It's the complexity of data that makes people who they are. In order to respond to what people truly want and need, we need to be capable of dealing with complex data, gathering it into data sets which we are able to process. That's smart. This kind of smart cannot be run by people.

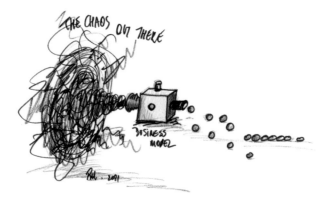

Artificial intelligence has been proven to show bias, not as a product of itself but as a result of the data it has been fed in the machine learning process. Prejudice against women, people of colour and people with different religious beliefs, among others, is an issue that is deeply embedded in our history, and thus our data. Things are slowly changing, but if we fail to pay special attention to promoting diversity, any progress we have made could quickly be reversed.

According to UNESCO, the gender biases found in data sets and algorithms may serve to further spread and reinforce harmful gender stereotypes. AI is made by humans and, as a result, it reflects any conscious and unconscious bias we may have.

There are several problems that must be tackled if we want AI to promote equality across the board, in terms of gender, ethnicity, religion and more. First of all, we need to ensure that we collect data from all segments of society and, rather than just collating it all together, make sure that it is disaggregated. In this way, we can provide better solutions for the *whole* of society, not just the average of the whole (we already talked about how averages can be skewed when we talked about old economic theory).

Another problem we must consider is the development and problem-solving team. STEM subjects are traditionally dominated by white males, but in order for the machine not to show any bias, it must be trained by a truly diverse team, made up of people from different backgrounds.

"Representation of the world, like the world itself, is the work of men; they describe it from their own point of view, which they confuse with the absolute truth."

Simone de Beauvoir

Given that we're talking about learning in ecosystems, inherent bias in AI and big data is an enormous hurdle that must be overcome, but bias is also a problem for companies as a whole. COVID-19 showed us that the system had broken, that we can't continue perpetuating an economic model that was good for profit but bad for people and planet. Now's the time for people, society and business to create a dynamic balance for the world of tomorrow.

Fluid, dynamic ecosystems will allow us to ride the wave of change. We can either wait on the beach, stuck in the old economic mindset, until the tsunami swallows us whole, or we can be a surfer riding the wave, ready to adapt and grow as the surroundings change. What we need in order to do this is data and not data that comes from the world view of a white male. No, we need data from many touchpoints. We will process this data to glean information that will influence the central brain. If we only have data from the perspective of a white male, then our brain will be one-dimensional. We'll be stranded on that beach watching the wave approach. Diversity is key to feeding a dynamic brain that allows us to build systems that grow faster and are more sustainable. Diversity matters.

Just like artificial intelligence, companies need to rely on a diverse team and data sets that cover all backgrounds to create a dynamic environment capable of responding to challenges. Every decision, no matter how small, can be the difference between standing on the beach and riding the wave. Diversity is crucial to making those decisions count.

If we don't tackle the prejudices that are inherent to our past (and thus the data we feed algorithms) then our history will only be replicated in the future and any progress we have made will be erased.

Our brains are wired in a certain way, the result of our upbringing, trials and successes. However hard we try, it is impossible for us to rewire those networks completely. But we can rewire the networks in our companies. We can welcome greater diversity, embrace different backgrounds, embody our varied trials, failures and successes. We can use information that is the product of diverse data sets. We can build sustainable and flexible ecosystems that help us respond to the needs and wants of society as a whole. We can make diversity a core tenet of our companies.

Find the passionately curious and empower the people in your company to question the patterns and the status quo. Recruit to become multicultural. The more diverse your organisation, the more curious your company will become by definition. Seek out open-minded people who want to explore, transform and activate. Diversity is vital to helping us ride the wave into the new tomorrow.

Optimisation is complex

Let's go back to the idea of smart cities that are able to optimise well-being as much as possible for every person in that city while reducing the footprint on the planet. This kind of city can never be run by people. It must be run by artificial intelligence, supplemented by the (emotional) intelligence of people to produce augmented intelligence. People are not able to create an optimisation, because they will always be influenced by their patterns and everybody's patterns are different. My patterns will clash with your patterns. My interpretation of the truth will clash with yours. We cannot optimise collective wellbeing when we are blinded by our own perceptions.

In the same way as we need a reward for learning, we need to define a reward if we want to build a city which optimises the wellbeing of all its inhabitants. How do we do that? Once again, it boils down to data. We need to create a system that is driven by data, that benefits from massive processing power, that is not programmed but instead trained by trial and error and imitation of human behaviour and interaction. We need to define wellbeing. We've already discussed how every individual's definition of wellbeing is different. We can make assumptions, but if we define the criteria we can figure out when people feel good and when they don't through trial and error.

The only way to do all this is to build an ecosystem – a web of sensors, applications, a network and a central brain – that can deal with all of this data. Humans only have five senses; that's all we're capable of handling. That's our limitation. Ecosystems need to go beyond that limitation. They need to be smart like an ever-learning human brain driven by complex data. We cannot make abstractions when it comes to running a smart city, smart mobility, smart healthcare or smart food. These topics cannot be tackled individually. When we address smart agriculture, we also need to consider the implications for food, supply chains and healthcare, because it's all interrelated.

Healthcare is the perfect example. If we want to set up good healthcare (not just sick care), we need to talk about food and mobility. Human health cannot be separated from food and exercise. If we don't eat well, we cannot be healthy. If we don't move our bodies, we cannot be healthy. In order to provide optimised healthcare, we need to look at the comprehensive set of factors that influence our health, regardless of industry lines. We now have the tools to build ecosystems so we are going to start doing exactly that, crossing industry lines until they blur and fall away into the red ocean that we have helped to create and will need to survive. All of our patterns will float away in the red ocean until all we have left is one giant data lake made up of data and happenings. Without our patterns, companies will become children again and learning will need to start fresh.

Complex problem solving

We need to start again, gathering data and formatting patterns. However, we need to ensure that we have a constantly learning process, which is definitely not one-off or programmed, which helps us build up and renew patterns. We still need patterns, because it's impossible to process every happening individually. Imagine a city that uses cameras run by artificial intelligence to monitor the city. These cameras don't recognise people or faces, but rather patterns and behaviour. As a result, they can identify anomalies in the patterns. For example, they could alert to someone lying down where they shouldn't be. They could recognise a fight breaking out, overcrowding or a mugging. As long as the happenings they see fit the patterns of normal life, the artificial intelligence only sees the patterns.

With the evolution of technology comes growing fears surrounding privacy. Surveillance cameras are criticised as an intrusion on our privacy. However, artificial intelligence could allow us to improve safety with a higher number of cameras and respond to privacy concerns by hiding our faces. The patterns protect our privacy. The artificial intelligence monitors the patterns, fitting incoming data with patterns and thus doing nothing. The more data it collects that fits the patterns, the better it becomes at identifying any anomalies. It's an abstraction. The technology doesn't look at faces, it looks at patterns. However, when it identifies an anomaly, it can use facial recognition. If someone is attacked in the street, that doesn't fit the pattern. Humans, however, are not able to just look at patterns; we are trained to see faces. Furthermore, we would never be able to monitor enough cameras to cover a whole city. Artificial intelligence can. It has the processing power that we do not.

Artificial intelligence can be used in other ways too to boost wellbeing. When was the last time you waited for a bus, only to have two turn up at the same time, one that's bursting with people and the other one empty? Buses follow a schedule but if the first bus is running late, there's nothing to change the schedule of the second bus. However, if artificial intelligence were active on both those buses, it could respond to and improve the situation. It could tell the second bus to slow down and wait for a few minutes to allow for new passengers waiting at the bus stops. It could tell the first bus to not stop at a few stops, so that the bus behind it can pick people up. It could tell the first bus to stop, let half of the people off the bus so they can get on the second bus and thus run with two comfortable buses. There are various options, but in order to do this we need to have sensors on the buses, connecting those buses via the central brain which makes the decisions.

The small is the same as the whole

We've drawn parallels between ecosystem components, interaction with the outside world and the body. This is no coincidence. We have looked at ecosystems as if they are people. A company is made up of people. I believe that if your company's interaction with the outside world resembles your smallest unit, i.e. people, then your interaction will be easier. I call this fractal theory: the small is the same as the whole and the whole is the same as the small. Companies struggle to implement digitisation and new technologies to run a better company,

THE BIG is THE SAME AS THE SMALL is THE SAME AS THE BIG

but if you think of a company as a body, as a human being, then you know exactly where technology can enhance your work. Your company needs to interact with the outside world just like your smallest unit.

This can also be translated to a larger canvas. Big ecosystems and companies should have similar structures. This makes it easier for companies to become part of the bigger structure. It's no longer about the big eating the small. It depends on your constellation, your infrastructure. There are concerns that large organisations cannot work with small ones without swallowing them up. This is the answer. If the structure of your big company is the same as the structure of the small one, that won't happen. Russian nesting dolls are all the same shape, they all have the same basic structure. The only difference between each doll is their size. This allows them to fit together perfectly. Companies, and ecosystems, can apply the same principle. When we talk about ecosystems, we tend to talk about large ones. We don't call a company or a person an ecosystem. However, if we can plot people or companies or larger entities on the same ecosystem canvas, they can fit together like those Russian nesting dolls.

I'm late, I'm late for a very important date

Entrepreneurs ask me time and time again: "Rik, how can I know when the market is ready for our product?" They want 100% certainty that the market is ready for their new product before they launch it. When Apple launched the iPhone, they sensed that the market was gearing up for a new type of product, but by bringing the product to market they were able to influence the market. Consumers weren't able to predict that they wanted a mini computer in their pocket. The market cannot be ready for a product until it is there.

That's true interaction with your environment, with the context. If you're not too early, then by definition you're too late. We are no longer in a world where innovation can be plotted on a slow curve. Everything is much faster now. If you wait, you will enter a market that is already taken and by then you are too late. You can enter the market but the price and specifications will already be defined. All that will be left for you is to eat the remains. That business model is all right. You could get by. But it's no way to run your business if you want to develop something new. This is also applicable to ecosystems. If you wait to build an ecosystem, or to become part of an ecosystem, then you might be too late. If your place in that ecosystem is already taken, then you are definitely too late. The ecosystem doesn't need a second option. An ecosystem is not about having two suppliers you can play off each other to get a lower price. That's a classic supply chain, not an ecosystem.

A Belgian supermarket chain has been implementing this sort of thinking. They have started to buy land for farmers to grow potatoes. The supermarket owns the land, the farmers work the land and grow the potatoes. The farmers no longer carry the risk of high overheads and can benefit from access to big data on weather and growing practices. They can work with other farmers, rather than competing against them, to grow the best crops. This is not about one versus another. Instead we're all in this together. If the harvest is good, it's good for all of us. If it fails, we're all in the same boat. The supermarket won't simply switch

suppliers and buy elsewhere. The farmers' problem is the supermarket's problem. It's no longer supplier versus purchaser. Farmers have
an important role in this ecosystem. Farmers who are not members of
this ecosystem will have no chance of supplying the supermarket with
their potatoes, even at a cheaper price. What's important to the supermarket is the survival of the ecosystem they have created.

Smart ecosystems

In short, smart ecosystems are based on two key principles: learning
and complexity. Smart ecosystems need to be capable of gathering
complex data, learning from that data and making connections. They
need to learn by imitating human behaviour and through trial and error
using different and constantly evolving patterns. This must be a continuous process of improvement, of adapting to the changing reality and,
as a result, cannot be programmed by humans who inevitably bring
their assumptions and perceptions to the table. Humans will add value
by defining the result, harnessing the power of artificial intelligence to
provide optimal solutions that humans alone are not capable of identifying. We need to be smart: intelligent, hungry for development, connected and driven by real data.

MEETING TONY HSIEH FROM ZAPPOS

DELIVERING HAPPINESS

A couple of years ago.
(i couldn't tell you exactly when
I am bad with dates.....)

I was in the US for a keynote presentation, I remember
the place, the people, the scene; i remember it was
not summer or winter; i remember having to leave the
room to take a walk, because the company was pretty
bored with stuff, from a progress i was not privy to.

Participate

"Give me six hours to chop down a tree
and I will spend the first four sharpening the axe."
ABRAHAM LINCOLN

featuring:
a chance meeting
breakfast bliss
open arms
the ice age
seeing the skeleton
finding the superfluous
the power of exponential

Meeting Tony Hsieh from Zappos

A couple of years ago (I couldn't tell you when exactly, I'm bad with dates), I was in the US for a keynote presentation. I remember the people, the place, the venue; I remember that it wasn't summer or winter; I remember having to leave the venue to take a walk, because the company was presenting brand new stuff, facts and figures I was not privy to. I walked to the iconic university grounds I had seen from the hotel, in an attempt to fight those post-keynote blues, when the adrenaline is still rushing but there's nobody to share it with. Being the opening keynote has an advantage – you set the tone for the day – but the disadvantage is that you're on your own afterwards. You have two options: either you open your laptop and start reshuffling your slides, even making new ones, or you get out of there, go to the bar for a drink or take a walk.

That day I took a walk. I remember it wasn't hot or cold, but I also remember having a high temperature. A few hours later, a feverish sweat ran down my spine as I queued to get on the plane. During my keynote, I had a sore throat. During that walk, however, I stumbled into the university's arts museum. I was nearly alone in there. There was an elderly lady marvelling at a Van Gogh and a small group of students talking with a professor, but that was it. It felt unreal. I wandered around until it was time to grab my suitcase to catch my plane to Amsterdam, where I was giving a keynote the next day.

That whole trip seemed surreal; maybe the fever had something to do with it. I had arrived the day before as my final dress rehearsal was at 7pm and I was opening the next day. The room was huge, a very American setting: at least 100 large round tables to seat at least twelve people each, an impressive podium and a sizeable screen. There was woven casino carpet lining the floor and crystal chandeliers hanging from the ceiling. At the end of the not-so-perfect rehearsal, punctuated by servers preparing the room for dinner and the band tuning up on the podium, I uploaded my slides onto the main computer and called it a day.

That evening, I was invited to eat dinner at the table with senior managers and other speakers. The band was loud, forcing you to speak to the person directly next to you. The guy next to me, sitting between me and the CEO, was fairly quiet and extremely friendly. Then I noticed his name tag: Tony Hsieh, Zappos. I found out that he had been the closing speaker on the first day. A few years earlier, at an event for the same company in Miami, I referred to Tony Hsieh in my keynote when discussing the importance of value-driven behaviour and company culture, the importance of customer experience. Evidently, the CEO had told Tony Hsieh about my keynote.

When Tony stood up to retire for the night, the CEO said: "It's a pity you can't see Rik speak tomorrow. You should see how his onion model explains what you were talking about from a different perspective. He mentions you and your book." Tony replied: "I will be there at the opening keynote, for about the first 30 minutes." Then he turned to me: "They're picking me up at 9.45am. Do you speak about me before then?" In that split second, I decided to say yes.

We talked for another five minutes or so. The CEO asked Tony why he wanted to be best-in-class in terms of customer-centricity. His answer is crucial here: "Because there is no other option. You cannot put the customer in the centre just a little. If the customer is not in the centre, they're not central. One day, another company will come along and make them the centre. That's when you'll lose that customer and all your other customers to the other company. I want to be that company."

Tony went to bed and I went to work. I spent the rest of the night adapting my keynote for two reasons. First of all, I usually talk about Zappos in the last section of my keynote, when Tony would already have left. Secondly, I had not included Zappos in the deck I uploaded to the main computer just a few hours earlier. The organisers had urged me to switch up my keynote from the last time, in Miami, as many of the same people were there. So I had created a new deck without the Zappos example.

By the next morning, however, I had completely reshuffled my deck, optimised it, and learnt it by heart. I headed downstairs, gave my USB stick to the technicians and enjoyed a hot cup of coffee before kicking the day off with Tony Hsieh in the front row. That day, I opened with what Tony had said. He gave me a thumbs up and I was on a roll. He ended up staying for the whole keynote and left during the questions. We exchanged a few messages on Twitter before he died in 2020.

I do believe that the world will evolve into a place where one eco-system will fight another. If there's one ecosystem that allows me to reach my destination within fifteen minutes, and that's it, then I'll choose them (in a way it already exists – Uber). However, if I have to decide between Uber and the city's smart mobility system, I'll choose the latter.

Think about it in terms of companies. For me, there has always been a massive rift between Uber and Lyft – their original mindset. Uber wants to create Uber. That's it. Lyft, on the other hand, tries to connect to the city and involve city mobility management in what they're doing or, conversely, tries to integrate Lyft into what the city is doing, rather than just seeing that city as new ground to conquer. Of course, Uber is conquering the world much faster be-cause they don't care whether the city is in tune with them or not. Lyft is much slower because they try to connect to the city, to make sure they are in tune with the city's organisation of mobility and to try to integrate Lyft into that. Uber doesn't care.

I once visited both companies in San Francisco on the same morn-ing. You feel the difference. One is hard and macho, talking about how fast. The other is softer and friendly, talking about how well. Even the logo is different: one's black and one's pink. When they talk about their successes, their stories are miles apart: one talks in terms of numbers and the other talks in terms of positive impact to commute times. I didn't need to explain the difference to the group I was guiding – it was crystal clear. If you were going to in-vest in one of these companies on the stock exchange, which would it be? If you're just thinking about the benefit to your wallet, it would probably be Uber. But if you think about the benefit to your wallet and contributing to a better world, you'd choose Lyft.

Ultimately, people will decide what works for them and what fits with their values.

Building a platform designed to serve people

Swiftly[79] is a smart inter-city mobility platform that improves real-time arrival information for users and allows (transport) providers to access data. Swiftly doesn't charge end users for their use of the platform, but instead makes money from cities and the transport companies that use it. Users contribute by feeding their data into the platform and enriching available information, which cities and transport companies can then use to improve their performance. These cities and companies also feed data into the platform, using their vehicles and other infrastructure as sensors. Swiftly doesn't use these companies as a link in the supply chain to build value that they can sell later on to end users; they allow companies access to the same information that is available on the platform.

Every city will want to use that platform, which is the advantage of it. All cities need to do is feed the platform with data, so they simply have to create the sensors that will feed data into the algorithm. The more cities use the algorithm, the cleverer it will get, which will subsequently increase the benefits gained by each city when they use the platform. Using this kind of platform is like having a super intelligent person running every aspect of mobility in your city using an overview of everything that is happening.

The automotive industry should no longer be thinking about the car of the future, but the mobility of the future. This transformation can only be made possible by ecosystems that unite mobility, infrastructure, utilities, networks and sensors. It will need to involve car, battery and tyre manufacturers as well as many more players with different areas of expertise.

Transport in the future will be fully fleet owned. As a result, cost of ownership will become a key consideration. As individuals, we are lousy at dealing with this concept. If we really thought about how much it costs to own a car, we would never even have one. However, once all vehicles become fleet owned, cost of ownership will be a key concern that one company alone will not be able to cover. Companies will work with a number of other companies to share services and consequently drive costs down. Toyota and Uber have collaborated in this way. As part of their partnership agreement, drivers are able to lease cars from

Toyota and use their earnings from driving to pay back the car.[80] Toyota and Uber are not the only ones who have embarked on such a collaboration, fully aware that they cannot build a platform alone.

But it's not just about ensuring that every partner shares the same values and goals. How can the city identify which pavements should be widened, where service should be increased to cater to rising passenger numbers or where extra public transport stops could be useful? That's where data-driven companies like Swiftly can step in. According to their website, "Swiftly analyses billions of historical and real-time data points from your transit vehicles to surface the most impactful improvements to your service." The idea is to establish a single platform for the whole city's transport data, working with existing systems and operators to collect and analyse data.

Swiftly plays the role of the central platform. They collect data from sensors, analyse it and send information back to the sensors.

Traditional companies laid the groundwork for platform companies to step in

My body has infrastructure, sensors, applications, a network of nerves and a central brain. When I go to pick up a glass of water, my body subconsciously notices things about that glass of water. My eyes check the colour: is it clear? My fingers check the temperature: is it too hot? My nose checks the smell: does it smell normal? My taste buds check the flavour: does it taste normal? My body uses all of these sensors automatically to check that the water I'm drinking is not going to make me sick or burn me.

We were born with these senses, but ecosystems need to develop them. Platform companies – such as Uber, Airbnb, Booking, Spotify and Netflix – didn't come into existence by reading my book or looking at a glass of water and saying that they needed to become a platform. Something else happened, something that made them sit up, take notice and say, "Hey, we can fill a gap here."

Let's go back to the beginning and my dad walking into his local bank. At first, all of the infrastructure was very close together. The bank teller who my dad talked to was part of the front-end infrastructure. He

ensured sales and customer interaction. He was also the back-end infrastructure. Everything was very direct: my dad walked in, had a conversation with the teller (front-end) and the teller did something (back-end). There was a direct connection between the product/service and the customer interaction.

However, when the bank scaled, this changed. The customer interaction was turned on its head and turned into a process and, in doing so, a gap was created between the customer and the infrastructure. The very moment you start to scale and you turn your operations into a process that you can scale, your front-end and back-end infrastructure stay connected but you lose touch with the customer. A rift forms between what you do and a potentially changing environment with changing customers.

At the bank, when it scaled, the customer became a customer number and the bank teller was no longer the same person but a different person every day. The personal contact was lost. All of the elements still existed – customers, front-end infrastructure, back-end infrastructure – but there's no direct connection any more. If I walk into another branch of my local restaurant in another city, I see a similar environment, the same concept, but there's not the same personal touch. When my local record shop became part of a chain, I was offered more choice but I lost the personal recommendations. The happenings in the bank, restaurant and record shop were no longer connected to me. They went from being outside-in, driven by the customer, to inside-out, driven by the process.

Good customer experience is highly personalised and dependent on context. The more one tries to scale that happening into a controllable process, the higher the chances that the customer experience will become impersonal, boring or even bad.

What does this have to do with platform companies? The answer is simple. That gap that incumbent companies created by scaling represented an opportunity. It's in that gap that platform companies were able to establish themselves, using the front-end and back-end infrastructure of existing companies as their back-end infrastructure and creating applications that were closer to the customer. Platform companies effectively used that gap and what already existed to respond to customer frustrations caused by scaling.

Let me give you an example. Booking used what already existed – hotels, B&Bs and other accommodation – and created an application which made it easier for the customer to choose. They identified the idle capacity and went and established themselves there. Hotels had scaled and, as such, were no longer in tune with what the market wanted. Booking used that gap to position themselves through applications. They used the infrastructure provided by hotels, not to steal it but to use the data from that infrastructure on the platform and they used the platform to feed the applications. The more small data they collected, the more big data they gained and the better they could feed the platform. The more they fed the platform, the better it could help and do clever stuff for every customer.

Spotify is another example. It's so close to what my local record shop used to do. In some ways, it's even better than my local record shop was at keeping track of what I like to listen to and when. Spotify filled the gap between music producers, music shops and customers.

The ice age of customer engagement

Of course, in order to feed a platform you need sensors and a network, but you can get this from the analogue world. Companies have been scaling and, by scaling, they have created the ice age of customer engagement. This ice age of customer engagement created frustrated customers but companies weren't even aware that customers were frustrated. That's where the danger lies. That's where the idle capacity is created. And that's what other companies, like Spotify, used in order to build applications that are built on data. You can only build applications based on big data if you start doing it with a platform that steals data from the analogue world, turns it into digital 1s and 0s and uses it to feed the platform and build applications.

In this book, I use a lot of the same examples – Amazon, Uber, Spotify, Waze, Booking, Airbnb – but that's not to say that you have to imitate them. If you want to create a music platform, there's nothing to say that you need to replicate the image of Spotify. When I talk about eco-systems, the important takeaway is what's underneath, not what you see on the outside. Uber and Spotify are both platform companies but they don't resemble each other. However, under the surface they both share the same basic structure.

When you look at a platform company, they all have infrastructure whether they built it themselves or hacked it. They all use sensors. In fact, they make it all about sensors. If you have sensors integrated into your infrastructure, but especially if you have sensors in your applications and you use the sensors that your customers already have, then you can feed the platform even more. It's always about sensors, the platform, and building a network through which you can lean on all participants to contribute to and build the network.

Participants come in many shapes and forms; they're not just companies participating in the network, they're also users. When you use Waze or Spotify, you participate in the network. You're not a constant participant, because you only participate when you are connected on the app, but you are a participant. With platform companies, it's not just the building blocks that are the same but also the mechanisms.

These are all crucial points you need to understand if you want to create an ecosystem. Companies must look at what they already have, what their existing building blocks are, and rethink how they use them and how they put them together. The new world might look a lot like the old on the surface, because we're going to reuse a lot of those old elements, but the difference will lie in how we use them.

What is a double flywheel? How do we create one?

A traditional business model in its most basic, essential form is simple. It starts (think back to fragile) as front- and back-end infrastructure which is close to the customers. Think about a local bakery. You don't need to ask whether that business model is inside-out or outside-in. It's organic. The shop (the front-end) is closely connected to the oven (the back-end); customers walk into the shop to buy goods which creates short feedback loops. The front-end is influenced by the back-end and has an effect on the goods and services offered, and thus on the customers who influence the front-end which influences the back-end. The brain holding it all together is the baker.

HOW TO CREATE A DOUBLE FLYWHEEL

If that bakery becomes a chain, that connection is broken. The scalable part of the business (the back-end) starts to become the dominant factor while the front-end becomes a formula that is the result of the back-end and the formulation of the happening between the shop and the customers (the happening being turned into a formula). As a result, there is no longer a short feedback loop. There may be feedback, but in economies of scale direct feedback is a factor which may disturb and is thus avoided. Customers change in line with a variety of factors, so the gap between the front-end (which is becoming one with the back-end and turning into infrastructure as a result of the scalable formula) and what customers are actually looking for continues to grow.

If that gap becomes large enough, there is room for the so-called "disruptors" to come in from outside of the business. Given that you are locked inside the business, you don't even notice the growing gap, because you're far too busy optimising the formula (which has made you rigid). You may as well have laid out the red carpet for outsiders: all they have to do is dive in, between your infrastructure and the customers who are looking for something that you haven't even noticed (and that they might not even see), to turn your customers' frustrations into delight and Uberise your business. They don't have to invent a business (it's still a bakery) but they focus on the interaction with customers, gaining their attention (and money and, most importantly, data). The real "trick" when it comes to Uberising a business is to hack the existing infrastructure. The in-between disruptor, that focuses on customer delight, doesn't have to be a baker because you already are one and you're good at it. Your speciality is no longer about being close to the customer, but about being an efficient bakery. If that's the case, the chances are that all other bakeries are the same and that their customers are also frustrated. Consequently, the disruptor can scale fast. They have got all of your customers for free, they don't have to invest in infrastructure because they have yours so they can focus on what they do, the core of their business: building a data-driven platform between you (the infrastructure) and the customer, as well as building one (and later maybe more) applications on top of that platform and feeding the platform with data collected through interactions with customers.

As a result, in between the infrastructure and the customers, we get a platform and an application (think the Spotify or Booking of bakeries).

I have seen slides saying the same thing thousands of times: Uber is the largest taxi company but owns no taxis; Booking.com is the largest hotel company but owns no hotel rooms; and so on. But those statements are wrong. Uber is not a taxi company, Booking.com is not a hotel company; they are platform companies. They apply the TREE principle; they're a different breed.

This is the start of Uberisation and a highway to being able to scale fast. There are millions of frustrated customers, an existing business model and millions of bakery chains that are good at making their products but lousy at being in tune with the customer. Beware, those bakery concepts have lost themselves in the trap of operational excellence which can only lead to them being squeezed out of the market. However, there will always be a market for those who have not given up on the most important element: the relationship with the customer.

The real secret of Uber, Booking.com, Netflix and Amazon lies in the double flywheel, in dealing with (or, even better, involving) *people* (who are empowered and engaged) rather than *customers* and engaging them to make sure that they become a part of the ecosystem (not just customers).

By creating an application that is Faster, Easier, more Accessible, Simpler and more Tempting than the traditional business (the FEAST interface), those platforms are engaging the customer to become more than just a customer, using all things digital to escape the "normal" boundaries of the interaction. They "ask" the customer to share their smartphones and use their network connections and they "ask" customers to become quality controllers, supervisors, ideators, co-creators, sales and marketing departments and co-workers free of charge. In many cases, people even pay money to be part of the team, so blinded by the FEAST and the engagement that they don't notice or don't mind.

It may sound like magic to some, but it's all down to the double flywheel. The better the application, the more people will use it and the more they will feel like the application is something that they need and that brings value. The more they use it, the more data the application gathers and feeds to the platform. The more the platform is fed by data, the more performant it becomes and the better it understands the customer. As a result, the brain is better able to react and be proactive with the small data of each interaction. In turn, the application keeps getting better and better, more and more personalised so the platform collects more and more data to be processed and activated.

You can see the mechanism. It's easy to see how one leads to the other and round in a circle. Just imagine how easy it is to keep this model going once the platform is up and running, in addition to the two fly-wheels. Just imagine how you can now build new applications on top of that platform, in turn collecting more and more data to feed back into the platform to make both the original and the new applications better. That is the double flywheel. That is the core of the ecosystem, which is why I call it an ecosystem.

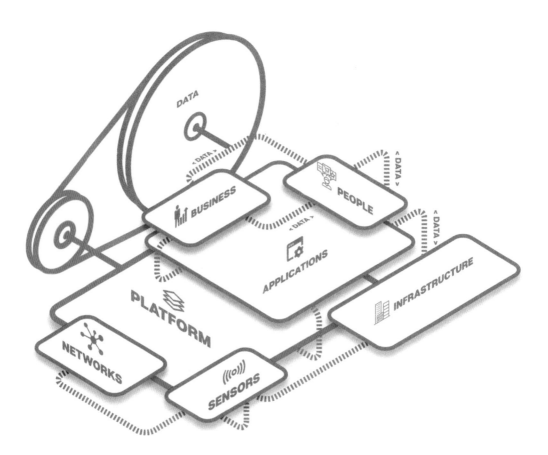

The heart of an ecosystem is the double flywheel dynamic.

Utilising the idle capacity

In many business models, you can identify what is not being used to its maximum potential and that's what I call idle capacity. If you look at your customers and all they're doing is buying your product, that's idle capacity. If they buy your product, they must also contribute to feeding the platform. That's how you can maximise their input but, in return, you also have to maximise your output because otherwise they won't want to participate in the ecosystem. And if they don't want to participate in the ecosystem, then the game is lost.

If you know that Spotify is using your data, but you don't get anything in return and on top of that you're paying for the service, then you'll leave. Once again, that's idle capacity. The music catalogue is there, phones are there, users are there – how can you connect them and contribute to their very existence? If you think about Spotify, what would you miss? Personalised suggestions and user-generated content. Everyone can generate content, upload their podcast or other people's music. My podcast is on the same level as Prince's discography, because it's all available on Spotify.

Don't look at the appearance, delve into the structure

This is the key to platform companies and what traditional companies must understand if they want to become an ecosystem: it's about look-ing at what you are and thinking about how you can transfer it to those building blocks and that underlying canvas. It doesn't have to look like Spotify or Amazon or Uber. You don't have to imitate them. In fact, don't. Instead, think about the skeleton underneath. Compare ecosystems to humans: we all look different on the outside but on the inside we have the same basic infrastructure (our skeleton, blood vessels, muscles, ligaments, joints and so on). It's the same for the ecosystem economy. Every one will look different even though they have the same basic skeleton.

I fear that companies wanting to become an ecosystem will just look at the outside and try to replicate that, without understanding the un-derlying skeleton. But if you just try to emulate the appearance, you're bound to make a mistake. If you just look at the appearance and try to recreate the appearance of an ecosystem without understanding the underlying skeleton, you may build something that looks like a human being but doesn't work like one. If you ask it to walk or run, you'll realise that you recreated a statue and didn't foresee that it may need to run. If you just think about the appearance, you'll recreate the look but you'll be missing the skeleton and muscles that make it function.

Don't Spotify your model, unless you intend to imitate the underlying skeleton rather than how Spotify looks. It's a mistake I see far too often in banks, insurance companies and start-ups to name a few. They're good at recreating the looks, but they fail to understand the underlying dynamics and, as a result, they fail. The ecosystem will only be healthy on the outside if it is healthy on the inside. The looks are the result of what lies underneath, not the other way around.

An ecosystem must be built on exchange with the outside world, just like in nature ecosystems need minerals and sunlight. Ecosystems draw from the outside world but they also contribute; it cannot be a one-way street, otherwise it would receive nothing. It's all about exchange of whatever it may be – money, energy, data – with the outside world, because you need to feed the ecosystem and you need to offer something in return.

Building an ecosystem starts with identifying customer frustrations, that idle capacity. Then you turn it around. How do you build applications? The aim of an application is to detect and solve customer frustrations. The bigger the gap between what customers want and what we do, the bigger the chance that customers will be frustrated and the bigger the gap we leave for companies to come in and build an application that solves that frustration, building a platform between your infrastructure and what customers want. By being a platform and using as many sensors as possible to build that platform, the platform quickly becomes more and more clever than whatever company was there in the first place. As it grows, the platform can push the old industry to the dump pile and position itself between the customer and the dump pile.

The TREE formula

To understand an ecosystem, you need to look at all of its parts, the whole circle: customer frustrations, how to build an ecosystem, applications, the link between the ecosystem and the outside world, how it's all connected. In an ecosystem, big data is connected to extreme customer-centricity which is connected to platform thinking which is connected to ecosystems.

To put it simply, it all boils down to my TREE formula: Technology first, Red ocean of frustrated customers, Engaged people, Ecosystem economy. We are diving into that third dimension, we're no longer living in a purely analogue or a purely digital setting. You need to stop what you were doing before, because the tsunami that is artificial intelligence is fast approaching.

Put technology first. You need big data, artificial intelligence and robotisation. Start collecting whatever data you can right now. Look at what data you can extract from existing records. Don't just count what money is coming in, count what data you have. Without data, artificial intelligence will be useless and you never know what data you might need in the future, so just collect as much as you can. Data can come from anywhere – your interactions with key partners, customers and the outside world. Every day that you fail to optimise the collection, storage and processing of that data into information and actions is a day lost.

Take Spotify again. Spotify does more or less what my local record shop used to do for me, but it does it better: it creates my very own music universe, it recognises me, listens to me, inspires me... I feel engaged. If Spotify were no longer around, I would miss it as much as I missed my local record shop. My Spotify fits me like a glove and is different than yours. Spotify is able to do that for millions of customers. They are able to crack the magic formula: connect to many and engage individuals.

Develop a red ocean strategy. See the red ocean of frustrated customers. Why are they frustrated and how could you help? Don't focus on new products and new customers in new markets, focus on your existing customers and how you can optimise their customer experience. Use your technology, your data, to create something that brings value to the customer, that turns customer frustration into customer delight. Make the customer the centre of your interactions and peel back the onion from there. Disruptors positioned themselves in the old model, between your so-called perfect solutions and the desired customer experience. Don't let that happen again; play the part yourselves.

Don't make the same mistake Kodak did. They didn't harness the power of digital because they believed that the picture quality provided by their cameras and film roll would win. It didn't. Customers wanted to share their pictures, their memories, instantly and on various platforms. Digital didn't offer quality, but it fulfilled this need. Kodak's mistake was to focus too much on their solution: the film roll. They were in love with the solution, not the problem. It needs to be the other way around: don't fall in love with the solution, fall in love with the problem.

Engage people. The difference between bad and good customer experience is engagement. Engaged customers buy more, buy more often and stay loyal. They serve as your sales and marketing department – they will tell other people how good you made them feel.

Transform your model into an ecosystem. The only way you can create this constant performance with customers and crack the c2MxEi formula is by transforming your business model into an ecosystem.

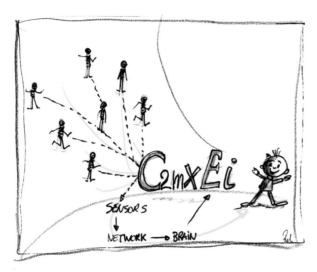

When many companies come to me asking about ecosystems, they're concerned about the investment, both of time and money. Yes that's needed, but only to get the flywheel turning. If you build good apps that turn people into sensors and infrastructure and give people value in return for this data, you will bring more and more people in to the ecosystem. The more people you bring in, the more you grow and the cheaper it gets. The more you engage people, the less you will have to pay out on things like sales, marketing and quality control. Engaged people do all of that for you. If you look at Airbnb, we are their quality controllers. If you look at Tesla, we are their marketers. Once you have that flywheel turning, people will keep it growing. So don't just count money, count data.

Creating an algorithm that works for your customers

Getting an ecosystem off the ground is a hard job for one massive reason. The heart of an ecosystem is the platform, the "place" where data is processed by a "learning algorithm" which gets better and wiser the more it eats data.

The problem is that people have zero tolerance for all things digital. As humans, we are willing to accept mistakes made by human beings, we forgive and offer second or third chances, but we don't offer the same clemency to artificial intelligence or robots that make the same mistakes. In 2019, Belgium saw 646 road traffic fatalities[81] and across the European Union, this figure was estimated at 22,800.[82] In Belgium, that's almost two people per day who die because of a road traffic accident, nearly the capacity of two Boeing 747s crashing. However, just imagine if a self-driving car had an accident on public roads. In Germany, self-driving cars will be allowed onto public roads from 2022,[83] but just imagine that first accident. There will be an uproar, a national enquiry; how dare a robot kill a human being even though humans kill other humans in traffic accidents every day? But like I said, humans have zero tolerance for digital failure.

That's why, when you release an algorithm for use by the public, you need to make sure that it's good, even better than good. An algorithm in training is not at its best and our customers expect the best, better than the best. But an algorithm in training makes mistakes, many mistakes, before it can perform at its best. The customer, however, couldn't care less. They don't want to deal with the algorithm's mistakes. Can you really blame them?

Consequently, companies face a paradox when starting an algorithm. You need people to interact with your ecosystem and your platform, so that they can feed the platform and help it mature. However, people will not accept an immature platform that is bound to make mistakes. Don't despair, there are a couple of options available to you. Let me tell you about them, their advantages and disadvantages, the things you need to be aware of when making your choice.

1. Buy an algorithm that has already been created and trained.
2. Build an algorithm yourself.

Buy/hire an algorithm

The first option you have is to buy or hire an algorithm. This is absolutely feasible; in the future, algorithms will likely be the new product to buy. For example, I have visited companies that are developing virtual assistants, run by artificial intelligence, to make telephone calls (you know those annoying types of recurring calls to follow up on interested customers). People don't like making these calls again and again, but a robot can do it. These robots are often given a name, usually female for some reason, and sometimes even a job title, age and birthday, to make "her" a part of the company. Once you've set the AI up, it will start doing business for you in that one specific skillset. These robots run by AI are pretty good. They won't start out as your best employee, but a fairly good one. Within a couple of weeks, however, they'll probably be the best option you've ever had.

Buying an algorithm is thus a fairly good option. But you need to be aware of a few things first. One of them is that this algorithm will only be helpful in very limited areas of your business. The AI has to be trained in these highly specific areas because they need to know the vocabulary/terminology and the language of that sector, to make the most of speech and language recognition. Nevertheless, within the boundaries of a particular sector, the algorithm can perform fairly well. That might be a shortcut you can take. There are more issues you need to be aware of, but let me first explain the second option to you.

Build the algorithm yourself

There are different ways in which you can build an algorithm yourself. The first method is an option if you already have a large data set, a large quantity of historical data in a particular area. If you have that data you can use it to train your algorithm before you release it to the outside world. This is particularly helpful in an industry which isn't moving very fast, because that old data will be a good test laboratory for the algorithm of real circumstances. But, in order to be able to build an algorithm and train it using old data, there are two prerequisites: it must be a slow-moving industry and you need to have historical data.

Trial and error using historical data

Let me give you an example, a real example I was involved in. (For confidentiality reasons, I will not disclose the name of the company nor its true industry – the story however is true.) Imagine a company in the construction industry with years and years of historical data regarding their tender offers. Writing an offer for a big tender is an extensive process, which involves lots of people, time and money. It's also comparable to sticking your finger in the air and making your best guess as to the direction of the wind. There are so many products and product combinations you could offer, you simply have to hope you're offering the right thing. Anyway, this construction company wanted to automate tenders, so they showed me their CRM system. I was blown away. Never before had I seen so much data, data about every tender offer they had made, data about their competitors' offers and data about whether they won or lost. So much data that they had been keeping for more than ten years. The CEO told me that they weren't exactly sure why they kept all those records, but they just kept doing it. In the beginning, they hoped sales representatives would be able to use it to make better offers, but it was just too much data for them to process. They were drowning in it, but they continued to make the records none-theless. If you have so much data that you don't know what to do with it, then you're lucky.

The construction company contacted a couple of platform-producing companies in San Francisco to get an algorithm built for them, based on their data and trained using their data. The result was an algorithm that was as performant as any algorithm that had been training for ten years. This meant that when they released the algorithm, it worked well from the outset. It was as good and even a bit better than human be-ings. It kept learning and growing, so the company started retraining sales representatives to be the eyes and ears of the algorithm, the data collecting machines to feed the algorithm. The company's hit rate went up in no time; the effect on their bottom line was simply astounding.

However, the company also wanted to bring this success to the part of their company on the other side of the Atlantic, in Europe, where they also had an extensive operation and the same problem with tenders. They took the empty shell of their algorithm to Europe, they trained super sales representatives, but there were two problems. First, they were unable to retrain the algorithm because the historical data they had in the United States simply didn't exist in Europe, so they used the algorithm trained on American data. The second problem was a result of the first. The algorithm was a complete bust in Europe, because it had been trained in an American context.

This is something you must also be aware of if you're buying or hiring an algorithm – you need to know how it was trained. If you're operating in Europe, and you hire an algorithm that has been trained with Asian data, you may have a problem not because of the data itself but be-cause of the different context. If you don't have the historical data to re-train and adjust the AI that you're using, it might do completely wrong things. So either you need to have your own historical data or, if you don't have that, you need to know what data has been used to train the algorithm. Do a trial first to check whether it works or not.

Trial and error through internal training

Another method is to build your algorithm but not release it to the public immediately. You can train it, raise it, help it mature, internally, by asking your employees to interact with it as if they were customers, thus training it to become good with the number of people you have and the number of interactions you can give it. Of course, this may take a while. If you have a few million customers but only 100 employees who can train it, it will take a while to train the algorithm.

Imagine a bank that creates a chatbot, which is run by artificial intelligence. The bot would be accessible to all customers to help answer their queries and resolve their problems. The bot would be built with the best technology, to help guide customers through what they need to do to resolve their problem and how to do it.

The problem is that a bot needs data. Like any chatbot, when first released, the technology is still rather juvenile. It hasn't had the time to collect the data it needs to improve. Of course, as a company, you don't want to release something that's not going to be truly helpful to the customer yet, so when and how do you launch it? Imagine the bank to decide to launch the bot with its employees and early adopters first, before making it available to the big public, all the bank's customers. Those first users would thus be entrusted with raising this AI child, giving the bot the data it needed to improve and mature.

In short: the bot would have the computing power, but would need the data in order to become truly useful and valuable to the customers. Artificial intelligence is fairly simple: the more people use it, the more information it gets, the better it gets, the more useful it gets and the more applications it can create. Once you get that flywheel turning, it becomes exponential.

Shadow learning

Another method you can use to train the algorithm is shadow learning, which is what Tesla has been doing to train a self-driving car. There are some aspects that you can program: learning to read and understand traffic signs (e.g. speed limits), learning the rules of the road (the high-way code), teaching the algorithm that for a bend of x degrees, it can travel at a maximum speed of x mph.

The one thing you can't do with a self-driving car is trial and error, which is the option we have been looking at until now (testing out old or new data sets). Trial and error involves the algorithm running operations time and time again and learning from every single mistake it makes. That's what makes it so much better than human beings. We think humans learn from mistakes, but in most cases we don't. Algorithms learn from every mistake and that's why they get better all the time. That's why algorithms often outrun human beings.

Nevertheless, there are certain things, like self-driving cars, that you can't possibly train with trial and error. In that case, you can use shadow learning. Tesla does this through the auto-pilot system installed in their cars. Even when the driver doesn't turn the auto-pilot mode on, it is on, it's watching and learning from what the driver does, what they do with the steering wheel in certain circumstances. It learns where you drive, how you drive, how you interact with other traffic, how you perform complex manoeuvres that can't be programmed. By doing this, not just in my car, but in the millions of cars they have on the road, Tesla gets quite a lot of information that they can use to develop a super driver. The central brain learns from every other Tesla car, every kilometre I drive, every mile my colleague drives, and gets better and better. At a certain point, they'll say that the central brain has been trained enough and they can release the self-driving option in a car. Of course, they won't release that option for free, you'll have to pay for it, even though you're the one who helped train the brain.

Be clear about the reward structure

As a company, you need to be aware that these are your options: you can buy an algorithm or build it yourself and to train it you can use trial and error (historical data, internal training) or shadow learning. I think that, in the future, most companies will opt for the build-it-your-self option, but it's important to be aware that you'll need to change the make-up of your company to do that. You won't just need coders, you'll need experts in a range of domains. You can explain to coders what you want the AI to accomplish, but first you need to understand the reward structure, which is much more important than the actual programming of the AI.

You have to program what it needs to do. Imagine if you programmed an AI to save planet Earth, but you fail to give it that extra vital instruc-tion: don't kill human beings while doing so. I know, and I'm sure you know, what the AI would do, because the shortcut to saving planet Earth is to kill off the virus known as the human race. In most cases, whatever you ask the AI to do, its task will be complicated by human beings. Self-driving cars are already more than capable of driving you from Brussels to Berlin, if there were no human-driven cars on the road. Humans make it difficult. So if you don't expressly tell the AI that it needs to learn to interact with humans, to love and respect them, it won't. In order to do this, we need psychiatrists and sociologists in our organisations to train the algorithm and tell it what to do.

The second big difficulty is what we have discussed in terms of training. When you start using an algorithm, it won't be mature at all. At best it will be like a toddler, but most likely still a baby. You can't expect cus-tomers to welcome you sending them a baby to interact with. That's an issue you have to solve. I'm still on the lookout for other options but for the moment the only ones I see are trial and error, using historical data in a slow-moving industry or training the algorithm internally; or shad-ow learning, imitating what users are doing and learning from them.

Rather than create your own, you can participate in one to get off the starting line

There is another possibility, but it may not be what you had in mind. What if, rather than trying to start out and create your own ecosystem, you became part of an existing one? There are already ecosystems that are up and running; some of them are closed, like Tesla and Uber, but oth-ers are open, like Amazon and the Dutch bol.com (we'll look into them in more detail in chapter 11). By joining an existing ecosystem, you can start to use the platform, and by using it and accessing it you can access some of the data to get your flywheel turning thanks to the energy of the larger flywheel you're linked to. If you're a sensor in the ecosystem, you can get your data flywheel turning by using the ecosystem's flywheel. If you're an application, you might use the ecosystem's flywheel to make your application better and build up your own flywheel.

This option is a perfectly good option that I think many companies will see the merits of. It's what KBC, the Belgian bank, is trying to do: create the double flywheel in banking but also become a partner for life for customers, and allow other companies to link into that ecosystem and benefit from it. Are you running late for your train and don't have a ticket yet? Ask Kate to get you one. If the KBC app, and its AI Kate, are linked in an ecosystem to the national rail service, that's possible.

The more companies become small ecosystems themselves, the better they will feed the big ecosystem and the better the big ecosystem will feed the small ones. The better small companies become ecosystems the better they can feed the customer because the customer is an ecosystem. It's the fractal theory, where the small is the same as the whole and the whole is the same as the small. Resemble your smallest unit.

Patience is a necessary virtue

In the next chapter, we will look at the building blocks of the ecosystem, but I can't give you a recipe on how to create one. What I can tell you is that you need to start with the essential tools. If you want to bake a cake, you need an oven and a cake tin. If you want to build an ecosystem, you'll need data and an algorithm. Data is the juice of the ecosystem, and the algorithm allows you to extract all the nutrients from it. So what do companies need to do right now, even if they're not ready to create an ecosystem? Gather data. Know why you exist, what your purpose is, and gather data like crazy. Think of that construction company. Using the data they had available they were able to feed the algorithm, but without data the algorithm was useless. It's an important lesson to

PATIENCE ...... EXPONETIAL

learn. If you don't have historical data, you can't kickstart the algorithm; you'll have to start from scratch and that could take years.

You will need patience to get the flywheel turning but once you get it going, really going, it will be a thing of wonder. It will be exponential. Imagine a watertight football stadium in which you're seated in the top row. One raindrop falls in the middle of the field; the next minute it's two, the minute after that it's four. Every minute the number of raindrops that land on that field doubles. After 45 minutes, only 7% of the stadium is filled, just a slightly flooded field. However, it will only take four more minutes for the stadium to be filled completely. That's the power of exponential. I'm sure that, sitting on that top row, you weren't worried for those first 45 minutes and by the time you realised what was happening, it was too late.[84] Companies expect results fast, but the first part of your journey will take time, money and resources. There will be no results, until it becomes exponential. However, if you train your algorithm with historical data, you may be able to get a head start, you may already be at that 45-minute mark. In any case, historical data will help you get there much faster.

It's hard for people to imagine the impact of exponential, which we have seen clear as day during this pandemic. Nevertheless, we must realise that once we get that flywheel turning, we will have to go through that first flat part of the curve for a long time before it starts to become exponential and really get going. I fear that most companies will give up in that first part. It's a paradox you need to be aware of: you'll be pouring money, time and resources into the algorithm but will see no results, because, while the algorithm is young, you can't involve the general public and, as a result, the journey will be even slower because you can't feed it.

Many companies tell me: "Rik, first we need to know what we're going to do with the data, then we'll gather it." That's the old way of thinking. That construction company I told you about gathered data, even though they didn't know why. They just felt they needed to and it paid back big time. Ecosystem thinking, algorithms, data… it's not just for companies like Amazon and Alibaba. I'm talking about a construction company, which used this power to augment their tenders. It's not a very sexy business, but the results and the impact on their bottom line are flabbergasting.

THE ULTIMATE QUESTION
(no the answer is not 42)
What would users(*) of the ecosystem miss if the ecosystem weren't there?
((*) read users + participants in the ecosystem)

Build

"If I have seen further, it is by standing
on the shoulders of giants."
ISAAC NEWTON

---

featuring:
finding ingredients
tapping into the untapped
seeing true
connecting the dots
being human
double-sided
a spider web

No magic recipe, but a set of ingredients mixed with one basic principle

When I first started to write this book, I wanted to talk about the ingredients and the recipe you need to follow to create an ecosystem. However, as often happens when writing, I realised that my vision was not to be. Yes, there are ingredients that are crucial to an ecosystem, but the method used to create it does not involve a set order of steps. A recipe has a beginning and an end; building an ecosystem does not. It's not a matter of where you start, but more about when and why you start. While building an ecosystem, you need to maintain a holistic overview. By doing so, the system itself will tell you what it needs.

Nevertheless, there is one key ingredient, one fundamental principle if you will, that is needed to build the ecosystem. This principle is overarching. Like in baking, no matter the recipe, there are some things that don't change: don't overmix the batter once you've added flour or you'll remove the airiness; don't open the oven while the cake is baking or the cake won't rise. These are principles that every good baker knows, but once again we can't compare them fully to the principle of the ecosystem. In baking, these principles are relevant at a specific stage of the baking process. In ecosystems, our principle is continuous. It is the all-encompassing question that must be revisited continuously. It is not a one-time thing designed to be applied at a certain point in the process. It is more like a constant guiding star above our heads.

What would users* of the ecosystem miss if the ecosystem weren't there?

* by users, I mean both outside users and participants in the ecosystem

The answer to this question is the original why, the raison d'être, of an ecosystem. If there's no reason for outside users or participants to use the ecosystem, if they gain nothing from it, that's the end of the ecosystem's raison d'être and thus the end of the ecosystem itself. It's the bedrock that underpins the whole of the ecosystem, a question that must not be asked just once but should be asked again and again. That's why an ecosystem must maintain a constant feedback loop; it needs to be reactive. Are we still relevant? What would people miss if we weren't there?

In a way, this question is the beginning, the middle and the end. If you develop an ecosystem but don't ask this question from the outset, the ecosystem doesn't stand a chance. If at some point during the ecosystem's existence, the reason why you developed the ecosystem is no longer in tune with what people would miss if it were not there, then the ecosystem will die. Why? Because it is no longer being fed by the outside world. An ecosystem's energy – whether that be money, resources, data, or anything else – doesn't stem from the ecosystem itself but from the outside world. The outside world will only grant you access to those resources, that energy, if there's something in it for them, some sort of higher purpose – the answer to that question. The question isn't the first step of the recipe, it's the higher purpose that is omnipresent. The ecosystem must always be in tune with that perspective. If the outside world changes, by definition the ecosystem must react.

Connect with the outside world

As I said, and I cannot stress this enough, there is no set order to developing an ecosystem. There is a series of ingredients, what I call building blocks, but the order of these building blocks is not defined. One thing I would recommend when building an ecosystem is that you translate that ultimate question into at least one application – one interface between the ecosystem and the outside world. If you want to do something for the outside world, you need to create a connection with it in one way or another. That's an application and, in most cases, literally an app. You know that your customer spends their life on their smartphone; the most expensive square metre of real estate is made not of bricks but of clicks.

Start with what you have

An ecosystem is not built from scratch. If you want to transform your existing business model into an ecosystem, I would start by filling the infrastructure box. Look at what you do today and, for the time being, throw all of those existing building blocks (people, knowledge, buildings, patents etc.) into the infrastructure box. Ultimately, your infrastructure box should be as light, as asset-free, as possible. The more assets you have, the harder it will be for you to be flexible. But for now let's put them all in that box.

Rather than purchasing or generating more infrastructure, try to rely on external partners to fill up that box insofar as you can. This is known as "hacking stuff" in San Francisco. Uber "hacked" existing technology and resources – they identified idle capacity in the analogue world and created a digital space to make use of that capacity. So, rather than developing it yourself, where can you find idle capacity in the old analogue world that you can use as infrastructure? If you are an existing company, you can turn this question on yourself: where is the idle capacity in my own business? How can I make better use of that idle capacity? Use as much of that idle capacity as you can. Make it as light as you can. Make it as asset-free as you can.

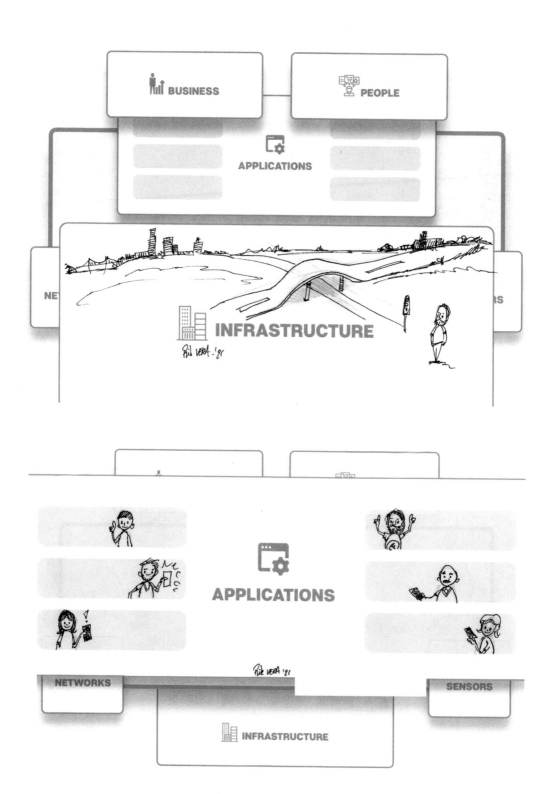

BUSINESS

PEOPLE

APPLICATIONS

NE...

...RS

INFRASTRUCTURE

APPLICATIONS

NETWORKS

SENSORS

INFRASTRUCTURE

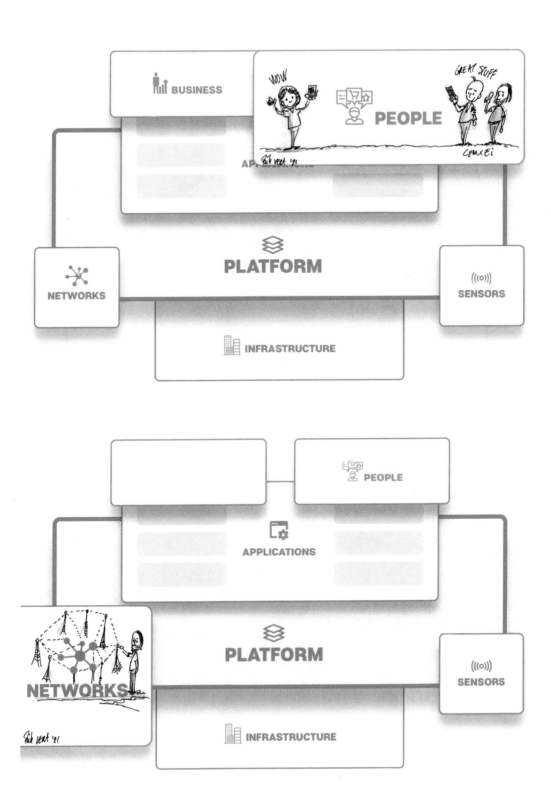

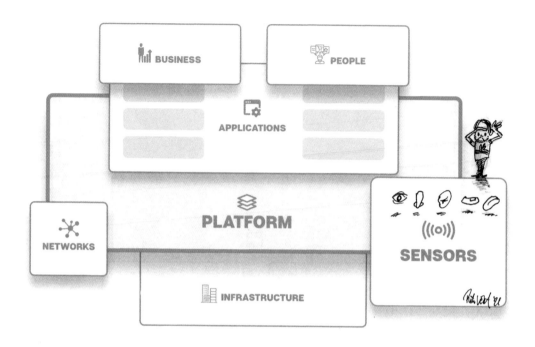

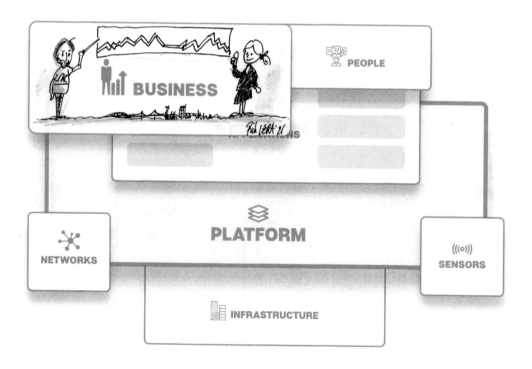

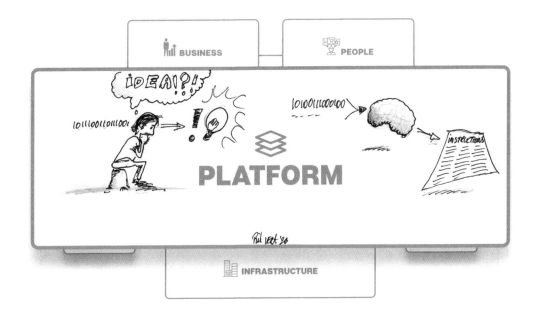

Build an army of data collecting machines

Once you have that figurative box of infrastructure, you need to try to get as much stuff out of that box as you can so that you can use it in another box. Let's say that we want to develop smart mobility in a city. Everything that already exists – cars, traffic lights, trams, trains, buses, roads, and so on – goes in the infrastructure box. You don't need to produce these things or buy them, they're already there. Now, how do you make that infrastructure box as light as you can? If a train is just a train, it stays in the infrastructure box. But if you equip that train with sensors, it's no longer just a train, just infrastructure; instead it becomes a data collecting machine. By equipping that train with sensors, you move it out of the infrastructure box into the sensor box.

I recently read an article about a food ecosystem being developed in a city. Their infrastructure is all the land potential in the city, from that one square metre of balcony space to the hectares of land owned by a farmer. If you want to create a smart food ecosystem, all of these individual parcels of land are your infrastructure. You don't need to buy them, they already exist. Somehow, you will have to collect information about all that ground and what happens there. To do that, you'll need phones or the internet, but that also already exists. Once you've identified these points, you realise that you don't need to develop much infrastructure, because most of it is already there, already available.

This is what I mean by infrastructure: it's necessary, but insofar as possible the infrastructure you use should already be there. Later on, you may notice that you need more infrastructure. In that case, you can partner with someone to get it or produce items that count toward infrastructure but in the beginning, you start with what already exists.

Utilise any idle capacity

Although this infrastructure may already be available, that doesn't mean that it is being used to its full potential. That's what I mean by idle capacity. If you look at how you could maximise the use of that land, it's clear that you'll never be able to maximise output if you don't organise use of the land on a platform. If everyone tries to create their own balcony garden, that's good but it doesn't optimise the output of all the square metres available for the population. If you consider all of that available ground as one large piece of land, you can maximise its use and optimise the output. To do that, you need to know what is going on there.

Data is like the gift of sight

This brings us to the crux of what enables an ecosystem: collecting, processing and activating data.

An ecosystem gets input from the outside world as well as from participants in the ecosystem. It's what makes an ecosystem different: it connects all the dots; it enables interaction with every dot. The whole ecosystem must be in tune with the outside world and feed the outside world just as the outside world feeds it. If the ecosystem weren't there, participants would miss that interaction, just like users.

There is an order when it comes to using data; you have to start by collecting data. If you want to create smart city mobility, you need to start by collecting data about where your travellers are and when, where your trains and cars and other vehicles are and when. It's like our bodies: you can have a brilliant brain but if our sensors (sight, hearing, taste, feel, smell) don't feed our brain, it leads to nothing. Once again, it's a case of the chicken or the egg. In a smart city, smart mobility requires having as many sensors as you can integrate into your infrastructure. Without these sensors, you are blind.

The same goes for building smart food ecosystems within a city. If you don't know what people are doing with their balcony gardens and you don't coordinate what they're doing, it's useless. You need to have feedback loops, but not all sensors have to be digital. I can't imagine that smart food ecosystems would involve having a camera watching every square metre of space. What's important is what is happening there, so the sensors in this case might be people who collect the data and use digital methods to communicate and share that data. It's then about the platform, which needs to use that data to see how it can be optimised to help you. How can the data about individual balcony gardens be used to optimise food production so that people would miss that ecosystem if it weren't there?

One of the biggest challenges for companies when building an ecosystem is to equip as much of the infrastructure with sensors as they can. The more sensors they have the better. The second but more difficult challenge relates to how best we can feed our brain. The more sensors we have, the better we can feed our brain, but we must not limit ourselves by defining what we're going to do with the data and then letting this define what sensors we need. If we did that, we would once again fail to optimise the potential of our infrastructure. The more we can measure, the more data we can collect, the better we can feed our brain, and the more we can process.

We still think in terms of a controlling mindset: first you define what you want to do, then you define what data you need which then defines what sensors you need. But it has to be the other way around. When a child learns, their brain doesn't dictate what data it will or will not absorb. It just absorbs as much data as it can, which then formats the brain. If you are born without one of the senses, you develop another method of dealing with reality – if you are blind, you may develop a heightened sense of hearing. Perhaps, if we were born with more senses, we would develop our brain in a different way.

"Two thirds of her cognition is outside of her brain, in her arms. Her entire being is thinking, feeling, exploring. She's got 2,000 suckers and she's using all of them independently."

Craig Foster, *My Octopus Teacher*

Think of your sensors like the suckers of an octopus, constantly searching for information, interconnected by a central brain.

Be like a child. Don't limit what you learn, what your sensors will see, to what you think you need to know. Acknowledge that you don't know what you don't know. Be open to data showing you a new direction. But data can only do that if you let it, if you collect enough of it and, most importantly, if you don't limit it.

Think about your goal

Consequently, when we build our sensors we must not start with assumptions about what sensors we need to collect what types of data so that we can do something that is pre-defined in a way. If we started with assumptions about what we needed, we would not be maximising the potential of the data. Of course, I'm not saying you shouldn't think about the end goal at all – it can help you to start with a basic framework – but you should not let that define what sensors you need. If you want to build a smart food ecosystem in a city, you might say that your goal is to be able to produce enough food to feed everybody in the city, while limiting the consumption of water and energy needed to produce that food. Think about what you would need to be able to do that? And don't forget that why: what would people miss?

Say you want to develop smart city mobility, your goal might be to make sure that people can travel from any point A to any point B within the city in no more than fifteen minutes. That's a starting point that you can use to explore the type of sensors and infrastructure you might need, but it doesn't define the sensors you need. Imagine that you achieve that goal. If, as a user, I lived in a city like Paris and was able to travel anywhere I liked in that city within fifteen minutes, without using my own vehicle, I'd miss that if for some reason it was no longer possible. That's the raison dêtre of your ecosystem. The more sensors you can build in, the better you'll be able to achieve that goal. You may even be able to go beyond it, but you have to start somewhere.

What sensors do you already have?

When you're filling that box with sensors, don't forget to look at your existing sensors: are you using your existing sensors to collect data? Are they serving as a sensor? Do you gather any data they might collect? Do you maximise the data you (could) collect from your sensors? This is a good starting point when thinking about sensors. Once you've answered those questions, think about how you could increase the number of sensors you have, but that's only step 2. First you need to look at what your existing sensors are and if you're using them. People count as sensors, but we tend not to see them as such. However, if you want to optimise travel time in a city like Paris, you'll never be able to achieve your goal if you don't follow people. Let's face it – people are crucial sensors.

In a company, we often forget to treat our sales representatives as sensors. I know of companies who send out 400 sales representatives every day who each meet with seven or eight (potential) clients. What they learn during those meetings is invaluable information, but it is not used. That's a colossal amount of data that is not being collected or transformed into information that can inform the company. Sales representatives tend to be sent out simply to sell. By not learning from their interactions, we're missing a trick.

Subconsciously, we collect data with every conversation we have. Sales representatives gather data in their brains but rather than sending that data to the central brain, the platform, it is kept in each individual brain. Imagine if those 400 sales representatives were connected robots. At first, those robots would be quite stupid in comparison with human beings, like those waiter robots I mentioned earlier. However, every time they have an interaction, data is generated and shared. This means that not only would the central brain become 400 times better with every iteration, each robot would too. That makes it exponential. In just one iteration, a single brain would become 400 times cleverer. Such a system would outrun humans in no time.

Nevertheless, robots are limited. Humans are much better at learning than robots. But what we don't do is connect all of our brains and feed them into a central brain. If we did, it would create augmented intelligence. We already use this to some extent in our daily lives. Many people say that having all the knowledge of the world on the internet has made us more stupid, less capable of using our memory, but in reality it has made us more intelligent. We may not be doing things ourselves, but by relying on an external brain we are being clever. It's how nature works: if something is available, if there is idle capacity, why wouldn't we use it? Why would I use my brain to do a calculation that the calculator on my phone can do? The more we rely on external systems to relieve some of the pressure on our brains, the more capacity we free up for other activities.

Using data to connect the dots

If you have a garden, you know what's happening in the garden so you are the sensor. You have the data. That data exists but if we don't connect all the people in the city who have a garden, if we don't gather all their data and feed it to the central brain, then we can't use that data effectively. In trying to build a smart food ecosystem in a city, we might ask questions like: how many calories and ingredients do we need to feed our population? Do we have enough land to do this? Who will benefit from participating in the ecosystem? You can only answer these questions if you connect everybody, share or collect all that data, turn that data into information and feed that information back to each individual user.

In order to solve a complex issue like smart city mobility, we need to use a super-brain because we need the computing capacity. All the super-brain needs is data. You also need to tell the super-brain what you want to get out of it (i.e. your higher purpose). If you tell the super-brain that you want every journey to be a maximum of fifteen minutes, the brain will find minuscule time advantages – let's save three seconds here instead of two seconds there and ten seconds here instead of seven seconds there. By making all of these incremental savings that human beings wouldn't even notice, the super-brain could achieve our goal.

Two-way communication

There are a couple of tricks that you can use to build an ecosystem. First, make sure that your applications don't just give out information but also collect information. They should double as two-way sensors with the outside world. If they're not doing that, they're making you blind. We have created that extra dimension that goes beyond the flat analogue earth; we need to use it to get information about how people use whatever interface we have with them. In the past, we had that interface but couldn't collect that data – we were blind. If we wanted to find out what our users thought, we had to do market research. However, in most cases, we simply considered that if people were buying our product it was a success. We didn't know anything about how people used it or what people did with it. That information would have been useful – we could have learnt from it. Now we have the means to do that. Your applications must also be sensors.

Engage and use (but don't abuse) your customers

The second trick is to try to engage your customers and turn them into infrastructure and/or sensors when they are using your interface. They probably won't be sensors all the time; if you use Waze or Uber, you only share your data with them when actually using the platform. If I walk into my local restaurant, I'm only part of their ecosystem when I'm there. I'm part of the happening on the evening I go to the restaurant, but that evening would be different if I weren't there. Even in the same restaurant, with 99 out of 100 of the same customers, the happening would be different if one thing were different, if one person weren't there. That's why it's important to involve your customers in the ecosystem, to learn from them, because even the smallest difference can be significant. If I use an app for smart city mobility, I'm not just using the app and the algorithm, my information is feeding the app at the same time.

What do you get out of your application?

The third thing that you have to think about is how your application informs you and gives you data. How can users of the ecosystem not just use the ecosystem but also feed the ecosystem? As the creator of the ecosystem, you also need to get something out of it. It may not be money; it may be something else. It depends. In a city, it's not about making money but about providing people with the best possible transport to make them happy. What you measure is citizen happiness. What you get from users is data to make the ecosystem better. Of course, if you're a company you need to think about how you'll make money. You have a choice: do you charge consumers for using your interface, while simultaneously feeding it (think Spotify or Netflix), or do you make your interface free of charge and sell the information you glean elsewhere (think Waze or Uber)? People think that a company like Waze sells data but they don't; they turn data they get from their customers into information and sell that information. It's the same with Uber. If you want to set up a restaurant chain in a city, rather than wetting your finger to feel where the wind takes you, Uber can tell you where the best hotspots are: where people get out of or into cars etc. You can make a guess, or you can ask Google, Uber or someone else and pay for that information, which most likely will be good information.

Not all data will be relevant all the time

With so many sensors, you'll easily have too much data. But this is normal. It's like our brains. Our senses perceive much more data than our brain absorbs. When you're having a conversation with someone, most of your brain power is focused on that conversation, not on the environment around you. It still collects that data to use if it needs to notice something. Every morning, when I sit down to drink my coffee at my desk, my fingers automatically pick up the cup. My brain doesn't absorb that information, it's automatic. But if the cup were hot, my brain would notice and warn me.

This will be the same for whatever ecosystem we build: there will be too much data. Small data (what individuals do) produces big data (what groups do). You feed that big data into the central brain which then picks out the data it needs to make decisions. The central brain will never use all of the data that is being fed into it at any given moment in time, just like our brain will never use all of the data it is receiving at any given time. Once the central brain is clever enough, it will know which three or four data points it needs to make a decision. The rest of the data will be superfluous, unnecessary at that time, unless something happens, unless a hot cup threatens to burn its fingers.

Managing your networks

By now, you should have a good idea of what your infrastructure, sensors and applications are. We know that the platform is the central brain that manages all that data and creates information. So we're left with the network for which you will need external partners: network providers. Telecom companies are an essential factor of any smart entity that you wish to build. The good thing is that the network is already out there. On the flip side, you need to know that network providers have access to your data. They have access to your data for a fraction of a second and they use, or you might say abuse, their position by constantly turning that data into information.

When you want to build an ecosystem that is honest and transparent about what happens to data in the ecosystem, one of the first hurdles you must tackle is your agreements with the network providers, the telecom providers.

With all things digital, we tend to forget a second, but very important, type of network: the interhuman network. Companies often underestimate the power of the human network, of people talking to people, of people influencing other people. This human network can communicate orally or using those digital networks. They become a network on top of a network. They make connections. The platform can decide which connections to make between digital sensors, but people can do that too: they build the network, participate in the network and facilitate the functioning of the network.

With regard to the digital network, you need to make sure that your agreements with telecom companies are as watertight as can be, especially if you are a city or government. It's important that you are transparent with users about what happens with their data, and you must force telecom companies to be transparent with you. You can't be fully transparent if there's a black box that encases what's happening – the unknown – with telecom companies.

Every time I use Uber, I know that at that moment in time I am participating in Uber's network and ecosystem, but I'm not always aware that I'm also feeding the telecom company with my data. As a user, I pay money to the telecom company in return for access to the network, but I don't get anything in return for the data I also pay into the system. With Uber I do get that return and the same goes for Google; I use Google for free but pay with my data – something I'm happy to do for what I get in return.

In an ecosystem, you will always have participants who truly contribute to the existence of the ecosystem and others that provide. Participants play by the rules of the ecosystem; providers need to be managed with agreements between the ecosystem and the provider. Concluding these agreements is part of the platform's role; you can't rely on every single participant to establish these agreements.

The platform serves a dual purpose

A lot of confusion surrounds the role of the platform as it is simultaneously an orchestrator and a facilitator. In the eyes of the end consumer, the platform is perceived as the network orchestrator that provides them with the interface that does exactly what they need it to do. In the eyes of the participants, the platform is not the orchestrator but rather the facilitator, the engine behind the ecosystem.

The platform in the eyes of the consumer

We often make the mistake of designing our companies in the wrong order; we design the customer interface from the inside out. This is not helpful to the customer experience, it actually harms it. If we design customer interface from the inside out, customers feel and see the skeleton underneath. They feel and see the mechanics of the operation: departments, processes, roles etc but they don't want to see that. When I look at a person, I know that there is a whole skeleton inside supporting them and enabling their actions, but I don't want to see that. I'd rather not know at all. It's the same for customers. They don't want to know what goes on behind the scenes.

That's why applications must be designed from the outside in. When planning your applications, think about what you want the customer to experience. It should be simple to explain. What actually needs to be done to deliver that customer experience is secondary. The customer experience must be designed first so that the mechanics are not visible to the user. What the customer wants is an interface on which they can FEAST; an interface which is Fast, Easy, Accessible, Simple and Tempting. If they're using a smart mobility app to get to their destination in fifteen minutes, they just want to know the best route. They don't care about the sensors, infrastructure, networks, participants and whatever else is contributing to fulfilling their request. They just want their question answered. The platform to them is the orchestrator, their single touchpoint with the ecosystem. Users don't care how it does what it does, they simply need it to fulfil its purpose.

The platform in the eyes of the participant

Although the platform feels central to the user, it doesn't play the same role for the participant. To them, it is the facilitator that enables the functioning of the ecosystem. The platform is there to serve, like the long-forgotten original role of a government. The platform is not designed to be dominant, it is not meant to lead; it is at the service of the participants in the ecosystem. The platform has the responsibility of being neutral; it is the collective brain of all the knowledge distributed throughout the ecosystem. It must be guided with HEART; it must be Honest, Ethical, Authentic, Responsible/Responsive and Transparent. Building an ecosystem is like setting up a community and the platform facilitates that.

Part of its facilitating role involves enforcing the rules of the ecosystem (which we discuss in chapter 10). When we build sensors, whether they're in trains, cars, mobile phones or anywhere else, we need to establish rules that govern those sensors and the resulting data. To ensure a harmonious community, we need to set rules that manage each participant's role and behaviour. That is the role of the platform. It is the framework of the ecosystem. It is also the ecosystem's touchpoint with the outside world. It is the platform that makes agreements with the network providers, enabling all participants to benefit from those agreements and alleviating them of the task of having to do it themselves. Wouldn't it be messy if each participant had their own agreements?

One platform – two functions

Let me illustrate how this works in practice. When you use Waze, you become a part of the Waze ecosystem the second you open the app on your phone. When you're not using it, you're not part of the ecosystem. When I'm in that ecosystem, I'm in tune with both sides of the coin – the two functions of the platform. In that moment, Waze is my network orchestrator because it lets me find the quickest/shortest route to my destination. It uses my data and the data of every user at that moment in time as input to give me that optimum route. Simultaneously, it is the facilitator as it collects my data and the data of every other user currently on that platform.

The platform is at the heart of the ecosystem, because it is where all data is processed into information. But it must also be as invisible as possible, facilitating the ecosystem without making itself the leader.

Ensuring a delicate balance

An ecosystem, just like in nature, survives on a delicate balance between the elements using the ecosystem, the participants and the outside users. If that energy is ever out of balance, because the platform absorbs a greater amount of energy to feed the platform, the ecosystem will implode. This is nothing new; it's something we can see happening in any traditional organisation. They all have a tipping point where the balance between the energy given and the energy received (energy given to the outside world and received from the outside world) is thrown off, where the organisation is absorbing large amounts of energy just to keep it alive. At a certain point, the organisation becomes so large that all the energy goes to fuelling the organisation. I've noticed that organisations often only realise that they've gone past that tipping point once it's too late, by which time they can't find their way back (just like we didn't notice the tipping point signalling the end of the old economy). The same goes for ecosystems. If the balance between the giving and receiving of energy between the platform and the participants is skewed, the platform starts to absorb excess energy. That spells the beginning of the end of the ecosystem.

We can overcome this problem by decentralising the brain, by ensuring its role as the facilitator. When companies come to me and say they want to create an ecosystem, they tend to see themselves as the network orchestrator, at the centre, gathering a couple of participants around them. They tend to envision a scenario in which they are the central platform and, in the end, they win. But there's a problem with this thinking. If you look at a smart mobility ecosystem in a city, who wins? Citizens win, not the network. If you think about a smart food ecosystem, people and planet will win, not the ones behind the ecosystem. That's the point of the platform: the facilitator's role is simply to facilitate.

The platform isn't the money making central machine you might have expected

This is difficult for many companies to understand: there is no money to be had in the platform. The platform doesn't make money. It should be as free of assets and of costs as possible. In traditional business terminology, we could say it's the cost centre but not the profit centre. That's why we must ensure that the platform doesn't absorb more energy than it can produce for participants to use. A bank once came to me with their idea, which in essence was: we want to become the network orchestrator, we'll gather a couple of companies around us and then we'll make money by being the network orchestrator. However, if you use the platform to that end, it spells the end of the ecosystem. The platform should be as neutral as possible, being the facilitator, ensuring that the rules, regulations, dos and don'ts of the ecosystem are clear, managed and enforced. The platform is not the money maker; the money lies in the applications that you and your partners will produce on top of the ecosystem.

Let's look at Waze again. It is free of charge for users. Its infrastructure is made of maps and phones that already exist. All it needs to do is bring all that data together on a central platform that makes calculations for us. This can't be done for free, so how do they make their money? Everything that we, as users, do is the sort of data that they can sell to companies. For example, cities that want to implement smart mobility could get a head start by asking Waze for data. Waze can tell you how many people travel by car in your city and when and where and how. You can either collect that data yourself from scratch, or get a running start by using Waze's data to feed your platform. Naturally, you will have to pay for the second option.

THE ECOSYSTEM CANVAS

It's not about the spider, it's about the web

When I talk to companies about becoming an ecosystem, the majority – probably 99% – say that they want to become the platform. First things first – that's impossible. If all companies were to try to become a platform, we'd end up back where we started, in the old economy. The danger is that companies think of the platform as the spider in the spiderweb, the central component that sees all and knows all about what is happening in the web. But if you want participants to come to your web, they need to be part of that web. If they know that you are the spider and they are the fly, they will never come.

The platform is not designed to be the dominant force; it is there to serve the ecosystem's participants. And the more they use the platform, the stronger it becomes.

THE NEVERENDING STORY OF THE ENDLESS IDLE CAPACITY OF THE OLD WORLD

idle capacity

IDLE CAPACITY IS THERE
(IF ONLY YOU SEE IT)

Others have plenty of idle capacity. if you look at all the
resources they have available - housing, energy, food, water -
they the you can also see there is often enough, or are
more than enough to fulfil the needs of the population.

ENERGY   FOOD

MOBILITY

WATER

10

Guide

---

featuring:
immobility
good for people
a non-extensive list
preparation
building the foundations
finding the balance
survival

Idle capacity is there, if only you see it

Cities have plenty of idle capacity. If you look at all the resources they have available – mobility, energy, food, water – then you can also see that there is often enough, or even more than enough, available to fulfil the needs of the population. The problem however is the idle capacity, the resources that are wasted because they're not optimised, because we don't use the connections between the dots, the ones using and the ones providing those resources.

If you go to San Francisco, this may be one of the first things you notice when you step off that plane. You walk out of the terminal and see all that mobility. There are cars, Ubers, Lyfts, traditional taxis, public transport, scooters, bikes and more.

When you land, you may find a ride to the city centre straight away, but if it's busy you may have to wait a while. When you finally get a car, it's likely you'll be stuck in rush-hour traffic, surrounded by cars that have just one person in them, the driver. There's so much mobility that it often turns into immobility.

There's plenty of mobility, but you can only optimise it, make it truly mobile if you bring it all together as an ecosystem to make it work.

San Francisco suffered from congestion because there was simply too much... of everything – Ubers, Lyfts, shared bikes etc. How do you optimise that capacity? How much capacity do you truly need for a city of 4.7 million people? If you look at the answer to that in theory, and what you have available, you may have ten times more mobility than you actually need. Nevertheless, if it's not optimised that 'ten times more' means nothing; you're just throwing more mobility at the problem and creating the opposite effect – immobility.

Making mobility work for people

San Francisco is a city that has stolen my heart, not just because of the energy you feel in the air there but also due to its aim to make city life better for its residents. One example of this is their mobility network. You've probably experienced this scenario at some point: your train arrives a couple of minutes later than expected and, despite running to

the bus stop, you see the bus pulling away as it leaves at its scheduled time. The bus timetable was probably designed to coincide with the trains, but that's useless if the bus doesn't know if there has been a change. That's exactly what leads to this type of scenario. If the bus and the train were both sensors and, most importantly, connected, the bus could have waited just a minute or two to collect the passengers who were on the late train. San Francisco wants to eliminate this kind of problem. They want to connect all the available transport options in the city – buses, trains, planes, trams, scooters, you name it – using data and sensors so that everything works together in the service of the person.

Of course, in recent years we have seen our cities explode with new forms of transport. In addition to the traditional car, bus and train, we now have many more choices open to us. We can share vehicles, from bicycles and scooters to electric mopeds and cars. We can share rides through carpooling. We can hail rides through private hire services such as Uber or Lyft or catch a ride in an autonomous vehicle. Our workplace may offer a shuttle service and our online orders may be delivered to us through courier network services. There are so many possibilities, or at least this is the case in San Francisco where all of these services are available. As a result, cities are having to cope with a much more diverse offering on their streets and adapt to the surge of new and different vehicles. In response, they may have to increase the number or size of bicycle lanes, widen pavements, increase the quantity of transit and docking stations or re-evaluate the location of parking spaces.

Aligning goals across the board

Another issue that has arisen from this boom of new service providers is regulation. How can San Francisco, as the natural network facilitator, ensure that all the companies operating on their streets do so safely, ethically and in the best interests of the user? In response to this problem, the city established a set of ten guiding principles to ensure that "all potential transportation providers meet key safety, affordability, availability, interoperability and sustainability goals".[85] Any service provider who wants to operate in the San Francisco area must thus contribute to meeting the city's goals in these ten areas: collaboration, safety, transit, congestion, sustainability, equitable access, accessibility, labour, disabled access and financial impact. For example, this system allowed the city to restrict the number of shared scooters available in its perimeter, notably in order to limit congestion, by selecting five providers to supply 500 scooters each.[86] Only companies that fulfil the requirements and follow the rules are allowed to be a part of the city's transport ecosystem.

The rules of an ecosystem are crucial to the functioning of an ecosystem and if a company doesn't abide by them, they get excluded. It's the platform's job, as the network facilitator, to set these rules of good conduct and ensure that they are respected. This can't be left to the goodwill of the participants; it needs to be done centrally and it needs to be as clear and transparent as can be. The ecosystem's dos and don'ts, goals and objectives, rules and values need to be clearly established and wholly enforced. In this way, like San Francisco, the ecosystem is managed and closed to new entrants if they don't comply. Nevertheless, this is also what enables the ecosystem to remain open to new participants who wish to join and contribute in line with the established principles.

The "rules" I will set out in this chapter are by no means an exhaustive list; they are simply issues that I have encountered so far. I'm sure that there are more that I haven't yet experienced.

If you know me, then you must also be saying, "This doesn't sound like Rik, talking about rules." Or you might be saying, "But if you have to let an ecosystem happen, rather than build it intentionally, how can there be rules?" Yes, it's a paradox.

What I have tried to come up with is a set of guidelines, a sort of charter that I am calling "rules" of the issues you must address from the start. It should be a minimum set: if you take one rule away, the ecosystem would fall apart, but if you add one more rule, the ecosystem would become too complicated. As I said, this list isn't exhaustive, but neither should it become exhaustive, otherwise it would no longer be workable. Too many rules would make the ecosystem rigid, rather than dynamic. Nevertheless, you have to establish some sort of charter as to how you will work together.

So, this chapter isn't about *the* rules that you must apply, it's more about me sending out signals to make you aware of the potential issues you may encounter. If you start building an ecosystem and don't think about these issues and how to deal with them before-hand, you'll run up against them during the process. If that happens, the people – forces – within your company who don't like change will use it to stop the change, and that could kill your project.

Let this chapter give you food for thought so that you can avoid these problems from the get-go. But also avoid any excessive control; it's not necessary and would even be detrimental to what you are trying to achieve. Be aware of the issues and have a plan in place to prevent them.

Solve problems before you start

Before you start creating an ecosystem, you need to think about the rules of the game. Who's the owner of the data collected? What happens to the data? How do we know that the data is being handled in the right way? How do we know that the data is being fed to our platform and not another platform? Data will soon be, or perhaps already is, more valuable than money, which means that there are people who are out to do wrong.

When creating an ecosystem, you are creating new rules for a new type of game. It is crucial to think about them and discuss them before

even involving another party. Data needs to be used correctly, its use must be transparent to every participant, and we need to make sure we're doing right by that data.

Basic rights such as privacy, security and freedom are intuitive elements of a data-driven world; they should go without saying but nevertheless it is important to clearly define them for successful implementation. Certain rules must be embedded into the very foundation of an ecosystem to make it connected, free, sustainable and democratic.

Protect data while making it available to all participants

In an ecosystem, end users expect solution-driven, understandable and user-friendly applications that guarantee that their data is 100% protected. Data is an essential part of making this possible. Data guides the interaction. As a result, that data must be available to all participants. Companies that may already have access to this data must grant access to other participants. Thanks to the rules laid out in this chapter, you will be able to build an ecosystem that is completely at the service of the end user's wellbeing, both in the quality and speed of service provided by participants and in the prioritisation of users' and participants' digital rights.

The ecosystem's purpose is to work together, to collaborate digitally, so that the whole of the ecosystem determines what is done with data, not just the company that collected it in the first place. This doesn't mean that participants have to open access to all of their databases straight away, but it does mean that the ecosystem must seek to achieve a healthy data economy based on digital rights, where data is shared and used on a central platform where every participant has a say. This is the fundamental role of the platform: to implement and continue to develop fairness and responsibility in order to enrich and share the knowledge, experience and skills of the ecosystem. Without the insights, creativity and expertise that are already available to a large extent in the ecosystem, we cannot achieve our goal of offering wellbeing to our end users. Working together is essential to identify what users need and the effect of our interactions; this in turn is crucial to further develop and improve these interactions in the future.

- In order to have a say in how data is used, it must be crystal clear to everyone what data is gathered on the platform and who by.
- Data must be processed securely in a way that fully complies with data protection rules.
- In the end, we want to move toward a data economy that is not simply driven by profit but also by other values, such as the protection of digital rights and the promotion of a healthy workplace. To do this, we need to combine our strengths to make and share tools that boost the data economy.
- We must make it easy for participants to hold the platform accountable if data is unfairly collected or used.
- The platform must inform participants about how the algorithm uses data, creating a record of what data the platform supplies to the algorithm and why. This record must be constantly updated and participants kept informed.

There is one key factor without which a data-driven ecosystem would not be functional nor benefit fully from the opportunities offered by data. This key factor is: relevant data must be available to all participants.

Establish the infrastructure needed to fulfil your goals

The ecosystem needs to benefit from modern infrastructure and organisation for processing data. Access to data is not granted automatically, so someone needs to establish and define who gets access to and is able to use the data. Given that data sets are growing larger and more complex, and because data collection often relies on expensive and specialist equipment, ecosystems tend to lean towards companies that are specialised in the collection of certain types of data. However, if a company occupies a dominant position, it can easily set its own requirements in terms of cost or data use, thus limiting the platform's access to the data. We may also see companies that know more about the users of the ecosystem than the ecosystem itself and that might want to use that knowledge to set up their own similar tasks. The ecosystem must therefore search for solutions that do not rely on putting data collectors in a dominant position. This also implies that the ecosystem may decide simply not to collect certain data, if there are other options available which would allow the ecosystem to achieve that specific objective.

Implement the following principles to ensure equal access to data:
- When negotiating new contracts or agreements with suppliers, partners or other collaborators, it must be agreed that the rights to any data collected or created under said agreement belong to the ecosystem. This ensures that data created with the tools of the ecosystem is used in pursuit of the ecosystem's objectives and tasks.
- Make the open data policy more user friendly. Sought-after data sets often become available online. We can set up an independent internal open data watchdog, whose job it is to make information publicly available and ensure that information becomes available when participants request it. An external advisory group should also meet regularly in order to discuss pain points and priorities.
- Make more data available. The ecosystem should come up with creative solutions to anonymise data and enhance its value for data enrichment.

Don't sit still, grow with the changes

The options available to us regarding how we analyse and use data are constantly being developed. However, it is important for the systems and organisations within the ecosystem to evolve in tandem with these developments. Use state-of-the-art analysis environments and tools to process data more quickly and securely.

For participants in the ecosystem, this means:
- Investigating whether a "digital rights test" can become a compulsory part of large technology projects to ensure that the ecosystem's collective digital rights in terms of data use are respected.

· Developing and investing in more open source material, as a result of the sourcing strategy to give more transparency to how the ecosystem handles data.

This ecosystem strategy will allow participants to better prepare themselves for the future. While some organisations and companies may be new to data collection and processing, this is the core task of the platform. Responsible management of data is the utmost value of the ecosystem, so that data can easily be combined with other data in order to draw new conclusions. Data also presents another advantage: it makes it possible to answer end users' questions more quickly and to measure which activities work well and which don't. To do this, it is important for ecosystem participants to know how to find the data that can help them and to implement it effectively and legally. Responsible and effective use of data is not something that the platform can do alone. That's why the platform must develop a cooperative and responsive ecosystem. In practice, this implies maintaining constant contact with participants and upholding a balance of varying interests.

Large technology companies know more and more about their end users. It's important that we develop more regulation on a national and international level in order to protect the customer. We need to develop new initiatives that present a fully fledged alternative to the current data economy, because current data collection methods used by technology giants have restricted the equal opportunities and free will available to customers. We need an alternative for a more inclusive and fair digital landscape.

The three dogmas for the ecosystem to live by

Every ecosystem is governed by three dogmas that ensure its survival and success:

1. Survival above all else. The raison d'être of an ecosystem is the very survival of the ecosystem. One thing that will not change in the business world is competition; in the new world, ecosystems will compete with ecosystems. The highest-performing ecosystems will be the ones to survive.

2. No winners, no losers. Within an ecosystem, everyone is on a level playing field. There can be no winners, because that would risk destroying the dynamic and delicate balance of the ecosystem, thus undermining its performance as a whole. By definition, if there are no winners there can be no losers. Participants in an ecosystem are in it together, they cannot be out to get ahead. In San Francisco, those five companies with 500 scooters each are all on the same page; no company is going to eat the market share of the others.

3. Data is everything. Data is the glue that binds the ecosystem together and allows it to perform. Data is a fundamental component on many levels, from the quantity, quality, diversity and accessibility of data to the computing power, knowledge and skills required to process that data and transform it into information, and the creativity, imagination and belief given to the outcome as a tool to generate new products, services and business models. Data is *the* tool you need in order to speak digital.

In short, rules are an essential part of a data-driven ecosystem. They may seem complex, but they are governed by the understanding of what an ecosystem is really about. It's a collaboration between parties that is framed by rules outlining the desired behaviour and embedding mutual agreements.

Potential problems you need to be aware of

As with all collaborations, there are some problem areas that we must pay particular attention to:

1. Trust and trustworthiness. Data is accompanied by fear; fear that data will be misused, maybe even abused, or end up in the wrong hands. There are many factors that could play into data misuse: outdated technology, bad governance and data leaking. All of these can lead to data not being deployed as originally intended and as agreed by participants.

2. (Transactional) cost structure. Every data transaction carries costs that may lead to problems of a technological or procedural nature. In terms of technology, the following issues must be avoided: bad connectivity, mismatching standards and a lack of data compati-

bility. With regard to procedure, the problem once again lies in our differences which must be aligned: knowledge, skills, organisational structure and internal rules. Best practice in this case is to gather technological challenges together on the platform in order to outline and implement governance collectively.

3. **Fear of mutual competition.** Most participants will be new to this type of collaboration among peers. The whole data landscape is largely untapped territory and, as a result, it can seem like new (potential) applications and even business models are being developed every day. It is thus logical for companies to fear losing their competitive advantage by sharing their data. Participants from the old economy in particular are averse to throwing the door wide open in case new rivals, who tend to be better technologically armed, benefit and do clever things with that data. Digital participants, on the other hand, suspect that more traditional players will want to steal their technology and people. To top off this culture of distrust, all participants in the ecosystem fear that the "owner" of the platform will draw too much of the value created toward themselves (this is one of the reasons why I don't like the term "orchestrator").

4. Missing financial opportunities Data continues to be largely unfamiliar territory. Consequently, companies may not see the potentially profitable nature of data, and may simply focus on sharing it with the rest of the ecosystem instead. As a result, individual value creation within the ecosystem may not be optimised. Conversely, this also presents a danger if value is created by just one participant, as this value would be partly absorbed by the ecosystem and thus not fully beneficial for the concerned party.

If these four crucial topics are not well managed within the ecosystem, the potential dangers presented by the ecosystem will thus continue to outweigh any potential value drawn from it. Subsequently, the ecosystem will be doomed from the outset, barely making it off the starting line.

Lay the groundwork for a healthy and sustainable ecosystem

When creating an ecosystem, there are two factors that must be cemented. They are the foundation upon which the ecosystem can be built:

1. Define the ultimate goal of the ecosystem. This objective must establish a dynamic balance between all participants in the ecosystem. It must also contribute to creating both a better society and profit, while putting people and planet first.

2. Establish clear agreements surrounding (data) governance and collaboration among all participants in the ecosystem.

The purpose of an ecosystem is always to use shared data and a shared customer base to develop new products, services and concepts, and perhaps even new business models, free from the constraints of traditional industry lines as we know them now.

Understand the components that make up the ecosystem

To make sure we're all on the same page when we get to the rules, let's recap the elements of an ecosystem. There are two data streams, four roles and five features.

Data streams:

1. The internal data stream. This ensures that the basic infrastructure of the ecosystem runs as fast and efficiently as possible, while allowing it to improve continuously. The internal data stream applies to all data measured throughout the infrastructure and concerns internal movements and operations, which enable the ecosystem to function better when collected on the platform.

2. The external data stream. This measures all external data and feeds it into the platform where it is collated and enriched for better insight and information, thus creating a richer breeding ground for new products, services and business models.

Roles:

1. The brain (also known as the platform and the network facilitator/orchestrator). This is where data is collected and processed into enriched data, otherwise known as information. The platform is also the producer of rules and guardian of governance. The aim of the platform itself is not to create further value, but to process and enrich the data that is used to create value. As

PARTICIPANTS

THE BRAIN

ENABLERS

NETWORK ENABLERS

a result, the platform is a uniquely neutral entity. In traditional economic terms, it is a cost-centre rather than a profit-centre. How this cost-centre is funded must be determined in advance when establishing the ecosystem; payment can be made on the basis of a set distribution framework, the value of the enriched data (minus the cost of data input) or a combination of the two.

2. Participants. They feed the platform with the data they collect as a **sensor** and they use the enriched data, the new information, to develop new **applications** (including products, services, concepts and business models) which generate new value. Participants can be members of several ecosystems; they are not restricted to just one. The applications they create often become new sensors in turn, which continue feeding the platform through short feedback loops.

3. Enablers. They look after the **infrastructure** of the ecosystem (such as the hardware, security and computing power) and are duly compensated for their work. Participants can be enablers too. Enablers can also contribute to the ecosystem by feeding external data in from their sensors, but not all enablers have to be participants in the ecosystem. They can quite simply be utility providers. However, due to their access to the ecosystem and the importance of their data, agreements must also be made with "external" parties regarding data management and use. This is of special importance with one enabler in particular: the network enabler.

4. Network enablers. This specific enabler is responsible for connectivity, ensuring that data travels quickly and efficiently from sensors to the platform, from the platform to applications and back again. Network enablers are often not true participants in the ecosystem; they are utility providers. Nevertheless, clear agreements must also be established with these enablers due to the fact that they have access to the ecosystem's data. A fast, safe and clear network is of vital importance for a well-functioning ecosystem.

Companies participating in the ecosystem can provide several **features**. These are the building blocks we have already discussed:

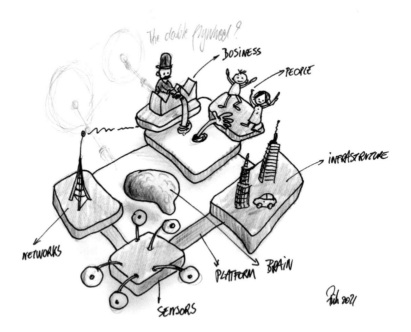

1. Infrastructure – the hardware and basic necessities for the functioning of the ecosystem.

2. Sensors – all possible touchpoints that gather external data to feed into the ecosystem.

3. Platform – the place where all data is collected, processed, combined, enriched and transformed into information.

4. Network – the web that connects all the dots as efficiently as possible.

5. Applications – the new or improved products, services and business models. They can be B2C, B2B, B2E (ecosystem), E2E or P2P (platform to people) applications.

THE ECOSYSTEM CANVAS

A well-governed ecosystem maintains the balance between autonomy and collaboration

What's important is that the brain/platform/orchestrator/facilitator understands how to create and maintain the right context in order to keep the data-driven ecosystem together. Participating companies must be aware of the potential value, possible risks and latent sources of conflict that are unique to ecosystems. Good governance is needed to manage these unique issues.

The rules needed "to govern" an ecosystem can be split into two different categories:

1. Autonomy. The rules that fall under this category ensure that participating companies are able to be as autonomous and empowered as they need to be.

2. Collaboration. These rules ensure that participants understand the complexity of the ecosystem and the need to work together with other participants. The aim is for the functioning of the ecosystem to become as important to them as the results thereof. Furthermore, specific rules are needed regarding data ownership, in addition to the availability and use of that data.

These two categories of rules must be maintained in dynamic balance by the platform. Just as we saw how it is impossible to have absolute freedom and absolute equality, autonomy and collaboration are seemingly opposing forces that must be maintained in equilibrium. Absolute autonomy would make collaboration impossible while absolute equality in collaboration makes any sort of freedom impossible.

The ground rules of autonomy

There are three ground rules to enable autonomy:

1. Understand each other. In order to build up trust within the ecosystem and prevent any mutual competition, participants must know and understand each other's objectives, enablers and barriers. This gives the platform the means to develop rules that enshrine the mutual motivations of participants rather than focusing on their actions.

2. Strengthen the bridge builders. The ecosystem's platform and enablers must actively seek to integrate all parties. They need to bring all participants together and, in this way, encourage the processes of the ecosystem. They must be able to dismantle obstacles between participants and adequately explain why that is necessary. They are also responsible for establishing data standards, ensuring a shared interpretation of definitions and making sure that the architecture is understood by all.

3. Strengthen insights. It is important to give the necessary decision-making powers to certain people while ensuring that nobody feels like their autonomy has been diminished. The rules and values that outline how data is handled determine whether participants trust that their data will be used correctly now that that data is in the hands of the platform. To obtain the necessary transparency, it is vital to be open about data sources and the use of data as well as to encourage involvement by participants, giving them a role in data management.

I can say without a doubt that ecosystems will occupy very pronounced strategic positions in the market. One way to eliminate the risk of mutual competition and foster trust among participants is to get all participants in the ecosystem to sign a non-compete agreement. Participants will only agree to share sensitive data with each other if that trust is formally embedded. Moreover, the platform can also assure participants that their data will be used correctly by implementing automatic privacy tools that protect data sources while they are being processed on the platform.

The platform cannot make its attitude to data clear, expressed and documented enough. Any leeway in interpretation would undermine trust and thus undermine the ecosystem. What is deemed misuse or abuse of data must be clearly defined; this could include collecting or sharing data without authorisation or sharing data outside of the ecosystem. These are obvious examples, but they must also be included in the definition. It must be crystal clear. One of the platform's fundamental roles is to monitor these rules closely.

The ground rules of collaboration

In addition to the three rules of autonomy, there are three rules to ensure collaboration:

4. Increase reciprocity. The goal of an ecosystem is the very survival of the ecosystem. The success of each participant in the ecosystem thus depends on the success of the other participants. This is why the platform must be extremely clear about that shared ob-

jective, the progress being made by the ecosystem and how the data offered to the ecosystem contributes to that goal. The clearer the objectives, the more participants will be encourage to work together to bring about collective results. This shared aim will help counteract self-interest, which would only undermine the interest of the whole. Traditional "contracts" between participants are not an option, as they would undermine motivation and the ecosystem would subsequently fall apart.

5. **Be extremely clear about the progress of the ecosystem.** A well-developed reporting model is needed to share updates with participants and keep them informed of how their contribution, and the contribution of others, is serving the whole of the ecosystem.

6. **Reward every contribution.** Every contribution of data must be rewarded by the ecosystem through the platform in some shape or form. One option is to financially compensate data. A second option, which is more sustainable but harder to implement, is to provide some sort of non-financial compensation for the data collected, such as a share in a barter scheme to use the information created by the platform. Whichever system is chosen, the value and subsequent compensation must be clearly defined.

Rules aren't enough, you must share a set of values

In addition to the rules that govern the ecosystem, participants and the ecosystem as a whole must share a set of **values**:

· **Inclusive.** Data must contribute to inclusive cooperation between companies. Differences between participating companies need to be taken into account while also maintaining equality. Data must contribute to making the ecosystem stronger as a whole; it must be available to everyone and never shut any participants out. Data management should never have a negative impact on participants.

· **Managed.** Data management increases the freedom given to participating parties and the impact they can have. Management is important to determine how data is collected and used. It allows parties to be independent and free to decide what to do with the data.

- Tailored to people. Data creates insights but it never has the last word. Data always only represents a part of the reality. When using data, the unpredictability that is in our very nature as humans must be taken into account. The user of data must take the lead, rather than the technology. Any errors in data use must be tackled on a human level. Responsible data use is fuelled by humanity, combining the strengths of humans and technology. But the person always has the upper hand over technology/data.

- Legal and monitored. The platform works with participating companies to ensure a fair and secure data landscape. In order to maintain a balance of power structures and avoid any abuses of power, data streams must be well managed and secured. Data is gathered in one context; it should be used honestly and implemented as effectively as possible.

- Open and transparent. Transparency and openness are the foundations, the bedrock, of an ecosystem. By being transparent, the platform shows what it does with what data. It is clear to see whether access to data is granted correctly. The ecosystem can strive for sustainable accountability by making the computer system open in the long term. Dealing with data openly makes for a healthy data ecosystem. Shared standards are very important, mainly because they allow for easy reuse and foster openness. By dealing with data and information openly and transparently, everyone is able to participate on an equal basis of information, benefiting from the same knowledge and insights.

- Of and for every participant. Data collected by participants is designed for use by the whole of the ecosystem. The impact, sustainability and manageability of data exchange must be well organised so that participants feel the benefits. How technology is managed, how what is and what isn't allowed is determined must be safeguarded so that it is meaningful for everyone. Of and for everyone also speaks to the way in which we develop our policies. When implementing new data systems, we need to make it crystal clear who is involved.

Working together for the survival of the ecosystem

It's the role of the platform – the facilitator – to notice if something has gone awry, to notice that if they don't intervene now, the ecosystem will fall apart. It's easier for cities, like San Francisco, to become the facilitator because that's what they are by definition. But it's also a role that companies should adopt. If you want to become an ecosystem and play that central role, it isn't about making money but about ensuring that everyone abides by the rules of the ecosystem so that the ecosystem can keep existing.

The rules, dogmas and values set out in this chapter are vital to ensuring the survival of the ecosystem. There can be no winners or losers – they could ruin the ecosystem. In an ecosystem there are just enough rules to hold it together. Take one rule out and the ecosystem will fall apart, but add an extra rule in and the ecosystem will come to a standstill and risk being eaten by the chaos around it.

It's all about transparency, data and playing the rules of the game because, ultimately, the raison d'être of an ecosystem is the very survival of the ecosystem.

when days comes we step out of the shade
afraid and unafraid
the new day as we free it
For there is always light
if only we're brave enough
to see it
if only we're brave enough
to Be it

(The hill we climb, Amanda Gorman)

11
Exemplify

"When day comes we step out of the shade,
aflame and unafraid,
the new dawn blooms as we free it.
For there is always light,
if only we're brave enough to see it.
If only we're brave enough to be it."
EXTRACT FROM "THE HILL WE CLIMB" BY AMANDA GORMAN

---

featurIng:
the (dis)advantages of scale
double flywheel
white spots
something for nothing
using what's wasted
hyper-personalisation
TREEcosystem

But I'm just a one-person business, I don't want to grow

You may have reached the end of this book and be wondering if this is really an option for you. Perhaps you're thinking: "But I just run a local bakery in a small village, so how does this relate to me? How am I going to be able to develop these two flywheels and win the ticket to eternal life? I don't want to grow, I just want to keep my business alive and well."

I can't promise that I have the magic formula to protect you from whatever evil may come along to disrupt your business, but I can tell you this: you already are a small and very agile ecosystem. You have the infrastructure: your shop, your oven, your recipes. You have a flow of goods: you buy ingredients and transform them into products that you sell for money. Any money you make, minus the cost of running the infrastructure and paying for the ingredients, is your profit. That's not what makes you an ecosystem though; there's something more to it than that.

The flow of goods is something that is fairly easy to scale: buying ingredients and processing them in your infrastructure to create a product that you can sell at a profit. That's what we call economies of scale: the bigger the scale, the greater the profit. That was the driving force of the old economy which ended up eating people and planet. Scaling to become bigger should allow for more efficient production, lower prices for bulk-bought products, reduced logistics costs, cheaper capital, reduced marketing costs and a better spread of risks. However, these are the types of companies that became rigid and which risk breaking when the outside world changes too fast, simply because they are unable to react. What's worse is that they are unable to feel that something is going on, because the other side of the original process isn't scaled: interaction with the customer. Scaling the process is easy, because it fits a formula. Scaling customer interactions, on the other hand, can only be done if those unique happenings are reduced to a formula which, by definition, turns into one-to-many communications with subsequently reduced marketing costs. By turning the customer happening into a formula, it becomes a one-directional stream of data and information from the inside out. The company thus becomes comfortably numb, even senseless. When the happening is reduced to a rigid formula, there are no feedback loops.

When companies start to grow larger and scale, they grow into another breed. The very origin of an ecosystem company is what you, as a small bakery, do. Exactly, your bakery is an ecosystem. Your shop and what happens there is your application, your interface with the customer. You interact with customers in a two-directional conversation and the information learnt from those interactions is fed directly to the central brain, which is you. You know your customers, you sense what is going on and you can use that knowledge not only to adjust to the happening, but also to adjust to the context in which the happening takes place (the infrastructure). You connect to many, to all the people who come in to buy your products but you also personalise that interaction and engage with the person. Your tone, expression and language may change depending on whether you're talking to a man, a woman or a child (you are a human being, after all). You may notice that your customer is feeling upset that day and decide a croissant on the house may lift their spirits. At a certain point, you may decide to change the organisation of the shop or the layout of the products you offer or the type of service you provide, and you'll quickly realise if it was a good decision or not by listening to your customers. You don't want to lose customers, but you have the power to make fast adjustments if something's not working.

So don't worry about the "new" ecosystem economy, because you are the very foundation of it. Of all creatures, big and small, you have the upper hand. You are an ecosystem by definition. The only problem that you must be aware of is the fact that you are human. It's also your greatest advantage. Nevertheless, just be aware that, whether you want to or not, your vision is based to a large extent on assumptions. You may not see what you don't see or may not know what you don't know, because your brain is not processing all the data that it could process, whether that's because it's not trained or interested, or simply because the scope of your "lens" is limited.

Whatever your size, you have the advantage (and disadvantage)

Turning your business model into an ecosystem is not a walk in the park for any company. Small companies, like a local bakery, have the advantage of being close to the customer, but the disadvantage of not being able to get big data. Medium-sized companies might find it easier to

get rid of the old skeleton and go for a new one with different types of dynamics, but also struggle with big data. Large companies, on the other hand, have the advantage of big data but the disadvantage of their size, which may make it more difficult to break down their business model and use the building blocks to create a new one.

In the end, an ecosystem has nothing to do with the size of the company, but rather how you look at your company and organise it. No matter your size, you can be an ecosystem – you'll just organise it differently. Large companies need to look at how they can combine the best of both worlds and benefit from the advantage of scale. I'm not talking about the traditional economy of scale – let's forget about that – but rather the scale of big data. Small companies, however, aren't doomed because they can implement the dynamics much more easily than the larger one. That's their flywheel, the platform flywheel, while large companies have the flywheel of data.

I say that small companies have the flywheel of the platform, because if they think about it they already are the platform. They don't need AI to run it because they're still small and have access to the knowledge they need, but they can improve their knowledge further and become more curious without having to become a large company. Large companies, on the other hand, can get the flywheel of big data turning, employing an algorithm to use their data, either building their own ecosystem or linking into a larger ecosystem to do so. They need to become **driven by technology**.

Let the data guide you

With this data comes a change of mindset: let the data speak. In data I trust. Trust the data and what it does for you. You may still be in the early stages, using a fragile algorithm, or you may have scaled and are managing risk through a rigid algorithm. In both cases, you need to make that algorithm antifragile. Let the algorithm learn. Don't decide what you want it to do, let it speak for the data. You can create a learning algorithm, a genetic algorithm, by letting one flywheel influence the other and vice versa.

The double flywheel is the key to making an ecosystem antifragile. Employing a double flywheel is crucial to running an antifragile algorithm, which allows large companies to spin the flywheel of data while smaller companies have the flywheel of the platform. If you have the platform flywheel, think about how you can use it to generate data so that your platform can become stronger. If you have the data flywheel, think about how you can use that data to create a learning algorithm rather than a rigid one. Let the data speak, let the data influence the algorithm.

Bol.com – from retailer to platform

Let me give you an example of a company that has evolved over time from a retailer to a platform. I'm talking about bol.com, a Dutch company that, for those of you who don't know it, could be compared to Amazon and has built its business drawing on Amazon for inspiration, translating the lessons learnt to the Dutch market. It started as an e-commerce company, selling books online in 1999. They started in a digital environment, which meant that they started collecting data from the start, perhaps not all the data but some at least. Over time, they moved on from books to more and more different types of products.

Then came the moment - the same moment that a lot of other digital companies noticed, around 2010 and 2012 – that they realised that there was another dimension they could use. This was around the same time that Uber and Airbnb were born and it was no accident. Circa 2010 and 2012, the driving forces came together: the force of the internet and the force of people carrying the internet with them on their smartphones. Before this point, there were smartphones but not enough people had them or used them; indeed, at that time it was far too expensive to have the internet working on your phone around the clock. However, the tipping point came when the internet became less expensive and more people carried smartphones, essentially a sensor and a network, in their pockets. These were the necessary forces; Uber could never have existed without customer frustrations, but it also couldn't have existed if it weren't for people having smartphones and being connected to maps and the internet. It's very simple: I can't order an Uber without the internet. That's when we became sensors and platform companies were born.

Companies like Amazon and bol.com started to realise that there was something they could use there, in becoming an ecosystem. They already had what it takes: customers (or end users) and suppliers. They were the in-between party with the data and, as a result, they could become a platform. They used customer data and supplier data, connecting and brewing all of that data on the platform and, as a result, the platform grew and grew and grew.

There came a point when they opened up the platform as a marketplace, so that it was no longer restricted to their own retail activities but was open to any retailer that wanted to join. Bol.com wanted people to open their bol.com app whenever they were looking for something and the more products they had to offer on the platform, the more likely people would be to use their app when looking for something, from furniture to clothing, and from televisions to books. Bol.com couldn't handle more than 20 million products all alone, so they decided to become a platform that other retailers could use to sell their products and, as a result, bol.com would become the go-to place for people looking to buy something. In their original model, Bol.com made money on every transaction but then the marketplace, which began as a side business, started to grow.

The marketplace grew to such an extent that bol.com realised that it had become more important than their original business model, that of a retailer. Being a retailer was an old business model that had been digitised; being a platform was a whole new technology-driven business model. Consequently, bol.com started to no longer consider its old model as their main business model, and made the platform the priority. Bol.com also realised that there was a plethora of other business models that they could run on top of it, many of them B2B.

One of these applications is the white spot analysis. Thanks to the millions of products available on their platform and an average of two million people visiting the site every day, Bol.com has access to a multitude of information. This really is many connecting to many. What the algorithm can "see" in those data are white spots, identifying what people are actually looking for even though they don't realise that's what they're looking for. People can't see what the algorithm sees because we can only imagine what already exists. The algorithm, on the other hand, is so stupid that it's clever - it can see something we don't see. Using bol.com's massive platform, the algorithm can thus find white spots that bol.com can sell to companies. Companies will pay good money for that information and for bol.com it's an additional business model built on data that they already have. Either the end user or the supplier has already paid for that data, and bol.com is using that same data to create something they can sell to companies for a lot of money. Of course, it's a lot of money but it's less money than those companies would have to invest to find something that they didn't even know they were looking for. The white spot analysis replaces the traditional process of coming up with a product and then checking whether it would resonate with customers through market research, because the white spot is already the result of market research.

Using a digital twin to enhance market research

Other retail platforms are doing something similar, using a digital twin, but in reverse. They're offering companies the opportunity to come up with a product and test it with a virtual audience made up of fictional people that are the digital twin of the real world. Digital twins can test whether people would be interested in the product and how much they would be willing to pay for it. Again, this method is much faster, cheaper and more efficient than running real-life market research, because those consumers are not biased.

Pharmaceutical companies are also using digital people with lots of different types of DNA to run clinical trials. In this way, they don't have to risk making real people ill or, worse, killing them because the people they are testing don't really exist. This allows them to speed up market research and real clinical trials. These digital trials are not yet legally accepted, but they speed up the legislation process nonetheless, as the pharmaceutical companies can be fairly confident about the results they will achieve in real life.

Food delivery platforms work in the same way. They make most of their money not in the transactions between end users and restaurants, but in providing restaurants with information: where do people eat, what do they eat, where are the best places to open a restaurant. All of that information, gathered as part of their main model, is then sold as an additional model. Ride-hailing apps do exactly the same thing, selling information to companies, governments and cities. These are the new business models, we just don't often hear about them because most of them are locked under NDAs. It's more than a free lunch for these companies; in effect, they are paid for the ingredients that they make, without incurring any costs, and then they sell a very expensive lunch.

If there's one thing you mustn't forget, it's to put the customer first

For all of these business models, one ground rule stays the same: you need to start with a customer case. Never forget the **red ocean strategy**: turn existing customer frustrations into delight. Not long ago I had a meeting with a bicycle company that was trying to convince people to build sensors into their bikes. The business case seems obvious: if everyone has a sensor in their bike, the company will get data about when and where people use bikes and can bring that data to the platform to make information they can sell on to other companies. Right. However, what they want to do isn't really working because they can't convince the end user to build a sensor into their bike. Why would they? What's in it for them? They had only considered half of the flywheel: having sensors, data and a platform so that they can sell information. They hadn't taken into account the other half, involving the end user and what's in it for them. Would the end user pay for the sensor? What is in it for the customer? What frustration is being tackled? Perhaps, if they get something in return, like an insurance company insuring their bike, they'd be happy to install a sensor. But in order to do that, you need to involve an insurance company in the ecosystem.

To become an ecosystem, you need to start with some sort of customer friction, dissatisfaction, frustration that you can solve and turn into delight. If you don't do that, you have no raison d'être. The user wouldn't miss your ecosystem if you weren't there.

But you don't need to be an ecosystem; you can contribute to one. In Belgium, we have an electronic ID card with a chip. We can use this online to digitally sign documents and verify our identity. However, every Belgian knows that getting that card reader out every time, inserting your ID card and downloading a seemingly different type of software for every website is a pain and a hassle. That's where itsme comes in, a simple and efficient app that allows you to quickly and safely confirm your ID using just one pin code or a fingerprint scan. By itself, this app isn't all that interesting, but it's the number of websites, companies and platforms you can use it with that makes it a star app. Need to submit your tax return? Itsme has you covered. Need to check your bank account? Itsme makes it easy. Need your COVID vaccination certificate to travel? Itsme has your back. Itsme is a simple application that has the potential of being a cornerstone in every future ecosystem. It doesn't need to be an ecosystem itself, and nor do you; you can make yourself a contributor.

KBC has a very good banking app with an AI app called Kate, but the problem is that I only open the app when I need to do banking stuff. Just like bol.com, the bank needs to make sure I open the app on a regular basis and that the app is something I would miss if it were no longer there. I need to feel **engaged**. However, if they want to be a customer's partner in life (for more information on being your customer's partner in life, I recommend Steven Van Belleghem's book *The Offer You Can't Refuse*), they need to be more than just banking. They can gather data about you and banking in order to serve you better, extend their applications and extend their reach, perhaps involving public transport, cinemas, shops and more. By expanding, they can gather more information as long as there's a benefit for you – the user – as long as it makes your life easier. If I worry about missing my train because I'm running late and don't have a ticket yet, Kate could make my life infinitely easier by getting the ticket for me and letting me bypass stopping at the ticket counter. That is, without a doubt, added value and if I can get that kind of value from the platform, I don't mind Kate having my data. That's an ecosystem. If NMBS/SNCB (Belgium's railway network) wants to be part of the ecosystem, but it isn't digitised, it won't work. But if it does, then they have a business case straight away. KBC is the one that started it all, but others can jump onto that platform and learn from it, and by learning from it and becoming a part of it, they can get a head start on becoming a platform themselves.

Nir Eyal's Hook Model[87] is a great method to engage people with your company, your product, your application. First, you need a trigger that sparks a certain behaviour. This may be a notification on your phone: time to check in with the app to see what people are doing. These triggers often start out as external triggers but, as we continue to perform the habit, we develop internal triggers: I'm sitting down with a cup of tea, let me check in with this app. The next thing you need is action, you need the user to do something. The trick here is to make it as easy as possible and to motivate the user. Third, you need a variable reward. Don't keep offering the same thing over and over again; have a dynamic feedback loop that will allow you to switch up the rewards. Finally, ask for investment. This doesn't have to be money; it's about asking the user to do something for you, such as invite a friend, leave a review or share their data, which can then be used to improve their next experience.

Don't step back and make the same old mistakes

An ecosystem is a system that benefits every user, whether they're an end user or a participating company. That was the problem with ReGen Villages, an example I gave you in chapter 6. As I listened to James Ehrlich speak, surrounded by CEOs and directors of large companies who were becoming more and more enthused, I felt marvellous, I was looking at the future. But it all came down to earth with a bang. It was like going to restaurant, having a wonderful evening, a magnificent meal, and then being served dessert covered with shit. Ehrlich finished his utopic presentation by asking companies for investment, which he called sponsorship. Crucially he failed to translate that request for money into something beneficial for the companies. It was a real pity. What he was actually offering them was a once-in-a-lifetime opportunity to become part of one of the most flabbergasting experiments in human history, one that could lead to another better society: thousands of households living together in a city that is completely off-the-grid and run by a learning AI. It would have been a wonderful starting point for any company that wanted to become an **ecosystem**, an investment in the future that would perhaps have cost a great deal less than if they wanted to start an ecosystem alone.

People want to cooperate, they want to go off-the-grid, have no negative impact on people or planet and grow their crops. People are interested; the number of people who applied for the ReGen spots in Almere in the Netherlands exceeded the number needed tenfold. Nevertheless, ReGen faces two major problems. First, they will struggle to find enough sponsors as long as potential sponsors are not interested in building ecosystems and as long as ReGen Villages can't convince them of the potential boost they could give to the double flywheel. Second, the longer it takes, the more time politicians will have to realise that "something's wrong". If you look at the model from the old perspective, you would see a neighbourhood run by a computer that dictates what people should and should not do to enable the city to create circular models for water and food and energy. It's effectively a state within the state.

ReGen Villages is what we could call a super ecosystem, but there's nothing to say that you have to go so big. You can run it in a smaller way. Perhaps cities want to become self-sufficient in terms of food supply, which they could do if they counted all the land available to them and invited everyone to participate and connected all of those small things together as one big thing – data. They could help people, give tips and advice, bring the harvested food together to share it out. Nevertheless, in order to do this they would need an application, a brain that could manage all the different parameters, bring it all together and make it sustainable.

There is idle capacity everywhere we look

There's a car sharing app called Turo that allows people to rent cars from others and for people to make money when they're not using their car. For $90 per day, you can rent a Porsche for the weekend. In the early days of Tesla, you could rent a Tesla on Turo for $150 a day. The idea behind Turo was to utilise the idle capacity of the car that we use 10% of the time and leave sitting there, parked, for the other 90%. If someone put their Tesla on Turo for ten days a month, they could make $1500 – enough to pay back some of the lease, insurance, maintenance costs and all the other costs that go hand in hand with owning a car.

Now that I think about it, Shelby Clark, the founder of Turo, was the first person I ever heard speak about idle capacity. And he's right. People own cars and, by definition, that is idle capacity. Often, in the United States, families used to have a car for every purpose: the pleasure ride, the off-roader, the van or truck for transporting large loads. All of those cars, sitting in garages, were idle capacity. The biggest problem Turo had was how to solve the insurance issue and the trust issue, but now that everything is connected, that problem is gone.

Companies can look at the idle capacity in their own workplace. How many business people do you have turning up to the office in a company car in the morning? Does that car then stay there in the car park all day until your managers go home? That's money just sitting there. You'd go crazy if your production facility ground to a halt for the day, so why are you leaving all that money sitting there, untapped? In the United States, those company cars are now on an app, Turo-style.

Do you have a production facility that produces heat? What if you turned that heat into electricity to load the batteries in the cars your executives will drive home? If they only have a short journey, they could then use that battery as a battery, feeding into their home so they can turn the lights on and cook. If you look for it, you will find idle capacity. I'm not talking about the future; companies are already doing this.

Think differently. Engage, don't oblige

We have enough of everything we need – enough water, food, mobility and energy – but it's not connected, it's not working like an ecosystem so we feel like there's not enough. As a result, we keep adding more and more and more, essentially creating more immobility and more idle capacity. Making use of that idle capacity, people's cars, was the original idea behind Uber, but somewhere along the way they lost it. The capacity is there. We talk about overpopulation, but if everyone were to live in an area as densely populated as Amsterdam, the whole human race could fit in New Zealand. That's theoretical, of course, but it shows us just how much we have – too much energy, too many cars, houses, crops, cattle – and we still feel like we don't have enough.

There is idle capacity everywhere we look; just think about all the waste we create. On a small scale, we can each do our part. In my garden, we have a vegetable patch where we grow food for us to eat and any waste goes back into fertilising the garden to grow new vegetables. On a small scale, it's easy to do this, you optimise without thinking and, as a result, there's not much idle capacity. However, on a larger scale, this needs to be organised and it can only be organised if it's turned into 1s and 0s; you need to make the data work for you.

The moment you start this optimisation, you can't expect everyone to just start using it. Like the company that wanted to put sensors in their bikes, there needs to be something in it for people. It's one of the problems that governments face, they impose rules on what you have to do. Companies can't do that, they have to incentivise people to use their platform. Governments could take a page out of their book. You can't force people to use an app to reduce waste, but if they feel there's something in it for them, whether direct or indirect, they will want to contribute. People will get involved if they have something to do in your app for which they get rewarded, and you don't have to be the one to reward them – they can reward each other. As soon as they're involved and engaged, they'll invest in your app and the flywheel will start turning. Don't punish people for not doing something; make it voluntary and give them something, an incentive to use it.

The same goes for shared mobility. Governments talk about getting people out of cars and punish them for using cars. That's not the way to do it. They need to make sure that people have viable alternatives that they are happy to use. When I meet business people in Europe, they walk in with their car keys dangling from their hands – often a BMW, Mercedes or Audi – like it's part of their appearance, their first impression. In San Francisco, on the other hand, it's fashionable to not own a car. You may have a classic car in the garage that you enjoy taking out for a spin on the weekend, but that's it and you may not even have that.

Gucci is a brand that is designed to be exclusive. To have a Gucci bag is to make a fashion statement. Does it matter if it's not real? An article, explaining how a virtual Gucci bag sold for more money than a real one, drew my attention to a gaming platform called Roblox.[88] (Yes, I seem to have just skipped over that nugget of information, but go back and read it again: a virtual Gucci bag sold for more money than a real bag.) Roblox is an "imagination platform", designed to "bring the world together through play" and "enable people to be who they want to be". They call themselves the "architects of play", creating a platform where users can develop games that other people can play, a truly collaborative space in which users can create things the way they see them and make money from it. These users are known as Roblox's "community of creators".[89]

Roblox is essentially a virtual universe where users can create, play and be whatever they want. It's attracting all sorts of partners to the platform. Warner Bros. worked with Roblox to launch their new film *In the Heights* and organise a virtual flash mob to celebrate and get people involved.[90] BMG music is partnering with Roblox to hold virtual launch parties, provide music and sell virtual merchandise.[91] Gucci planned something similar, creating a limited-time Gucci garden in the game and selling digital items to bring their "exclusive" brand to the digital, more inclusive universe.[92]

A few years ago, we may have thought that customers would never want to pay real money for something they could only access in a game. Now, however, users are becoming more invested in their virtual alter ego, with various game designers allowing us to create in-game personas and interact with other people's virtual personas. The digital world is soon going to be a new economy that will be just as real as this one, but in that world you can be whoever you want to be. In that world, we'll be able to build homes and decorate them, maybe even make money there. It's creating an avatar, perhaps somewhere we will want to cross over to and live.

Idle capacity is everywhere we look, even if we don't see it straight away. You may need to think outside the box. The thing to remember is: wherever you see idle capacity, there's a potential application. All you need to do is bring people, supply and demand together on the platform.

Managers The Day After Tomorrow, the shift in communications

We've progressed from the flat earth to an interconnected, multidimensional space. We are coming full circle, from the old one-to-one communication through one-to-many to many-to-one to many-to-many just to come back to a new, enhanced version of the one-to-one model. The shift in how we communicate with customers has been upgraded. What's important now is to nurture personal contact between the brand and the customer, using digital to support that relationship. Smart data analysis enables us to create a new kind of human contact.

I concluded my last book, *Managers The Day After Tomorrow*, with some of these thoughts and, despite the upheaval of a global pandemic, they are still largely relevant today. It's not about completely wiping the slate clean and starting again, but using digital to enhance what we're already doing. In your 4.0 communications, many to many, think about how you can empower customers. In your 3.0 communications, many to one, think about how you can make customers feel like they are at the centre of their universe. In your 2.0 communications, one to many, think about how you can move away from boasting about your size, your renown, your products and think instead about who you are, what your company represents. Use mass communications to share that personality with customers.

People are emotional by nature and they are using emotion to choose the brands they want to buy from, the initiatives and values they want to support. It's not about upselling, deep-selling or cross-selling, but about building a relationship with your customer and using data and technology to foster that connection. Make sure that you get that two-way data: what you are putting out there and how people are reacting to that. Learn from what works.

As people, humans, we naturally use algorithms in each interaction we have with other people. We learn and react, adapting to what the other person needs from us. Technology can do this too and the more data you give it, the better your algorithm will be. Data serves to feed the customer relationship with warmth and thus build a stronger connection. Your algorithm also needs a reward: create warmth, create engagement, create wellbeing.

Don't aim to mirror people and their values; create your brand's own personality, its own voice. Chemistry between people isn't the fruit of the similarities between them, but rather the result of a dynamic connection, in which each person has their own personality and shows respect for the other. More and more, people are seeing brands as people, so build that personality and make sure it is one that shows HEART: Honesty, Ethics, Authenticity, Responsibility/Responsiveness and Transparency.

At the end of my book *Managers The Day After Tomorrow*, I posed 14 questions to help companies identify whether they were ready to face the future. Those questions are still relevant today:

- Are your entire organisation's knowledge and skills mainly aimed at understanding your own products, services and solutions, or do you know the customer better than you know yourself (and maybe better than they know themselves)?
- Does your management think in terms of obstacles and how to overcome them or more in terms of opportunities and how to seize them?
- Is your management style based on control (the middle man) or trust (the network)?
- Do you look for customers for your products or products for your customers?
- Do you work on assumptions or do you use big data and AI?
- Are your processes bogged down in long-term plans or are they flexible, constantly re-evaluated and questioned?
- Do you strive for perfection or do you accept failure?
- Do you focus mainly on details or do you prefer to view things holistically and see the big picture?
- Is tomorrow a continuation of today or the first step to your Day After Tomorrow?
- Are your traditional KPIs inside-out or are they new outside-in measurement tools?
- Do you have overall customer processes or is every customer interaction the process?
- Do processes serve to make life easier for your company or for your customer?
- Are you mainly occupied with sending out messages or do you prioritise listening to your customer?
- Is your communication 2.0-broadcasting or do you let your networks work for you?

A journey with no beginning or end

There's no hiding the fact that this book was written during a global pandemic. The first ideas came to me in that room in San Francisco, and I developed them further through online workshops held from my home studio. These were far from one-directional and I watched as we realised that what we were doing before was wrong. This book was written as we went from one lockdown to another, as we went from a shortage of face masks to an abundance, all the while discovering more about ourselves and our strengths than we knew possible, developing vaccines at a speed never seen before.

Nevertheless, there is a part of me that wished that those lockdowns had lasted longer. The pandemic showed us that we could do the "impossible"; companies could adapt to having their workforce working from home. The pandemic showed us that we could make a difference and hit the brakes on climate change, pushing back Earth Overshoot Day by 24 days. The pandemic showed us that much of what we were doing, living in a globalised world governed by profit and constant growth, eating the planet for all that it had, was wrong. But the pandemic didn't last long enough for us to forget our old habits. This book's journey started more than a year ago in San Francisco. Now we're starting to imagine life "post-COVID", the "new normal", yet people are still talking about going "back to normal".

This whole book is full of one paradox after another. There is no beginning or end to the ecosystem journey, but I had to decide on a beginning and end for this book. There is no one thing that comes first, the chicken and the egg both depend on each other. There is no end to the insights I want to put in this book, but I have to stop at some point. I guess that is the biggest thing we can learn: there is no end to learning. I learn from every workshop I hold, every keynote I give, every article I read. I hope you will continue learning, and seeking new knowledge, too.

TREECOSYSTEM

Build your TREEcosystem so that you can continue learning:
- Technology-driven. Use data to connect the dots, to respond to happenings in the outside world, to be fully aware.
- Red ocean strategy. Identify customer frustrations and find a way to turn those frustrations into pure delight.
- Engaged people. Give people a reason to participate in your ecosystem, to share their data with you. Make it worth their while.
- Ecosystem. Build an ecosystem that is responsive and agile, that embodies the three previous ideas fully. Make it work for all three Ps: profit, planet and people.

Where will we be in five years' time?

If we want to create a city where wellbeing is optimised for every person, we have a complex web of issues that need to be solved. On the flat earth, they seem to be impossible to solve, because we overlook the fact that we have a hyperconnected world full of connected dots. If we add artificial intelligence on top of our hyperconnected brains, so that people can augment it or it can augment human intelligence, we should be able to solve those complex issues. Issues like climate change and mobility contain so many variables that people couldn't do it alone. We will need artificial intelligence to help us solve these issues.

Not long ago, I was having a conversation with Pieter Abbeel, a top expert in artificial intelligence who has worked with Elon Musk and teaches at Berkeley. Just a few years ago (perhaps three or five), he told me not to expect too much from artificial intelligence. Last time I saw him speak, however, he was being interviewed in front of an audience and he said: "Even I am surprised at the speed of change now. Artificial intelligence is going to reach its maturity, by which I mean that it's going to become a part of our daily lives, within five years' time."

We all know, without a doubt, that this is going to be momentous. It's going to be the next tipping point, the next iPhone moment, the next internet moment – the only difference is that we couldn't predict that the iPhone was going to happen and that it would be so significant. It's going to be as significant as when the internet came into our lives. The iPhone wasn't just a phone, it was *the* phone that everyone wanted and so it changed the canvas of our society. I think that artificial intelligence will be the next internet moment. We all know it will be important, but we can't imagine what the impact will actually be. We only know that it will be huge, perhaps even more so than the internet.

Abbeel talks about artificial intelligence, but I think more in terms of augmented intelligence: the power of artificial intelligence combined with the power of human intelligence. To be more specific, I don't think that artificial intelligence will just be assisting us, like it does now through assistants like Siri and Alexa; I think that we will be assisting it. We will be the ones guiding artificial intelligence in its interactions with humans, because we understand human nature like AI never could. And let's face it, we are the greatest plague that mother Earth has ever faced.

The journey to a world that is ever further intertwined with technology will be full of bends and bumps, punctuated by important decisions. It is up to us to decide whether we want to use technology to make the good, the bad or the ugly. Until now, it has largely been one of the latter two, but people are unsatisfied. They are looking for the good and we can use technology to do that.

If I could sit down again in San Francisco with that CEO I spoke to in chapter 1, more than a year after that conversation, what would I say to him? First of all, I'd tell him to read this book. When we spoke more than a year ago, I knew that the change needed to come, I knew that being an ecosystem was the way forward, but I didn't know exactly how. I didn't yet know about the double flywheel, the extent of the importance of learning from data or the values that would guide collaboration between companies.

If I were to give him a summary of what I have learnt, what this book is about, it would be this:

COVID-19 didn't break the system, it showed us that the system we were running – the old economy – was broken. It showed us that the race for Profit had cast aside the importance of People and Planet, creating a frustrated society and an emaciated planet. Continuous, exponential growth, at the expense of people and planet, is not feasible. It created a red ocean of frustrated customers. Companies have been trying for so long to manage risk, to avoid it, that they have created a rigid system of processes and procedures, where they have fallen in love with their solution rather than the problem.

We can turn this around by creating an ecosystem of partners all focused on generating wellbeing for the customer. Wellbeing is an optimisation by definition, because there is no one definition of what wellbeing means to all of us. As such, we need to combine the best of human intelligence with artificial intelligence to create a genetic algorithm that can keep learning and improving with each iteration. We need to look at what we already have, the idle capacity, and use that rather than constantly searching for and creating more… waste.

Use the building blocks that already exist around you, whether within your company or outside of it. Equip as much of your infrastructure as you can with sensors. Use the power of the network. Create applications on top of the platform that bring value to you and your customers. In short, create something that would be missed by all – members of the ecosystem and users – if it were no longer there. Manage this cooperation, this partnership, with a minimal set of rules and values. Keep the ecosystem responsive, in tune with the outside world, constantly learning, so that the gap between reality and your assumptions may never take you by surprise.

Be driven by technology. Employ a red ocean strategy. Engage people. Be an ecosystem.

11.5

Work

"The only place success comes before work is in the dictionary."
VIDAL SASSOON

---

featuring:
superpowers and kryptonite
a pre-mortem
the hard questions
a beer card
peeling the onion
innovating smartly
the future

Spring 2019, a rainy day. I am on my way to an estate in the Belgian Ardennes to work with the executive team of a large Belgian bank. The team is there for two days and this afternoon is reserved for my workshop on how to build ecosystems. In recent years, I've given several inspirational keynotes for their leadership training programme. Today I am adding new elements to my base keynote: Managers The Day After Tomorrow, crack the magic formula. My keynotes evolve constantly; over the last few months, the E for ecosystems (from my TREE principle for exponential growth) has been taking centre stage. I didn't realise when writing my first book that ecosystems would grow into a workshop and then into the book that I am writing now (and that you are now reading).

Since 2015, I have run sessions at least ten times a year at the London Business School. I have noticed that "We need to become a platform" and "We need to build an ecosystem" have become key concerns. I have also realised that there is no set definition for what people mean by this and that how to turn a company into an ecosystem or platform is unclear. I became inspired by the opinions resonating from my own keynotes and the input of participants in exercises. For months now, I have felt the need to design a canvas outlining how to build an ecosystem and the required building blocks.

I left early this morning. I wanted to use the journey and the extra time on-site to prepare my session. The marketing manager asked me not to prepare anything: "We just want you to be there and keep us sharp when we are talking about how to become a platform rather than a bank. Just be there and make us aware when we are too locked up inside our banking stuff. Just be the outsider looking in." I still felt like I needed to prepare something.

A few days ago, I wrote a newspaper article about the automotive industry and Toyota's woven city. I decided to use the woven city as a brief introduction to the workshop. It's the perfect example of an ecosystem. No slides, just a speech to set the scene. As I drive along the mud-covered slippery winding roads listening to Nick Drake's "Cello Song" on repeat, I realise that I've finally found the building blocks I've been looking for.

I stop the car, trying desperately to retain my thoughts, grab a Moleskine and start drawing the ecosystem canvas. The first attempt is muddled, but the second represents exactly what has been going through my mind for months, without me being able to picture it fully until now. I grab my Surface Book and start building a brand new slide deck.

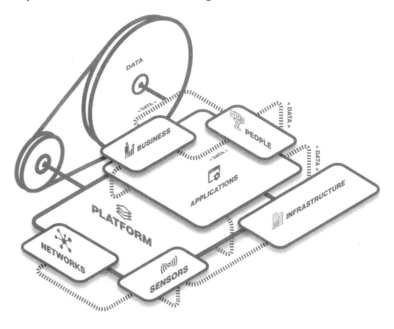

This workshop can be a hard task for companies that all of a sudden are forced to take a long, hard look at themselves... and they may not like what they see. To make the assignment a bit easier, but still reap the benefits, participants can be asked to "play" a smart city, with each team being given a specific issue such as energy, mobility, water or food. Their goal for the workshop would be to identify how to optimise that specific sector: how to make it sustainable, reduce the footprint, make it "circular" and get the double flywheel turning.

Pretending to be a smart city may be easier, because it means that participants don't have to look at their own business, which they see every day. It can be difficult to take a step back. However, if you look at something very complex and try to solve it, by definition you will find the building blocks, the dynamics, the need for sensors, networks, infrastructure, engaged people and more. Once you have discovered all those elements, you can then transfer what you've learnt to your own environment.

CHAPTER 11½
DAY 1

TREE PRINCIPLE

TECHNOLOGY

RED OCEAN STRATEGY

ENGAGED PEOPLE

ECOSYSTEM

1. Keynote : The Ecosystem Economy
The Truth behind The Hype

2. WHAT WOULD BE YOUR SUPERPOWERS ?

WHAT WOULD BE YOUR KRYPTONITE ?

TURN THE PAGE UPSIDE DOWN.

WHAT is:

PRESSURE COOKER METHOD

3 MINUTES IDEATION
5 MINUTES DISCUSSION
2 MINUTES PREPPING PITCH

1 LESSONS LEARNED

2 PRE-MORTEM

3 THE GREAT VISION

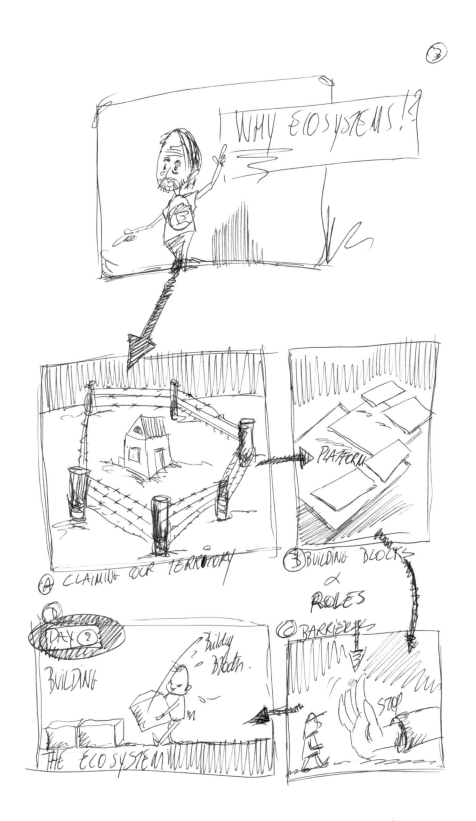

Day 1 – Setting the scene

*The Ecosystem Economy – the truth behind the hype **keynote***

The workshop kicks off with a poll. This is a new addition that I started using during the pandemic with the aim of boosting engagement on-line, but it translates well offline as well. The first question is: if you could pick one superpower, what would your ultimate business superpower be? The second is: if kryptonite takes away all your powers making you powerless, what would your kryptonite be? When I watched that first word cloud appear on the screen, I was slightly surprised but also re-assured by the similarity of answers. In response to the first question, most people described some variant of being able to read people's minds or being able to predict happenings. For the second question, most answers revolved around being blind or numb. Now the serious question: does your current business model embody your superpower or your kryptonite?

These answers present the perfect segue into my keynote, which I begin by delving further into the business model. Does your business model allow you to create current insights into your customers? Does it enable you to predict the future? Does it help you to read people's minds? Or is it numb and blind? Why? Why do we run our businesses in this way if we know that our ideal superpower is the exact opposite? Why do we run our businesses like kryptonite? If you've reached this point in my book, then you should already have most of the key points of this presentation in mind: the death of the old economy, the blurring of industry lines, the red ocean and so on. You know that you need to grab that superpower, to use sensors to read people's minds. After this essential introduction, we kick off with the first pressure cooker exercise.

WHAT IS A PRESSURE COOKER EXERCISE?

A pressure cooker exercise is more or less as the name implies. It's a brainstorming exercise limited to ten minutes – just ten minutes to spark ideas. When you run a lot of workshops like I do, you learn quite quickly that whether you give groups 10, 20 or 30 minutes, the outcome will always be more or less the same. Often, the out-come after ten minutes is even better than the outcome after 30 minutes. If you give groups 30 minutes, they will start wasting time, using up their energy before they even get started. They get bogged down in discussions, leaving more time for and wasting brain power on buts. If you give groups 20 or 30 minutes, they tend to start creating a group structure, developing some kind of hierarchy. However, with only ten minutes there's no time to do that. I tell them that they need to come up with something in ten minutes and I appoint a timekeeper, usually myself, to keep them on schedule.

Groups get ten minutes total: three minutes for trailblazing, five minutes for discussion and two minutes for preparation. In the first three minutes, groups should try to collect as many ideas as possible. This is not the time for judging or discussing. Just gather ideas. How you do this is up to you; you can write them on post-its, write a list, chuck them all on the table... whatever you want. Just don't discuss. It's easy to fall into the trap of hearing one person's idea and then commenting on it, but now's not the time. You have only three minutes to come up with ideas. It's difficult, so use a system. One suggestion I like to make is to go around in a circle. Person one gives an idea, followed by person two, three, four and then back to the start. If someone's idea has already been taken, they can pass their turn to keep the flow going. After three minutes of going around in a circle, you'll already have a lot of ideas on the table.

The second step is five minutes to discuss and cluster, while keeping the purpose of the exercise in mind. Once the 10 minutes is up, I want groups to present their outcome in 60 seconds, outlining no more than three elements. According to psychology, if you want to make an impression and have people remember it, you should mention no more than three elements. Nobody remembers more than three; more than three is just many. So reduce the number of elements to three and keep it to a 60-second crisp and crystal clear presentation. This is what I mean by "keep the purpose in mind": use the five minutes allocated to the second stage of the exercise to pick out the three elements you will present. There may be many more on the table, but you need to pick just three. You have five minutes to discuss, cluster and decide.

Finally, the last two minutes of the exercise is dedicated to planning who will present and how. Some groups choose to appoint a spokesperson; others prefer to present as a group. Whatever method you choose doesn't matter as long as you use those 60 seconds of presentation time wisely. I like to say, "Make it a purple cow. Present it in such a way that it makes an impression. You get 60 seconds of my time and 60 seconds of your colleagues' time so don't waste it. If there are 50 of us and you waste one minute, you're wasting 50 minutes by wasting one minute of 50 people's time."

In short, the pressure cooker exercise is a 10-minute activity – three minutes for ideation, five minutes for discussion, two minutes for preparation – followed by a 60-second presentation. I use this method all the time. It takes a little time to get used to; most people aren't used to working in such a limited time frame. That's why this type of exercise is ideal, especially if you slice the elephant. If you have a very complex problem, what you can do in only 10 minutes is rather limited. However, if you slice the elephant into snackable pieces, the pressure cooker method is ideal.

Lessons Learnt *pressure cooker exercise*

The pressure cooker method takes some time to adapt to, so I start off with an easy exercise: what are the lessons you have learnt from my presentation? This helps participants digest those first 45 minutes, giving all of the ideas and information I put out there time to settle. In groups of five to seven people, participants have the opportunity to put all the elements on the table and pick out the three most important to them. In some cases, all groups come up with more or less the same, but in other cases, a group will remember or highlight a completely different aspect that others had forgotten or overlooked.

Pre-Mortem *pressure cooker exercise*

After the first break, we continue with two more pressure cooker exercises. The first one is my favourite - it's the pre-mortem. I ask participants: why would your company no longer be relevant to people and society by 2035? 2035 may seem like a distant point in the future, but at the time of writing (in 2021) it's only been thirteen years since the financial crisis of 2008. In thirteen years, it'll be 2034 so 2035 is really just around the corner. My question is: why would you no longer be in business by then? Instead of writing your post-mortem in 2035, looking back at what you did wrong, I want you to write your pre-mortem now. When groups present the three elements they deem will be the company's downfall, I list them and hang the list on the wall. The list contains 10-20 don'ts that we must avoid. We will refer to this list throughout the rest of the workshop to make sure that we don't make the same mistakes.

Many groups present the results of this exercise like a real funeral, but I remember one group's presentation that really stood out. They gave each member a job title within the company, stood in a circle and talked to each other. Various people stood outside the circle – representing the supplier, customer, distributor – and were largely ignored. From time to time, a member of the circle would turn around to ask the outside parties a question, before turning back inward to continue their internal discussion. In the meantime, the people outside the circle started talking to each other, cutting out the middleman – the circle. This group accurately demonstrated how they were running their business. They were so obsessed by themselves, their processes and procedures, that they weren't watching the outside world. As a result, the outside world felt excluded, so they included themselves and excluded the middleman in turn.

The Great Vision *pressure cooker exercise*

"You can't go back and change the beginning, but you can start where you are and change the ending." – C.S. Lewis

The second pressure cooker exercise is the great vision: what type of company do you want to become by 2035? I've been doing this exercise for almost ten years and it's one of the main reasons why I started writing this book. I've seen thousands of variants of "We need to become a platform/ecosystem type of company." In nine out of ten groups, in one way or another, that's the outcome. When the group I mentioned previously came back on stage to present this exercise, they moved around instead of forming a circle. They mingled and started to connect with others. Rather than being the circle – the middleman – they became the platform that enabled communications to run swiftly and smoothly. Rather than being the spider in the spider's web, they became the web.

The Why of the Ecosystem *keynote*

Once we have completed these two exercises, I give a type of TED talk on the why of ecosystems. My earlier keynote was about the changing context, but here I go into why the answer to these changes is an ecosystem. Instead of commenting on the results of the two exercises, this presentation allows me to integrate the various elements that have been discussed, to say "This is what you've been talking about. This is the ultimate why of an ecosystem."

Claiming our Territory *pressure cooker exercise*

Before the lunch break, we round off with one more pressure cooker exercise: claiming our territory. Now we know that we want to become a platform company, what is our battleground? What territory do we want to claim as our web? Where does our web end? This exercise is about defining the playing field for the company.

Building Blocks and Roles in an Ecosystem *presentation + exercises*

In the afternoon, we move on to the practical elements – the building blocks and roles within an ecosystem – starting with a presentation followed by two exercises. We've laid the groundwork with the pre-mortem, vision and territory, giving us all the elements we need in order to identify which building blocks we have, need, must work on or are missing. Prior to the workshop, I ask the company to do some homework: build your own business model canvas. Most companies have already done this or know what it is so it's easy to do beforehand. We can then use it to break it down. During the presentation, we learn about the building blocks and roles in an ecosystem. In the exercises, we use the canvas to try to allocate the roles and building blocks. Which building blocks do you have? Which building blocks do you need to enhance? Which building blocks are missing? List the building blocks you need in an ecosystem and compare it with what you already have. You may be able to repurpose some features that worked for the old business model but don't here. The same thing can be done for roles. In the end, you may be left with a couple of building blocks or roles from your old business model that serve no purpose in the ecosystem model or that are on the list of don'ts from the pre-mortem.

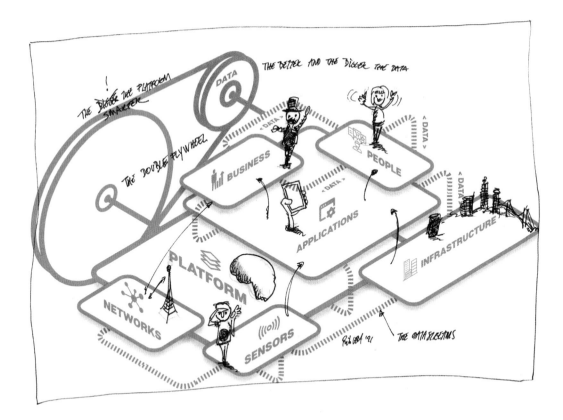

Potential Barriers *presentation + pressure cooker exercise*

We end the day with a final presentation about the potential barriers and dangers of an ecosystem. Day one – building an ecosystem – is very practical. Ideation can be uplifting and you may think it will be a walk in the park. But before we go any further, I share the potential barriers that companies may encounter in certain types of ecosystems so that you have the knowledge and information upfront. We finish with a final pressure cooker exercise: select three potential barriers and describe how you think you can overcome them. Day one is intense; it's time for some sleep.

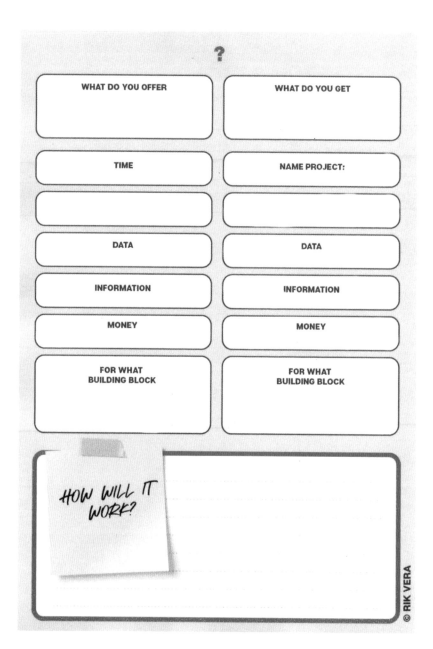

?

| WHAT DO YOU OFFER | WHAT DO YOU GET |

| TIME | NAME PROJECT: |

| | |

| DATA | DATA |

| INFORMATION | INFORMATION |

| MONEY | MONEY |

| FOR WHAT BUILDING BLOCK | FOR WHAT BUILDING BLOCK |

HOW WILL IT WORK?

© RIK VERA

Day 2 – Becoming an Ecosystem

Functions and partnerships *presentation + exercise*

Did you sleep well? I hope so. Let's refresh your memory about the day before with a 30-minute discussion, followed by a presentation introducing the functions and partnerships within an ecosystem. Essentially, what do you bring to the table and what can you gain from other members of the ecosystem? To allow this to sink in, we do a partnership exercise. If you want to become part of an ecosystem or you want to bring partners into your ecosystem, what is the trade-off? What can you offer and what can they offer you? Perhaps it's a building block or role that you're missing.

Ecosystem Values + Extreme Customer-centricity
presentations + pressure cooker exercise

After a short break, we jump back in with two presentations. First, we explore the importance of the values of an ecosystem and the sharing of those values. We continue with one of my most requested presentations on extreme customer-centricity and building the customer-centric model. How do you build applications? How do you turn information you obtain from the ecosystem into money-making applications? Customer-centricity is key, but how do you become customer-centric? Cue another pressure cooker exercise, the only one of the day, on how to turn customer frustrations into delight. Explore the customer experience. What are your customers' pain points? Pick one. How can you turn that frustration into pure delight?

Building Applications *exercise*

In the afternoon, we continue building on what we learnt this morning with two practical exercises. The first is the building applications exercise. We have already laid the groundwork: we know what kind of company we want to be and what red lines we need to avoid. Now we need to look at how we can do that. Think about companies like Airbnb and Uber. What can we learn from them? They didn't create a new business model, they didn't invest in infrastructure. They looked into transferring the old business model into the digital world using any idle capacity left in the analogue world. They asked if there were any

APPLICATION BUILDER CANVAS

NAME:

CUSTOMER FRUSTATIONS

FAST

EASY

ACCESSIBLE

SIMPLE

TEMPTING

CUSTOMER DELIGHT

HOW WILL IT WORK?

EXPERIMENT

HOW ARE YOU GOING TO EXPERIMENT

WHEN WILL IT WORK?
WHEN WILL IT NOT WORK?

CREATE VALUE

VALUE FOR ME

VALUE FOR BUSINESS

SCALE

THE FUTURE

what is your pitch?

© RIK VERA

customer frustrations that weren't being tackled by the old business model, because of idle capacity and analogue, that they could tackle and turn into customer delight. This is how you build an application. Looking at your existing business model, is there a customer frustration that you can turn into delight using technology and the framework of the new digital world? Can you develop a FEAST (Fast, Easy, Accessible, Simple, Tempting)?

Try to identify one customer frustration you could turn into delight and write it on a beer card. Don't write what you need to do to make it work, but how it would be experienced by the customer. If you were to describe the Uber experience as perceived by the customer, it would fit on a beer card. What Uber actually does behind the scenes is quite extensive and complicated, but that has nothing to do with customer experience. Make the customer experience so simple it can fit on a beer card. Then think about what you have available to make this work. What infrastructure can you use or repurpose? Uber didn't make anything new; they saw empty cars, drivers who wanted to make money, drivers and potential customers possessing a phone, phones having GPS and so on. All they did was make connections. We shouldn't be thinking about what we need to develop, but rather what we have available to us and how can we make this work by being clever.

The next step is to define how we experiment and how we make it as much of a minimum viable project as possible. You want to limit the impact. If it works, it works; if it fails, it fails. I see far too many projects ended too early or continued for too long because the measurement criteria were unclear. Lengthy discussions about whether or not to continue don't work. You need to define the criteria before even starting the project. This may be in terms of money or in terms of the features needed to make the product worth the effort. The type of criteria doesn't matter, but you must have them defined.

If the criteria are fulfilled, the project is working. Now, how do you scale? This isn't just an executive matter; how do you prepare the company for this?

What about the money? How are you going to make money? Companies like Waze, Facebook and Google don't charge users to use their applications; they make money in a different way, by gathering insights,

Work | **333**

collecting data and selling ads. Are you going to charge for using your platform? Can you collect insights and use that data to make money? At some point there needs to be money, but it might not be in that application. Some applications might just be designed to collect data that can be used elsewhere in your value stream to make money.

Customer-centric Onion Model *exercise*

The last exercise of the day is the customer-centric onion model exercise. Picture throwing a stone into the water; ripples spread out from that centre point. If something is in the way, the ripples are blocked. This is interference. Now imagine that centre point is the customer. This is your business model, based on the customer experience and then developed from there. The first ripple – the desired customer experience – is about building applications. To make sure that an application is customer-centric, it needs to be backed up by customer-centric values and company culture. You can't build a customer-centric application in a non-customer-centric environment. So ask yourself: what are the values we want our customers to feel when they deal with us? How do we build the culture to support that? What values do our people need to have?

Zappos, an online shoe and clothing retailer, is a perfect example. They don't talk about selling shoes, they sell happiness in a box. Zappos has a set of ten company values. New recruits receive four weeks of train-

ing in these values and how to translate them into value-driven behaviour. They need to unlearn process-driven behaviour because every customer interaction is different. Now that they have this value-driven company, they need to make sure that the culture is suited because it's not process or procedure driven. Value-driven can be less manageable, so you need to make sure that company culture backs it up. Pick out features that are already customer-centric and enhance them. Kill any that aren't customer-centric at all.

Day 3 – Next Steps

The Guide to Developing, Managing and
Leveraging the Ecosystem

The third day is all about what you do next. If you want to turn your traditional company into an ecosystem company within the next ten to fifteen years, you need to get moving as soon as possible. The problem is that what you need to start doing to achieve your goal is not always in tune with what you're doing today. So what do you do? How do you organise? On day 3, I teach participants to set up and use a strategy lab. How do you follow up on your third horizon projects? How do you measure them? These factors are not part of your current daily workflow, but they need to happen. That's why I created a template. In the first 45 minutes, I run through that template: how to set up a strategy lab, the dos and don'ts, the criteria to evaluate whether a project is worth handling in your everyday business and when it is ready to take to the innovation lab. We talk about the different stages, and how to measure those stages, to turn your project into reality. You can't wait; action is needed now – otherwise you'll never be ready by 2035. The whole morning of the third day is devoted to this. It's not a set tool that you need to use, but an idea of how it could look when adapted to your context, your company.

Innovation Mindset *presentation + pressure cooker exercise*

In the afternoon, we take it back to a human level by looking at the innovation mindset. If you want to drive innovation, you need to have the right mindset. Think about the surfer analogy we used earlier in this book. It's about becoming that surfer, ready to ride the waves and dream big. We use a group exercise to explore how you find the right people for your strategy lab. Furthermore, how do you communicate what you are doing in the strategy lab with the rest of your organisation? The most difficult part of innovation isn't coming up with the ideas; the most difficult part is preparing your organisation to accept those ideas. How do you make sure that what is being developed in the sandbox will be accepted by the rest of the organisation?

Back in 1939, Bill Hewlett and Dave Packard set up Hewlett-Packard in a one-car garage in Palo Alto, California. You may like to draw some inspiration from the "Rules of the Garage" that HP developed in 1999, the name referring to the company's birthplace. They might as well have been written in 2021.

- Believe you can change the world.
- Work quickly, keep the tools unlocked, work whenever.
- Know when to work alone and when to work together.
- Share tools. Ideas. Trust your colleagues.
- No Politics. No bureaucracy. (These are ridiculous in a garage.)
- The customer defines a job well done.
- Radical ideas are not bad ideas.
- Invent different ways of working.
- Make a contribution every day.
- If il doesn't contribute, it doesn't leave the garage.
- Believe that together we can do anything.
- Invent.

Rounding off *personal exercise*

My final exercise, to round off the workshop, is a personal exercise. I ask each participant to take an envelope and write a letter to themselves. In some cases, I even use three envelopes. What do you want to accomplish? Where do you want to be in the next three, nine or eighteen months? These envelopes are personal. I don't open them, I don't ask to see them. What you do with them is up to you. In some companies, we have asked people six months down the road if they want to share what's in their envelope, but it depends on the culture in your organisation. Participants have the right to say no.

Endnotes

1   Aurora. *Aurora is acquiring Uber's self-driving unit, Advanced Technologies Group, accelerating development of the Aurora Driver.* [Online.] 7 December 2020. [Last accessed on 23 April 2021.] Available at: https://aurora.tech/blog/aurora-is-acquiring-ubers-self-driving-unit-advanced

2   Campbell, Peter; McGee, Patrick. *Fiat Chrysler signs deal with Waymo as it steers away from Aurora.* [Online.] 22 July 2020. [Last accessed on 26 April 2021.] Available at: https://www.ft.com/content/228e2aee-6182-4d6b-8a69-e31cc19e4c9d

3   IsGeschiedenis. *Grote Paardenmestcrisis van 1894.* [Online.] [Last accessed on 23 April 2021.] Available at: https://isgeschiedenis.nl/nieuws/grote-paardenmestcrisis-van-1894

4   Avnskjold, Rasmus. *Geschiedenis van de auto.* [Online.] 14 May 2012. [Last accessed on 23 April 2021.] Available at: https://historianet.nl/techniek/machines/geschiedenis-van-de-auto

5   Kilcarr, Sean. *GM's Barra: Next decade to bring big automotive changes.* [Online.] 7 January 2016. [Last accessed on 23 April 2021.] Available at: https://www.fleetowner.com/industry-perspectives/trucks-at-work/article/21693729/gms-barra-next-decade-to-bring-big-automotive-changes

6   Thompson, Cadie. *General Motors CEO Mary Barra exclusively reveals grand plan to usher the company into the self-driving era.* [Online.] 12 December 2016. [Last accessed on 23 April 2021.] Available at: https://www.businessinsider.com.au/gms-mary-barra-interview-2016-12/amp

7   Toyota. *The Story Behind the Birth of the Prius, Part 1.* [Online.] 11 December 2017. [Last accessed on 23 April 2021.] Available at: https://global.toyota/en/prius20th/challenge/birth/01/

8   Okudaira, Kasuyuki. *The story behind the Prius.* [Online.] 22 November 2015. [Last accessed on 23 April 2021.] Available at: https://asia.nikkei.com/Business/The-story-behind-the-Prius

9   Graham Richard, Michael. *Traffic in Central London Moves at the Same Speed as Horse-Drawn Carriages.* [Online.] 11 October 2018. [Last accessed on 27 April 2021.] Available at: https://www.treehugger.com/traffic-central-london-moves-same-speed-horse-drawn-carriages-4856908

10 Wilson, Mark. *Car design is about to change forever. This video encapsulates how.* [Online.] 10 October 2020. [Last accessed on 23 April 2021.] Available at: https://www.fastcompany.com/90562654/car-design-is-about-to-change-forever-this-video-encapsulates-how

11 Johnson, Ben. *The Great Horse Manure Crisis of 1894.* [Online.] [Last accessed on 23 April 2021.] Available at: https://www.historic-uk.com/HistoryUK/HistoryofBritain/Great-Horse-Manure-Crisis-of-1894/

12 Wikimedia Foundation. *Ward Cunningham, Inventor of the Wiki.* [Online.] 23 May 2014. [Last accessed on 23 April 2021.] Available at: https://www.youtube.com/watch?v=XqxwwuUdsp4

13 Giuliano, Karissa. Watch Mark Zuckerberg's first-ever CNBC interview in 2004. [Online.] 29 April 2015. [Last accessed on 26 April 2021.] Available at: https://www.cnbc.com/2015/04/29/watch-mark-zuckerbergs-first-ever-cnbc-interview-in-2004.html

14 Ballmer, Steve; Gates, Bill. D6: Bill Gates and Steve Ballmer Condensed Chat 2. [Online.] 28 May 2008. [Last accessed on 23 April 2021.] Available at: https://www.youtube.com/watch?v=ze_7a-Dde8g

15 Cadwalladr, Carole. Google, democracy and the truth about internet search. [Online.] 4 December 2016. [Last accessed on 26 April 2021.] Available at: https://www.theguardian.com/technology/2016/dec/04/google-democracy-truth-internet-search-facebook

16 Smith, Dave. Google Chairman: 'The internet will disappear.' [Online.] 25 January 2015. [Last accessed on 23 April 2021.] Available at: https://www.businessinsider.com/google-chief-eric-schmidt-the-internet-will-disappear-2015-1?r=US&IR=T

17 European Parliament. 'Right to disconnect' should be an EU-wide fundamental right, MEPs say. [Online.] 21 January 2021. [Last accessed on 26 April 2021.] Available at: https://www.europarl.europa.eu/news/en/press-room/20210114IPR95618/right-to-disconnect-should-be-an-eu-wide-fundamental-right-meps-say

18 Hendricks, Scotty. Why Socrates Hated Democracy, and What We Can Do about It. [Online.] 7 October 2017. [Last accessed on 26 April 2021.] Available at: https://bigthink.com/scotty-hendricks/why-socrates-hated-democracy-and-what-we-can-do-about-it

19 Earth Overshoot Day. [Online.] [Last accessed on 26 April 2021.] Available at: https://www.overshootday.org/

20 World Economic Forum. The Great Reset. [Online.] [Last accessed on 26 April 2021.] Available at: https://www.weforum.org/great-reset/

21 Salem, Mostafa; Samaan, Magdy; Boykoff, Pamela; Krever, Mick; Reuters. Dislodging the huge ship blocking the Suez Canal could take 'days to weeks', as the traffic jam builds. [Online.] 26 March 2021. [Last accessed on 29 June 2021.] Available at: https://edition.cnn.com/2021/03/25/middleeast/suez-canal-ship-blockage-intl-hnk/index.html

22 Russon, Mary-Ann. The cost of the Suez Canal blockage. [Online.] 29 March 2021. [Last accessed on 29 June 2021.] Available at: https://www.bbc.com/news/business-56559073

23 Russon, Mary-Ann. The cost of the Suez Canal blockage. [Online.] 29 March 2021. [Last accessed on 29 June 2021.] Available at: https://www.bbc.com/news/business-56559073

24 Sanders, Marcus. Rodrigo Koxa Breaks Guinness World Record for 80-footer at Nazare. [Online.] 29 April 2018. [Last accessed on 7 June 2021.] Available at: https://www.surfline.com/surf-news/rodrigo-koxa-breaks-guinness-world-record-80-footer-nazare/23691

25 Kochkodin, Brandon. Everything We've Learned About Modern Economic Theory Is Wrong. [Online.] 11 December 2020. [Last accessed on 7 June 2021.] Available at: https://www.bloomberg.com/news/articles/2020-12-11/everything-we-ve-learned-about-modern-economic-theory-is-wrong?fbclid=IwAR1haMIRHlj97nb4y39Nd293OUNwCnPiokbNQnPhsPC_IldQNBRqhx3WLN8

26 Harrabin, Roger. Tata Steel windfall from carbon emissions permits. [Online.] 8 April 2016. [Last accessed on 7 June 2021.] Available at: https://www.bbc.com/news/science-environment-35994279

27 Bowers, Chris. *Rising awareness of Uber's harmful impact.* [Online.] 5 February 2020. [Last accessed on 7 June 2021.] Available at: https://www.transportenvironment.org/news/rising-awareness-uber%E2%80%99s-harmful-impact

28 Johnston, Matt. *Journalist An Uber Exec Reportedly Suggested Publicizing Personal Details About Has Responded.* [Online.] 18 November 2014. [Last accessed on 7 June 2021.] Available at: https://www.businessinsider.com/sarah-lacy-responds-to-buzzfeed-uber-report-2014-11?r=US&IR=T

29 Lacy, Sarah. *The horrific trickle down of Asshole culture: Why I've just deleted Uber from my phone.* [Online.] 22 October 2014. [Last accessed on 7 June 2021.] Available at: https://pando.com/2014/10/22/the-horrific-trickle-down-of-asshole-culture-at-a-company-like-uber/

30 Eurocities. *Parisians will live within a 15-minute radius.* [Online.] 3 November 2020. [Last accessed on 7 June 2021.] Available at: https://eurocities.eu/latest/parisians-will-live-within-a-15-minute-radius/

31 Masters, Jeff; Nuccitelli, Dana. *The Top 10 Extreme Weather and Climate Events of 2020.* [Online.] 23 December 2020. [Last accessed on 8 June 2021.] Available at: https://www.ecowatch.com/extreme-weather-climate-2020-2649628910.html?rebelltitem=5#rebelltitem5

32 Scranton, Roy. *I've Said Goodbye to 'Normal'. You Should, Too.* [Online.] 25 January 2021. [Last accessed on 8 June 2021.] Available at: https://www.nytimes.com/2021/01/25/opinion/new-normal-climate-catastrophes.html

33 Scranton, Roy. *I've Said Goodbye to 'Normal'. You Should, Too.* [Online.] 25 January 2021. [Last accessed on 8 June 2021.] Available at: https://www.nytimes.com/2021/01/25/opinion/new-normal-climate-catastrophes.html

34 UNFCCC. *The Paris Agreement.* [Online.] 8 June 2021. [Last accessed on 8 June 2021.] Available at: https://unfccc.int/process-and-meetings/the-paris-agreement/the-paris-agreement

35 Brahic, Catherine. *Turning a corner on climate.* The World in 2021. The Economist.

36 Revkin, Andrew. *Climate Change First Became News 30 Years Ago. Why Haven't We Fixed It?* [Online.] July 2018. [Last accessed on 8 June 2021.] Available at: https://www.nationalgeographic.com/magazine/article/embark-essay-climate-change-pollution-revkin

37 Grosfeld, Tom. *Rellen voor meer views op social media: 'Steek die Jumbo in de fik!'.* [Online.] 2 February 2021. [Last accessed on 8 June 2021.] Available at: https://www.parool.nl/ps/rellen-voor-meer-views-op-social-media-steek-die-jumbo-in-de-fik~bfd1feba/?utm_campaign=shared_earned&utm_medium=social&utm_source=email

38 Harris, Tristan. *How a handful of tech companies control billions of minds every day.* [Online.] 26 July 2017. [Last accessed on 17 February 2021.] Available at: https://www.ted.com/talks/tristan_harris_how_a_handful_of_tech_companies_control_billions_of_minds_every_day?referrer=playlist-the-race_for_your_attention

39 UNHCR. *The 1951 Refugee Convention.* [Online.] [Last accessed on June 2021] Available at: https://www.unhcr.org/1951-refugee-convention.html

40 WMO. *Climate change report is a wake-up call on 1.5°C global warming.* [Online.] 8 October 2018. [Last accessed on 10 June 2021.] Available at: https://public.wmo.int/en/media/press-release/climate-change-report-%E2%80%9Cwake-%E2%80%9D-call-15%C2%B0c-global-warming

41 Kemp, Simon. *Digital 2020: 3.8 billion people use social media.* [Online.]
    30 January 2020. [Last accessed on 10 June 2021.] Available at: https://
    wearesocial.com/blog/2020/01/digital-2020-3-8-billion-people-use-social-
    media

42 Freeland, Chrystia. *The rise of the new global super-rich.* [Online.] June 2013.
    [Last accessed on 10 June 2021.] Available at: https://www.ted.com/talks/
    chrystia_freeland_the_rise_of_the_new_global_super_rich

43 WEF. *Global Social Mobility Index 2020: why economies benefit from fixing
    inequality.* [Online.] 19 January 2020. [Last accessed on 10 June 2021.] Available
    at: https://www.weforum.org/reports/global-social-mobility-index-2020-why-
    economies-benefit-from-fixing-inequality

44 National Geographic. *Gentrification.* [Online.] [Last accessed on 10 June 2021.]
    Available at: https://www.nationalgeographic.org/encyclopedia/gentrification/

45 Statista. *Percentage of housing units with telephones in the United States from
    1920 to 2008.* [Online.] 30 September 2010. [Last accessed on 10 June 2021.]
    Available at: https://www.statista.com/statistics/189959/housing-units-with-
    telephones-in-the-united-states-since-1920/

46 Pew Research Center. *Mobile Fact Sheet.* [Online.] 7 April 2021. [Last accessed
    on 10 June 2021.] Available at: https://www.pewresearch.org/internet/fact-
    sheet/mobile/

47 United Nations. *68% of the world population projected to live in urban areas by
    2050, says UN.* [Online.] 16 May 2018. [Last accessed on 10 June 2021.] Available
    at: https://www.un.org/development/desa/en/news/population/2018-
    revision-of-world-urbanization-prospects.html

48 United Nations. *Growing at a slower pace, world population is expected to reach
    9.7 billion in 2050 and could peak at nearly 11 billion around 2100.* [Online.] 17
    June 2019. [Last accessed on 10 June 2021.] Available at: https://www.un.org/
    development/desa/en/news/population/world-population-prospects-2019.
    html

49 High Line website. [Online.] [Last accessed on 10 June 2021.] Available at:
    https://www.thehighline.org/visit/

50 Shear, Emmett. *What streaming means for the future of entertainment.* [Online.]
    April 2019. [Last accessed on 10 June 2021.] Available at: https://www.ted.com/
    talks/emmett_shear_what_streaming_means_for_the_future_of_entertainment

51 Pariser, Eli. *What obligation do social media platforms have to the greater good?*
    [Online.] July 2019. [Last accessed on 10 June 2021.] Available at: https://www.
    ted.com/talks/eli_pariser_what_obligation_do_social_media_platforms_have_
    to_the_greater_good

52 Elker, Jhaan. *World of Warcraft experienced a pandemic in 2005. That experience
    may help coronavirus researchers.* [Online.] 9 April 2020. [Last accessed
    on 10 June 2021.] Available at: https://www.washingtonpost.com/video-
    games/2020/04/09/world-warcraft-experienced-pandemic-2005-that-
    experience-may-help-coronavirus-researchers/

53 Shipman, Pat Lee. *The Bright Side of the Black Death.* [Online.] [Last accessed
    on 10 June 2021.] Available at: https://www.americanscientist.org/article/the-
    bright-side-of-the-black-death

54 CDC. *Influenza (Flu): 1918 Pandemic.* [Online.] [Last accessed on 10 June 2021.]
    Available at: https://www.cdc.gov/flu/pandemic-resources/1918-pandemic-
    h1n1.html

55 Joshi, Shashank. *Murder by numbers.* The World in 2021. *The Economist.*

56 Wikipedia. *Chernobyl disaster.* [Online.] [Last accessed on 10 June 2021.]
    Available at: https://en.wikipedia.org/wiki/Chernobyl_disaster

57 *Chernobyl.* 2019. [TV series.] Created by Craig Mazin.

58 Brand Minds. *Why did Nokia fail and what can you learn from it?* [Online.] 24 July 2018. [Last accessed on 10 June 2021.] Available at: https://medium.com/multiplier-magazine/why-did-nokia-fail-81110d981787

59 Vuori, Timo; Huy, Quy. *Distributed Attention and Shared Emotions in the Innovation Process: How Nokia Lost the Smartphone Battle.* [Research Article.] 18 September 2015. [Last accessed on 10 June 2021.] Available at: https://doi.org/10.1177/0001839215606951

60 Park, Will. *Nokia's CEO Kallasvuo says the Apple iPhone is a niche product.* [Online.] 17 April 2008. [Last accessed on 10 June 2021.] Available at: https://www.intomobile.com/2008/04/17/nokias-ceo-kallasvuo-says-the-apple-iphone-is-a-niche-product/

61 Wikipedia. *Dutch East India Company.* [Online.] [Last accessed on 10 June 2021.] Available at: https://en.wikipedia.org/wiki/Dutch_East_India_Company

62 Wikipedia. *Lottery.* [Online.] [Last accessed on 10 June 2021.] Available at: https://en.wikipedia.org/wiki/Lottery

63 Klarreich, Erica. *Computer Scientists Find New Shortcuts for Infamous Traveling Salesman Problem.* [Online.] 30 January 2013. [Last accessed on 10 June 2021.] Available at: https://www.wired.com/2013/01/traveling-salesman-problem/

64 Center for Creative Leadership. *How to Manage Paradox.* [Online.] [Last accessed on 10 June 2021.] Available at: https://www.ccl.org/articles/leading-effectively-articles/manage-paradox-for-better-performance/

65 For more information on business strategy, check out this article: Bennet, Jeffrey; Pernsteiner, Thomas; Kocourek, Paul; Hedlund, Steven. *The Organization vs The Strategy: Solving The Alignment Paradox.* Available at: https://www.strategy-business.com/article/14114

66 Wallace, David Foster. *Roger Federer as Religious Experience.* [Online.] 20 August 2006. [Last accessed on 10 June 2021.] Available at: https://www.nytimes.com/2006/08/20/sports/playmagazine/20federer.html

67 Regen Villages. [Online.] [Last accessed on 10 June 2021.] Available at: https://www.regenvillages.com/

68 Ehrlich, James. *The Future of Living: Self-Sustaining Villages.* [Online.] 6 July 2017. [Last accessed on 10 June 2021.] Available at: https://www.youtube.com/watch?v=QdNAEbAkThA

69 Cambridge Dictionary. [Online.] [Last accessed on 10 June 2021.] Available at: https://dictionary.cambridge.org/dictionary/english/ecosystem

70 Boroditsky, Lera. *How language shapes the way we think.* [Online.] November 2017. [Last accessed on 10 June 2021.] Available at: https://www.ted.com/talks/lera_boroditsky_how_language_shapes_the_way_we_think/details

71 Linguistic Society of America. *FAQ: Language Acquisition.* [Online.] [Last accessed on 10 June 2021.] Available at: https://www.linguisticsociety.org/resource/faq-how-do-we-learn-language

72 Kuhl, Patricia. *The linguistic genius of babies.* [Online.] October 2010. [Last accessed on 10 June 2021.] Available at: https://www.ted.com/talks/patricia_kuhl_the_linguistic_genius_of_babies/up-next

73 Okrent, Arika. *10 Language Mistakes Kids Make That Are Actually Pretty Smart.* [Online.] 16 October 2015. [Last accessed on 10 June 2021.] Available at: https://www.mentalfloss.com/article/31648/10-language-mistakes-kids-make-are-actually-pretty-smart

74 Mari, Lakshmi. *Hyperbolic discounting: Why you make terrible life choices.* [Online.] 2 August 2017. [Last accessed on 10 June 2021.] Available at: https://medium.com/behavior-design/hyperbolic-discounting-aefb7acec46e

75 Cytowich, Richard E. *What percentage of your brain do you use?* [Online.] January 2014. [Last accessed on 10 June 2021.] Available at: https://www.ted.com/talks/richard_e_cytowic_what_percentage_of_your_brain_do_you_use/up-next

76 Harvard University. *How Memory Works.* [Online.] [Last accessed on 10 June 2021.] Available at: https://bokcenter.harvard.edu/how-memory-works#:~:text=There%20are%20three%20main%20processes,through%20which%20information%20is%20learned

77 Valcour, Monique. *4 Ways to Become a Better Learner.* [Online.] 31 December 2015. [Last accessed on 10 June 2021.] Available at: https://hbr.org/2015/12/4-ways-to-become-a-better-learner

78 Popova, Maria. *Fixed vs. Growth: The Two Basic Mindsets That Shape Our Lives.* [Online.] [Last accessed on 10 June 2021.] Available at: https://www.brainpickings.org/2014/01/29/carol-dweck-mindset/

79 Swiftly. [Online.] [Last accessed on 11 June 2021.] Available at: https://www.goswift.ly/

80 Toyota. *Toyota and Uber explore ridesharing collaboration.* [Online.] 25 May 2016. [Last accessed on 11 June 2021.] Available at: https://mag.toyota.co.uk/toyota-uber-collaboration/

81 Statista. *Number of road traffic fatalities in Belgium from 2006 to 2019.* [Online.] 24 November 2020. [Last accessed on 11 June 2021.] Available at: https://www.statista.com/statistics/437883/number-of-road-deaths-in-belgium/

82 Woof, MJ. *Europe's road safety improved for 2019.* [Online.] 22 June 2020. [Last accessed on 11 June 2021.] Available at: https://www.worldhighways.com/wh12/news/europes-road-safety-improved-2019

83 Bellan, Rebecca. *Germany gives greenlight to driverless vehicles on public roads.* [Online.] 25 May 2021. [Last accessed on 11 June 2021.] Available at: https://techcrunch.com/2021/05/24/germany-gives-greenlight-to-driverless-vehicles-on-public-roads/?guccounter=1&guce_referrer=aHR0cHM6Ly93d3cuZ29vZ2xlLmNvbS8&guce_referrer_sig=AQAAAMWbuA-5DjXcauSq9ipBwVoFi0CnnudiuQK6hxbuhq_JQ040tqOysHJz76KgNYDwIyhoTA4uw6wLXLzZjTee5rcYJiv--HbZ2Jgzyi2fABxgPimCo6UhcR8CoJUTPY8JvNoCp6dQH2yyfCbsXeeIXKiOd8lQ0hTQOpQhRL7HIllr

84 Finstart Nordic. *Coronavirus proves we don't understand exponential growth.* [Online.] 27 March 2020. [Last accessed on 11 June 2021.] Available at: https://medium.com/finstart/coronavirus-proves-we-dont-understand-exponential-growth-52cd8b3b1a8f

85 San Francisco County Transportation Authority. *Emerging Mobility.* [Online.] [Last accessed on 11 June 2021.] Available at: https://www.sfcta.org/policies/emerging-mobility#panel-guiding-principles

86 Schweiger, Carol. *San Fran's mobility plans: a proactive approach to managing mobility.* [Online.] 24 August 2018. [Last accessed on 11 June 2021.] Available at: https://www.intelligenttransport.com/transport-articles/70742/san-francisco-mobility-guidlines/

87 Eyal, Nir. *The Hook Model: How To Manufacture Desire.* [Online.] [Last accessed on 22 June 2021.] Available at: https://www.nirandfar.com/how-to-manufacture-desire/

88 Kelly, Dylan. *A Virtual Gucci Bag Sold For More Money On Roblox Than The Actual Bag.* [Online.] 26 May 2021. [Last accessed on 22 June 2021.] Available at: https://hypebeast.com/2021/5/virtual-gucci-bag-roblox-resale

89 Roblox. [Online.] [Last accessed on 22 June 2021.] Available at: https://corp.roblox.com/

90 Roblox. *Roblox and Warner Bros. Pictures Bring In the Heights Launch Party to Roblox.* [Online.] 4 June 2021. [Last accessed on 22 June 2021.] Available at: https://corp.roblox.com/2021/06/roblox-warner-bros-pictures-bring-heights-launch-party-roblox/

91 Roblox. *Roblox Partners With BMG To Develop New Opportunities for Artists And Songwriters.* [Online.] 17 June 2021. [Last accessed on 22 June 2021.] Available at: https://corp.roblox.com/2021/06/roblox-partners-bmg-develop-new-opportunities-artists-songwriters/

92 Matney, Lucas. *Gucci brings digital items and experiences to Roblox in new partnership.* [Online.] 17 May 2021. [Last accessed on 22 June 2021.] Available at: https://techcrunch.com/2021/05/17/gucci-brings-digital-items-and-experiences-to-roblox-in-new-partnership/?guccounter=1&guce_referrer=aHR0cHM6Ly9jb3JwLnJvYmxveC5jb20v&guce_referrer_sig=AQAAAB7lNgffopFe1SYfoyEgbdoZFTY6qg0-Tld0DuDDPXOoyHQC50CsAXoJjEkrH6uYTcjN8aPLBV287HQSqfpy97RuvRuqb3DDrMfFarfXnNsiEBy4AfhBczfT4eloCL2v4JjHrWogOEeSp_kAFXQ1ST6kTYhsGtalhpJKcgTjoZCk